Tackling Complexity: Moving Up Levels of Nonfiction

Lucy Calkins, Series Editor

Katie Clements with Colleagues from the Teachers College Reading and Writing Project

Photography by Peter Cunningham

Illustrations by Jennifer DeSutter

HEINEMANN ◆ PORTSMOUTH, NH

This book is dedicated to my parents, for honoring and nurturing all my inquiries.—Katie

Heinemann
361 Hanover Street
Portsmouth, NH 03801–3912
www.heinemann.com

Offices and agents throughout the world

Cataloging-in-Publication data is on file with the Library of Congress.

ISBN-13: 978-0-325-07720-8

Series editorial team: Anna Gratz Cockerille, Karen Kawaguchi, Tracy Wells, Felicia O'Brien, Debra Doorack, Jean Lawler, Marielle Palombo, and Sue Paro
Production: Elizabeth Valway, David Stirling, and Abigail Heim
Cover and interior designs: Jenny Jensen Greenleaf
Photography: Peter Cunningham
Illustrations: Jennifer DeSutter
Composition: Publishers' Design and Production Services, Inc.
Manufacturing: Steve Bernier

Printed in the United States of America on acid-free paper
19 18 17 16 15   PAH   1 2 3 4 5

Acknowledgments

THIS BOOK GROWS OUT of the Teachers College Reading and Writing Project's (TCRWP) side-by-side work with teachers to develop strategies for supporting readers' work with nonfiction texts. That work has been enriched by the Project staff who lead a Content-Area Institute each February; by research in concert with Cognitively Based Assessment of, for, and as Learning, the research arm of Educational Testing Service, on argument; and by our involvement with a host of nonfiction authors, especially Seymour Simon. The Project's work with nonfiction has also been supported by collaborations with Steph Harvey, Kylene Beers, Ellin Keene, and Smokey Daniels.

A portion of this unit stands on the shoulders of the Project's work with strands of text complexity in nonfiction reading that began when Cory Gillette and Lucy Calkins led a study group of TCRWP staff developers to consider whole-book assessments. That research was updated in a new study group led by Lucy Calkins, Mary Ehrenworth, and Kathleen Tolan. This group created the "Strands of Text Complexity" document that undergirds the direction of this book. One group member, Amy Tondreau, rewrote the "Amazing Octopus" text to reflect the ascending levels of text complexity, and these texts weave across the minilessons. The group also developed the nonfiction text complexity challenge and strategy cards, which have quickly become a favorite of teachers and students alike. Thank you all for providing the strong foundation on which this book stands.

This unit has been nurtured by the contributions of so many colleagues, but there are a few for whom I am particularly grateful. Kelly Boland Hohne set this book into motion and wrote sections of it. Thank you, Kelly, for joining me as a partner across this journey. Thank you to Emily Butler Smith, Hannah Kolbo, Alissa Levy, Julia Mooney, Ryan Scala, and Amy Tondreau for your willingness to help out in any way. Thanks, also, to Jennifer DeSutter, chart maker extraordinaire. Your illustrations and charts bring the concepts to life and make content accessible!

This unit is what it is today because of the teachers who piloted versions of the unit, as well as the classrooms where the ideas contained within it grew. I am grateful to Dominique Freda, fifth-grade teacher at PS 107 in Brooklyn, who piloted the unit, and provided feedback and student work. I am grateful to Rachon Miller, K–6 Literacy Specialist, and Nichole Donahue and Lauren Aubry, teachers at Elmwood Elementary in New Berlin, Wisconsin, as well as Kay Reppen, fifth-grade teacher at Meadowview Elementary, in Oak Creek, Wisconsin, for sharing daily reflections, student work, and even video footage! Thank you to teachers and coaches who opened their classrooms to us for research, including Kerry Elias and Samantha Pujol at PS 101, Queens; Kathryn Minas at PS 158, Manhattan; and Barbara Rosenblum and Pat Faugno at PS 6, Manhattan.

The team at Heinemann is remarkable. My thanks go to Tracy Wells, who pored over every word, making the sentences cleaner. Your attention to detail and clear, crisp prose shaped this book into something beautiful. Words are insufficient for thanking Abby Heim who leads all of TCRWP's publications at Heinemann. She managed all the people, details, and deadlines with great grace. I'm grateful to Peter Cunningham, the photographer of Units of Study, and to David Stirling, who works with the photos to create pages that bring our beautiful children to life. As we hand these books off to Lisa Bingen and her team to carry them across the world, we are appreciative in advance of the work you'll do.

And, most of all, I am grateful to Lucy. I pored over *The Art of Teaching Reading* and learned from you at Summer Institutes, and your words filled my classroom long before we met. Thank you for welcoming me as a writer in your writing workshop, for conferring with me to lift the level of my craft, and for teaching me in ways that will impact my writing for years to come.

—Katie

Contents

BEND II Applying Knowledge about Nonfiction Reading to Inquiry Projects

An Orientation to the Unit

AS YOUR FIFTH-GRADERS near the end of their elementary school careers, step back for a moment to reflect on the incredible growth they have made. It was just a few years ago that your students were paging through *The Three Billy Goats Gruff*, learning how to use pictures to tell stories and discovering that they could use the first letter in a word to determine what that word might be. Now, they are tracking themes across complex novels and writing to develop their thinking.

The nonfiction texts your fifth-graders are reading are complex; they raise important challenges. These texts tend not to contain supportive headings and subheadings, nor the pop-out sentences that highlighted main ideas in the passages your students used to read. New words don't come with explicit definitions, and the definitions that are present often include yet more technical vocabulary. What's more, these complexities are often glossed over because of the engaging visuals and catchy fonts that make the texts appear deceptively simple.

This unit sets out to directly address these challenges. Across the unit, your students will study ways in which their texts are becoming more complex, and they will realize that the reading strategies they used to rely on are insufficient for these new challenges. You'll know this unit has paid off when your readers see that a text is complex and, rather than becoming discouraged, turn independently to the strategies they need for support. The far-reaching impact of what you teach in this unit will show itself in the ways your students deal with the difficulties they encounter in texts long after they have left you. As Peter Johnston reminds us, "Make no mistake, when we are teaching for today, we are teaching into tomorrow" (*Opening Minds*, 7).

At the same time, this unit supports students in building independent nonfiction reading lives outside of school. You will help students see that readers turn to complex nonfiction because those texts give them access to the knowledge they seek and open doors of opportunity. You'll make this crystal clear to students by giving them a broad choice of the topics they can crack open. Certainly they can continue to study traditional topics—castles, ocean life, kangaroos—but you'll also suggest they can study current events, their favorite sports team, or that singer they just cannot get enough of.

For students to truly be lifelong learners, they must see the value of embarking on a learning journey, one that feeds a passion or question of their own. In *For a Better World: Reading and Writing for Social Action*, Randy and Katherine Bomer write, "The ability to hook into something you want to accomplish and to pursue that desire across time is an essential attribute for a citizen to develop if he or she is to be capable of leading." Just like the pastry chef wanting to know the latest methods in baking, the scholar studying the latest science research on cancer, or the expectant parent wanting to know what on earth to do with a new baby, we create and take on learning projects that help shape our lives. Your students do not need to wait until they are adults to see the power of having interests and passions and pursuing those through research. As Dewey said, "Education is not a preparation for life; education *is* life itself." The end of this unit will affirm the importance of taking on a worthy project, and it will communicate to students that following interests of their own matters and is valued in your classroom. Being a strong reader of nonfiction and an independent researcher leads you to live more deeply.

Across Bend I, you'll help students inquire into the ways complex nonfiction gets hard, and you'll support them in developing skills and strategies to tackle those difficulties. You'll help students strengthen their skills in monitoring for sense, word solving, predicting, and summarizing, as they make sense of a host of complex texts. Then, in Bend II, you'll invite students to take on independent inquiry projects studying the topic they most want to learn about. Your teaching will support students in transferring everything they've learned about making meaning from complex texts to texts on their inquiry topic. You will extend this work, helping students to synthesize across texts and critically analyze author's craft.

SUPPORTING SKILL PROGRESSIONS

In the first unit for fifth grade, *Interpretation Book Clubs: Analyzing Themes*, you supported the major shifts from fourth to fifth grade in reading narratives. Those shifts have corollaries in reading expository texts, and this unit will help your students meet those expectations. Before embarking on this unit, you will want to read the Informational Reading Learning Progression for fifth grade and fourth grade as well, because your conferring and small-group work will need to shore up foundational skills on the fourth-grade learning progression, even while your unit advances into the new work of fifth grade. Many of the fifth-grade expectations will be advanced in this unit; others will be tackled in the later unit, *Argument and Advocacy: Researching Debatable Issues*.

By fifth grade, the nonfiction texts that your students are reading are becoming more complex. Students who read these more challenging texts will need to be ready to embrace complexity. No longer will students see the whole text working to support one fairly explicit and clear idea. Instead, it's much more likely that they'll need to be open to following different threads as they read an informational text. That means they will need to recognize that the text will often have multiple main ideas (some of which will be implicit, hidden between the lines). It is important that fifth-graders approach texts with the expectation that those texts will advance more than one main idea and that they can discern several main ideas in complex texts. This expectation is detailed within the "Main Idea(s) and Supporting Details/Summary" strand of the Informational Reading Learning Progression. This is also a critically important skill on the Common Core State Standards and on many other high-stakes assessments. Take a minute to read across the levels in the "Main Idea(s) and Supporting Details/Summary" strand. You'll see, for instance, that students in fourth grade might start trying to find more than one idea of a part, but readers in fifth grade are expected to figure out multiple main ideas.

This need to embrace more complexity crosses over and relates to more than just the "Main Idea(s) and Supporting Detail/Summary" strand. This unit supports essential comprehension skills, skills that fall within the "Literal Comprehension" portion of the learning progression, and you'll see these strands regularly mention the need for students to be more flexible as they read more complex texts. This need for flexibility will relate to students' work in the "Orienting" strand. When fifth-graders preview a text, it's important for them to recognize that the text might contain a long and winding introduction before turning to the focus of the text or that it might reveal its focus slowly in other ways. Your whole-class and small-group instruction across this unit will support students in the skills of previewing increasingly complex texts.

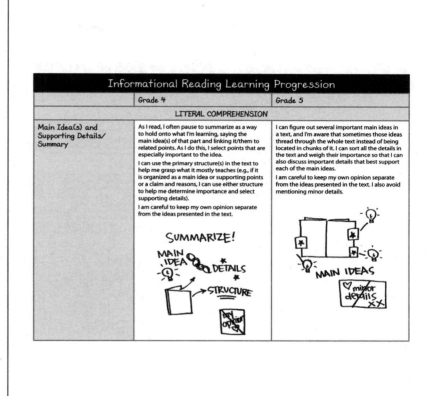

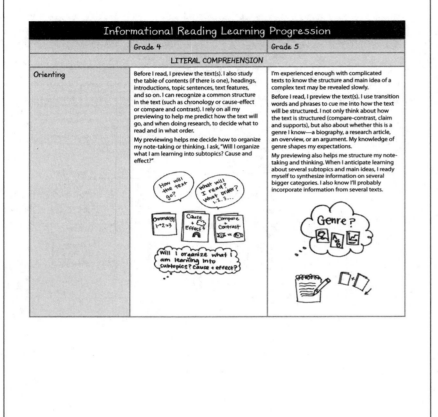

Informational Reading Learning Progression		
	Grade 4	Grade 5
LITERAL COMPREHENSION		
Orienting	Before I read, I preview the text(s). I also study the table of contents (if there is one), headings, introductions, topic sentences, text features, and so on. I can recognize a common structure in the text (such as chronology or cause-effect or compare and contrast). I rely on all my previewing to help me predict how the text will go, and when doing research, to decide what to read and in what order. My previewing helps me decide how to organize my note-taking or thinking. I ask, "Will I organize what I am learning into subtopics? Cause and effect?"	I'm experienced enough with complicated texts to know the structure and main idea of a complex text may be revealed slowly. Before I read, I preview the text(s). I use transition words and phrases to cue me into how the text will be structured. I not only think about how the text is structured (compare-contrast, claim and supports), but also about whether this is a genre I know—a biography, a research article, an overview, or an argument. My knowledge of genre shapes my expectations. My previewing also helps me structure my note-taking and thinking. When I anticipate learning about several subtopics and main ideas, I ready myself to synthesize information on several bigger categories. I also know I'll probably incorporate information from several texts.

figure out at the start (Is the author being sarcastic? Dramatic?), or may shift and change, and readers will need to notice clues and think, "How does the author probably want this to sound?" Taken together, a major thrust of your teaching across Bend I aims to support students in reading ever-increasing, more complex texts with strong literal comprehension.

Your fifth-graders will also need to add to their repertoire of ways to think interpretatively and analytically about expository texts, and your teaching across Bend II will particularly support this work. This fifth-grade unit (like *Argument and Advocacy*) will directly tackle "Comparing and Contrasting" and begin to focus on "Analyzing Author's Craft." In fourth grade, your students learned that they could compare and contrast texts in ways that included noticing the perspective of two authors and thinking about ways those different perspectives led to different ideas. In this unit, your teaching will support students in continuing to learn to analyze differences in perspective, particularly differences that tie in to the craft or structure decisions the author makes. You'll see that *Argument and Advocacy* continues work on "Comparing and Contrasting" and "Analyzing Author's Craft," and that unit also offers more teaching on "Analyzing Perspective."

This unit also supports fifth-graders in "Inferring Within Text/Cohesion." This strand is not about the structures of the text; rather, it's about the content of the text, the important through lines that hold a text together. It's about the relationships within a text—how one event can set off a chain of events; how one individual can significantly influence the outcome of a battle; how one scientist can make a contribution that can radically change what others in the field think. Or, in texts with more abstract concepts, it's about how concepts relate—how the idea that when electrons move, they carry electrical energy from one place to another can relate to why an electrical circuit is important or how a light bulb works. This is the *stuff* of the texts—the key, critical content—and it is built around relationships. In fourth grade, students learned that to discern relationships between things in scientific, historical, and technical texts, it helped to draw on structure. In fifth grade, you'll coach students to extend this work, so they generate their own ideas about relationships and interactions between two events, even when the author has not clearly laid out the relationships.

As fifth-graders begin to read across multiple texts on a topic, they will also need to continue learning to do "Cross Text(s) Synthesis" work. This work is particularly supported in the second portion of this unit as students read across texts on their personal inquiry topic. They will need to not only form

Students will need to carry this flexibility with them to their work in "Monitoring for Sense," recognizing that they may need to carry unanswered questions as they read, or do significant work to determine how two seemingly unrelated parts fit together. This mindset will also relate to students' work in the "Fluency" strand, because the mood and tone of a text may be tricky to

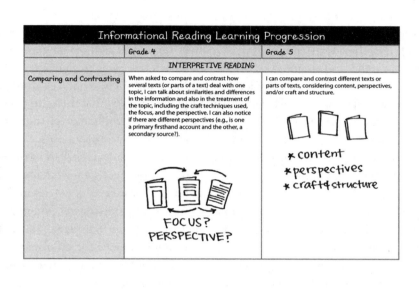

Informational Reading Learning Progression		
	Grade 4	Grade 5
INTERPRETIVE READING		
Comparing and Contrasting	When asked to compare and contrast how several texts (or parts of a text) deal with one topic, I can talk about similarities and differences in the information and also in the treatment of the topic, including the craft techniques used, the focus, and the perspective. I can also notice if there are different perspectives (e.g., is one a primary firsthand account and the other, a secondary source?).	I can compare and contrast different texts or parts of texts, considering content, perspectives, and/or craft and structure.

categories to capture their learning as they read deeply within a subtopic, sorting information from multiple texts into those categories but also notice contradictions within texts and think deeply about what might be causing those contradictions.

This unit places a spotlight on developing more active, critical citizens, and this work is deeply reflected in the "Critical Reading" strand of the learning progression. Fifth-graders are called to move beyond reading a text and taking its ideas at face value, and instead to think as they are reading, to make their own connections and spark their own ideas. Growing Ideas matters. In fact, we consider it some of the most crucial work that readers can do. And as students become more critical, they can not only raise their own questions, or grow ideas from texts or come to texts with ideas, but they should also be Questioning the Text.

All of your work with learning progressions will be informed by the performance assessments that are overviewed in the assessment section.

OVERVIEW

Bend I: Working with Text Complexity

In the first bend, you'll invite students to join you in a giant investigation into the ways nonfiction texts are becoming increasingly complex and the ways students' reading can shift in response to those complexities. As you gather students together, high-interest nonfiction texts in hand, you'll say, "I have a feeling that getting better as a nonfiction reader is a bit like getting better at video games. You need to master the higher levels—and those higher levels have harder challenges and require different strategies."

Once your students accept the challenge, you'll use contrasting texts to make these new complexities clear to them. One day, you'll lay out a simple nonfiction text—one your kids could have read years before—with clear headings and the main idea stated in a pop-out sentence. Then, you'll layer on a complex text and lead your students into an inquiry. As texts become more complex, how are they different? Your class will probably notice that in complex texts, main ideas aren't usually stated straight out. You'll remind students that it helps to chunk the text into parts and then pause after each part to say, "What does this chunk seem to be about?" After that, they can read on through another chunk and do that same pausing, thinking after a bit about how the chunks fit together.

Of course reading complex nonfiction also involves tackling increasing vocabulary demands. One day you'll guide students to study just a paragraph of a text that has been rewritten up the ladder of text difficulty, noting how the same word, *predator*, is supported differently in the easier version of the text than in the more challenging version. Another day, you'll expose students to research about word morphology, telling them, "What these researchers are saying is that as texts get harder, *more than half* the words you come across have parts that always mean the same thing in every word in which they appear. So when you find a difficult word, it will pay to look *in* the word, not just around it." In this way, you'll support students in looking *around* words and looking *inside* words to determine a word's meaning.

You'll wrap up your investigation into text complexity by helping your students read more analytically, thinking especially about the relationship between parts and the whole. You'll show students that even if a text appears at first glance to be a single, coherent text, it may well be a patchwork of pieces—containing, for example, passages that are written as narrative and passages that are clearly expository, or parts that are structured as compare and contrast and others structured as cause and effect. You'll teach students, "Just like you can connect and build a single row of Lego blocks, or a part of a Lego building, or an entire Lego building, the same is true of texts."

After students have investigated ways complex nonfiction gets hard, we suggest you introduce them to a tool you have been secretly building over the past few weeks: the text complexity cards, which list the challenges often found in complex nonfiction and potential strategies that can help unlock the complexities. You'll introduce this favorite TCRWP tool with a lot of fanfare and a word of caution, saying, "Readers, if you are reading along and you feel like your mind is on fire, then that is not a time to use this tool. But if, on the other hand, you are feeling a bit daunted by the text, then you might use this tool to think about the part of the text that feels hard." That is, the text complexity cards are intended to be a temporary scaffold, a message you'll make clear from day one.

As you draw the bend to a close, you'll help students orchestrate much of the reading work they have done as they summarize, crafting concise versions of a text's main ideas and key supporting details.

Bend II: Applying Knowledge about Nonfiction Reading to Inquiry Projects

In the second bend, you'll rally your students to become independent researchers, and you'll invite them to choose the one topic in the world they most want to research. Scanning your classroom at the start of this bend, you might have one student studying the Beatles, another Bigfoot, and a third diving into an inquiry of infectious diseases. We suggest you and your students spend the first few days of the bend conducting primary research out in the world. Students might interview a neighbor who works for a hospital to supplement their research on cancer, survey classmates to determine public perceptions of a soccer team, or observe their cat to get ideas for an inquiry into animal behavior. This primary research is important. Through it, students will discover the patterns and main ideas significant to their topics.

Equipped with a toolkit of strategies for tackling complex nonfiction from Bend I, after a few days of primary research, students will be guided by you back into their texts. You'll teach students, "Once you have some expertise on your topic, you are more knowledgeable when you come to your texts, you see more in texts when you look through your expert eyes." That is, a student researching guinea pigs, whose primary research revealed that these tiny pets can lead to big expenses, is more likely to note the significance of the line, "Guinea pigs may require several visits a year to the vet," than a novice.

Up to this point, it's likely that while your students are pausing and writing about their nonfiction reading, their notebook entries feel somewhat lifeless, and they lack the passion and energy that filled their notebook entries in the first fifth-grade unit, *Interpretation Book Clubs: Analyzing Themes*. You might teach students that "Informational writers *write* in order to understand what they are learning, angling their writing so it better explains the information." Marvel as your students move beyond boxes and bullets and summaries and begin creating charts and tables and making quick series of sketches. Later in the bend, you'll extend this work, teaching students that the very best writing about reading—and, we might argue, the very best writing—shifts seamlessly between writing with very specific details and writing about big ideas, themes, and issues and critical questions. You'll rally students to move up and down a ladder of abstraction, writing first about big ideas—theirs or the author's—and then to climb down the ladder and write about specific details.

Of course, Bend II supports other work. You will teach students to question what they read, inducting them into the ways you use Webb's Depth of Knowledge levels to strengthen your questions. Certainly, students will ask level 1 questions ("What year was Beyoncé born?"), and they'll read on in texts to find answers, but you'll also teach students to ask questions that extend across texts ("With so many challenges, is it worth it to be a famous musician?"). These questions that students ask will guide their ongoing research.

You will also support students in synthesizing information across different texts on a subtopic, noticing ways texts are similar and different in their content and presentation of a subtopic. As part of this, you will highlight not only what texts teach, but also how authors use dramatically different, strategically chosen craft moves to teach that information. You'll guide students to notice the author's perspective on a topic, however subtle, as well as to solidify their own perspective on a topic, thinking, "What is it I want to say to the world about my topic? What feelings do I want to instill in others?" This work lays the foundation for the deep critical reading work your students will engage in during the next nonfiction unit of study, *Argument and Advocacy: Researching Debatable Issues*.

In the last session of the unit, you'll gather students close, and say, "It's likely people started researching your topic long before you were born, contributing to a grand conversation on the topic." A few weeks ago, students were novices. "But now," you'll say, "you're ready to enter this conversation, to become a spokesperson for your topic, to articulate your own opinions." Across an exciting and fast-paced session, you'll teach students to plan for seminars that capture their key learning and perspective. Then you'll open the doors of your classroom and send students out into the school to share their knowledge. While this work will require some advance planning, we urge you to take on this session. A central tenet of real-world research is sharing your findings with an audience, as we see when conservationists share their research about animal habitats with city planning boards and when panels of doctors present their scientific findings to one another. Scurry from seminar to seminar. In one room, you might watch students present "Playing Football: The Risks and Rewards," another "Poisonous Dart Frogs Are Worth Saving," and a third on "New Advances in Moon Research."

As your students spread out around the school and teach one another, take time to marvel at what they know. Your students will come a tremendous way over the course of this unit.

ASSESSMENT

Your instruction will always be informed by assessments, and those assessments will be continual. You'll use running records and other observations of your students, examinations of reading logs and their writing and talking about reading, and performance assessments to track student progress and to align your teaching to what your best knowledge is of what they can do, can almost do, and can't yet do.

You have presumably taken running records at the start of the year, which yielded levels of text complexity that your students can handle. Hopefully, you gave a second informal running record to any student who showed signs of being able to progress up a notch during that unit. Many can do so after summer rust wears off, so it is wise to follow your first running record with a second one close on the heels of the first. For students who recently began reading books at a new level of text complexity, you will probably use those levels of fiction text complexity as a starting place for students' work with nonfiction. That is, assessing students is a time-consuming process, so it is reasonable to hypothesize that students can handle about the same level of text complexity in nonfiction that they can handle in fiction. Just keep an eye on your students as the unit begins. Students' reading levels for nonfiction are often below their levels for fiction. Be alert especially for signs of disengagement, and watch students' reading logs for possible declines in volume of reading. You may need to move students down a notch in nonfiction at the start of this unit, and then aim to provide enough support so they can quickly move back up.

You may have taught a unit you developed on your own between our first unit and this unit. If you didn't—if this is your second reading unit of the year—then your students who are entering the unit reading at standard will be reading level S or T. As you match students with nonfiction books, continue to aim for approximately 96% accuracy when they are reading without book introductions or other forms of support, although you may need to allow for a bit of struggle with domain-specific vocabulary. (This may mean slightly lower accuracy expectations for nonfiction than for fiction, because nonfiction, by definition, will introduce new domain-specific vocabulary, which will make accuracy a bit more challenging.)

You may ask whether it is reasonable for students to read nonfiction as well as fiction with 96% accuracy—how can they tackle informational books if they need to know most every vocabulary word before they are even given access to that book? This is a reasonable question. There are a fair number of experts on this topic who concur that you can almost take out the domain-specific words (the vocabulary words that the text aims to teach, for example: *barometric*, *meteorologist*, and *anemometer* in a text about weather), and then check that the kids are reading the rest of the text with 96% accuracy. The key thing is that readers need to have a strong enough grasp of the context so they can piece together what the text is saying enough to develop an approximate understanding of those challenging new vocabulary words.

If your school has access to a system that supports you in conducting running records of nonfiction texts (such as the Fountas & Pinnell Benchmark Assessment System), you might choose to use that system for administering nonfiction running records. Even if you don't have such a system, you can use any text that has been leveled, ask students to read a snippet of it (about 100 words), and conduct a running record. TCRWP's website does not provide leveled nonfiction texts for conducting running records.

Regardless of which approach you choose, this unit supports dramatic growth. Small-group work can reinforce this. The strands of text complexity in nonfiction (see *Reading Pathways, Grades 3–5: Performance Assessments and Learning Progressions*, Chapter 5) will be enormously helpful to you as you plan your small groups. That chapter detail major ways nonfiction texts become complex in relation to main idea, vocabulary, structure, and knowledge demands.

Know that in general, students can move to more challenging levels of nonfiction when they are reading about topics about which they have expertise. If a student is passionate about basketball, for example, she'll be able to tackle more difficult texts on that topic. For topics that are less familiar, it can help to provide students with several sequenced texts on the topic so that the reader dives first into the easiest text on that topic, say dolphins, and then reads progressively more complex texts as she gains background knowledge.

Of course, literal comprehension is necessary but not sufficient, and you will also want to assess your students' higher-level comprehension, looking specifically at all the skills comprised by interpretive, analytic reading. This unit begins with a performance assessment, available in the online resources, which is designed to highlight and support these comprehension skills. The performance assessment assesses four main skills that are critically important across this unit and on the high-stakes assessments your fifth-graders will be taking. In particular, this unit focuses on skills in the strands "Main Idea(s) and Supporting Details/Summary," "Comparing and Contrasting," "Analyzing Author's Craft," and "Inferring Within Text/Cohesion." More details pertaining to the assessment can be found in the Start with Assessment letter in this unit and in the online resources.

The biggest decision you will want to make right away pertains to the scoring of the performance assessment. In Chapter 2 of *Reading Pathways, Grades 3–5: Performance Assessments and Learning Progressions*, we describe ways in which you can hold a norming meeting with other teachers, so that all the teachers across your grade level can collaboratively score students'

performance assessments in roughly equivalent ways. The Informational Reading Learning Progression, combined with a big effort to calibrate your assessments, can enable you and your colleagues to come to a shared view on what constitutes good, better, best work in particular reading skills.

But what we think is most important is that you try to turn as much of the assessment as possible over to the kids. What you are truly assessing is the black box of what goes in a student's mind during reading, and no one is a better judge of that than the child. You'll find a letter detailing how this work might go in the classroom in Session 3 of the unit. To support your students with this work, you'll draw on the Informational Reading Learning Progression and on student-facing rubrics created from the progression.

A word of caution: If your students have not grown up within Units of Study for Teaching Reading and therefore have never before seen the nonfiction learning progression, you'll find their initial work on the performance assessment and their initial efforts to score themselves are very rough approximations. You would probably be more comfortable if you score their pre-assessment and then ask them to work in partners in Session 3, not to self-score but to understand how you scored them and to try revising their work. That would take a fair amount of your time, however, and if it postpones the unit or the unveiling of the learning progressions, it is probably not worth the trade-off.

Once students have studied the Informational Reading Learning Progression and gleaned an understanding of the indicators that might suggest they are doing higher-level work, this fills them with a sense of direction and resolve, and it puts a tincture over the whole unit. As students self-assess their work on analyzing craft, for example, you have almost painted the future teaching on that topic with a dye that makes that teaching stand out in your students' minds across the unit. They know it is a skill that will be assessed, so they sit up and look alert! At the point in the unit when you teach about analyzing author's craft, they're apt to think, "Oh, this is about author's craft. That was on the pre-assessment." By prioritizing this work on the assessment, you've demonstrated that you place a high value on this learning, and students will likely respond accordingly.

Giving students a sense of the end goals for the unit gives them a sense of agency and purpose, as well as a feeling that they can do what it takes to grow. Carol Dweck's research has shown that students who see hard work as valuable have a growth mindset and an empowered sense of themselves as learners. Mistakes are valuable because they lead to new learning, and a new challenge is something to be welcomed ... nts will feel empowered because they'll kn ... ves to be stronger. If they want to do bet ... to multiple main ideas instead of just one, for example. This is not hidden from the students—the goals are transparent, clear as day, and thus accessible.

GETTING READY

Gathering Texts

In Bend I, you will channel students to read high-interest nonfiction texts at their independent reading level. We suggest you scour your classroom library, school library, and local library, pulling high-interest books from anywhere you can. Whenever possible, group books into topic sets so that students can first read an easier text on a topic and then use that knowledge to access other books on the topic that are increasingly complex.

This unit incorporates one article, "The Amazing Octopus," that has been rewritten "up the ladder" to represent increasing levels of text complexity. You will probably want to study these articles with a group of colleagues before leading inquiries into these texts with your students. Notice the ways in which the version of "The Amazing Octopus" becomes more complex as you read up the levels. Spy on yourself as a reader, noting what you do to deal with those increasing complexities, and use what you notice to guide your conversations with readers. These articles will weave across your minilessons, conferences, and small-group work, and they can be accessed in the online resources.

In Bend II, students will embark on independent inquiry projects on topics of their own choosing, and they'll need to develop a collection of texts on their inquiry topic. These collections might include articles, books, and videos, as well as interviews, observations, and surveys. You will encourage students to be their own text collectors, but you will also want to support students in growing their collections. You might set up a time for students to visit the school or community library or invite students into the room to research and print articles outside of reading workshop.

Partnering Students

Across the unit, you'll want to partner students in different ways. For Bend I, you will find it advantageous to pair students in same-level partnerships.

Partners reading similar levels of text complexity will encounter overlapping complexities in the texts they read, and you'll recruit them to tackle those complexities together, trying out the strategies you teach and even creating their own. You will layer in additional support for partnerships by first channeling them into duplicate copies of high-interest nonfiction texts.

In Bend II, students take on independent inquiry projects on self-selected topics, and it is likely that no two students in your class will be researching the same topic. However, classes that piloted this unit found that students still benefited from being grouped together with a team of fellow researchers studying similar topics. This takes a bit of behind-the-scenes engineering, but it will be worth it. You might channel students studying music into one group, grouping together students studying the Beatles, Taylor Swift, and brass instruments. Another group might study unexplained phenomena and be made up of kids researching life in outer space, the Loch Ness Monster, and Bigfoot. A third group might include kids studying war and battles, with researchers studying different wars across time. The research teams provide company, certainly, but they will also likely lead to deeper investigations as researchers synthesize information across similar topics.

Conducting Read–Alouds alongside the Unit

The read-aloud text we recommend for Bend I is *When Lunch Fights Back: Wickedly Clever Animal Defenses* by Rebecca Johnson. There's much to love about this book. Your students will be in awe of the text, from the sections about the amazing defenses exhibited by prey about to be eaten for lunch to the compelling photographs and references to video games. You will likely admire the book's hybrid structure, the emphasis on how scientists work, and the multitude of embedded complexities inside the text. This book is sure to become a favorite. During Bend II, we suggest you read aloud a similarly complex nonfiction text. *Alien Deep: Revealing the Mysterious Living World at the Bottom of the Ocean* by Bradley Hague is an engaging text about hydrothermal vents deep below the ocean surface and the scientists who have made it their life's work to explore them. This text, too, weaves between narrative and expository chunks, is filled with complex text features, and moves seamlessly between facts and big ideas. Although you can choose to substitute other texts, know that these books are deeply embedded in sessions across this unit and play a prominent role in the teacher's research project in Bend II.

In Bend II, we recommend you take on the inquiry topic *scientists at work*, and use sections from *When Lunch Fights Back*, as well as *Alien Deep*. In addition, we suggest a few engaging digital texts on scientists, and you'll find links to these in the online resources. You will likely want to supplement this text set by, perhaps, adding a copy of *Extreme Laboratories* by Ann Squire or a favorite from the Scientists in the Field series. Articles and video clips can also be added to round out your text set.

You will want to carve out a separate chunk of time each day, outside of reading workshop, for reading aloud sections of these read-aloud texts and other informational texts you select for your text set.

✋ ONLINE DIGITAL RESOURCES

A variety of resources to accompany this and the other Grade 5 Units of Study for Teaching Reading are available in the Online Resources, including charts and examples of student work shown throughout *Tackling Complexity*, as well as links to other electronic resources. Offering daily support for your teaching, these materials will help you provide a structured learning environment that fosters independence and self-direction.

To access and download all the digital resources for the Grade 5 Units of Study for Teaching Reading:

1. Go to **www.heinemann.com** and click the link in the upper right to log in. (If you do not have an account yet, you will need to create one.)

2. **Enter the following registration code** in the box to register your product: RUOS_Gr5

3. Under **My Online Resources**, click the link for the ***Grade 5 Reading Units of Study***.

4. The digital resources are available in the upper right; click a file name to download. (For any compressed ("ZIP") files, double-click the downloaded file to extract individual files to your hard drive.)

(You may keep copies of these resources on up to six of your own computers or devices. By downloading the files you acknowledge that they are for your individual or classroom use and that neither the resources nor the product code will be distributed or shared.)

◆ START WITH ASSESSMENT ◆

Dear Teachers,

Before you turn the page and begin the journey of this unit of study, we want to remind you that it is enormously helpful to establish some baseline data on what your kids can (and can't yet) do as readers of nonfiction texts. The world today is rapidly escalating expectations for nonfiction reading and chances are good that your children will need to get into high gear soon in order to meet the exciting (and potentially overwhelming) expectations for nonfiction readers. These global standards may, for instance, require fifth-graders to read a collection of nonfiction texts, noting the authors' different perspectives on a topic and thinking about the vested interests that may inform those perspectives. Add to that the fact that on standardized assessments, kids are being asked to take on incredibly ambitious work, work that we, as educators, are often unsure that we could do. It is easy, then, for students to feel demoralized, overwhelmed, and paralyzed by the tasks ahead.

To counter these feelings, and to help fifth-graders make progress along these lines, you and your colleagues need the tools to communicate your literacy goals and pathways to children and to support them as they progress along those trajectories. Your children need access to low-stakes assessments that allow them to think about the progress they are (and are not yet) making toward that important work. To support these goals, you'll want to give a performance assessment before you begin this unit. This work will give you and your students a crystal-clear path forward.

You'll see that the assessment asks children to read more than one text and to do some high-level comprehension work. Much of what they're being asked to do is work they won't have been taught to do yet, so don't be dismayed if it seems hard for them. The hope is that by the time of the post-assessment, this work will seem more within reach. But if it still seems ambitious, you can find some consolation in the fact that research suggests that checklists and rubrics are especially helpful if they are challenging for kids, establishing a horizon for them. We're quite sure this work will be challenging for your youngsters.

The texts will be too hard for kids who are working well below benchmark to read. You could, of course, develop your own easier assessment, inserting these questions into easier texts. Alternatively, you could read these passages aloud, while letting children follow along. Certainly you will learn nothing about children's abilities to do higher-level thinking if they can't read the text at all! Your running records will tell you the level of text complexity a child can handle, and this assessment is meant to measure higher-level comprehension skills. So while reading the passages aloud isn't a perfect solution, it's better than the other options.

In a world where people rarely agree on anything, there is unanimous agreement that the biggest problem with most classroom-based assessments is that too often, nothing is made of the data. Please, please, don't neglect to score this for or with your kids within a few short days as they need the feedback, and they need the rubrics and learning progressions to be in their hands.

Best of luck to you with the performance assessment—and the unit!

Thanks,

Katie and TCRWP Colleagues

(?) How I approach Nonfiction Text with the genre in mind?

The More You Know, the More You See

~~Cause & Effect~~

IN THIS SESSION, you'll teach students that readers approach nonfiction texts with their knowledge of genre in mind, knowing the things that are apt to be important.

GETTING READY

✔ Before this minilesson begins, ask students to select and bring a high-interest nonfiction book to read to the meeting area. Also remind students to bring their reading folders (containing reading logs and pens) to the meeting area for every session.

✔ Have a fiction chapter book ready to reference to review what is worth attending to in fiction texts (see Connection).

✔ Prepare a chart titled "Nonfiction Readers Know it Pays Off to Think About . . ." and be ready to add students' ideas to the chart (see Teaching and Mid-Workshop Teaching).

✔ Have copies of the level 5 "Lessons from the Deep" article ready to distribute to students and prepare sections to reference. Enlarge the fourth paragraph on chart paper for students to mark up with a marker or project it using a document camera (see Teaching and Active Engagement).

✔ Leave flag notes at tables for students to mark up pages they want to share (see Link).

✔ Print a copy of the Informational Reading Learning Progression to carry with you across the unit (see Conferring and Small-Group Work and Share).

✔ Make sure students have new reading logs in their reading folders and that they are continuing to log their reading (see Link and Share).

T HIS SESSION OPENS YOUR UNIT on reading high-interest nonfiction texts with increasing complexity. Like most sessions that open a unit, it is broad, encompassing, invitational. You attempt to give students the big picture of what they'll be learning over the next stretch of time. You say to your students, "Note how you approach fiction texts, already knowing so much about what is worth seeing, noticing, in those texts." Then you add, "Skilled readers of nonfiction approach their texts similarly, equally aware of what merits attention." Then you proceed to remind students of all they have learned in previous years about reading with an awareness of text structure and of main idea. Quickly, you turn the reins over to the students and ask them to practice approaching nonfiction texts in the same way, drawing on all that knowledge to form expectations for those texts. Coming to texts with a nuanced understanding of genre moves students toward fifth-grade expectations for "Orienting" on the Informational Reading Learning Progression.

This instruction, then, is what one could call "high up the food chain." You aren't teaching them to eat protein—you are teaching them to maintain a balanced diet. That is, your instruction organizes and overviews a lot of more specific tips. Assuming that your students have received that prior instruction, given that this is fifth grade, the level of your teaching is apt to work. You'll be teaching students to transfer. If, however, your students have not been taught to read with an awareness of text structure or to read for the main idea, we suggest you support this lesson by borrowing a few lessons from previous grades.

The minilesson ends with those all-important words: *off you go*. The work that follows is the truly important part of today, and you will need to do some preparation for that work. Read the Welcome to the Unit to learn about the ways in which you can provision students' reading during this unit.

The More You Know, the More You See

CONNECTION

Launch this unit by suggesting it extends the previous one. Skilled readers see more in a text because they know what is worth noting, and that is true for nonfiction as well as fiction texts.

"Readers, gather close," I said. "Earlier this year, I told you the story about my friend Mary who knows nothing about baseball, and she went to her first pro baseball game ever—you remember . . ."

The students chimed in. "She thought it was boring. She thought, 'Nothing happens' 'cause no one was scoring!"

I nodded. "And you remember that part way into the game, her son Jack turned to her and said, 'This is so exciting I can't stand it!' and Mary looked at him with that 'Huh?' look on her face. Then he jabbered on about all that he was noticing: the pitcher's fastball and the heads-up plays by the shortstop and ways players were stealing bases. Listening to him, Mary realized that Jack was noticing so much more than she was about the game, and he was doing that because he knows more about it. To an expert, things others might take as inconsequential all of a sudden become important.

"Listening to Jack, Mary realized that for a baseball expert, everything matters.

"We talked about Mary and Jack's experience at the baseball game way back at the start of this year when you were getting ready to begin your year of reading fiction. Since then, you all worked hard at becoming more expert as readers of fiction. As a result, I bet I could pick up any chapter book in our library, and if I asked, before I started to read it aloud, 'What should we be looking for?' you'd already have a fistful of ideas that you knew would pay off to study."

Accentuate your claim that your students know what is worth attending to in fiction by creating a miniature exercise in which they can display their prowess with this.

"Let's try and see if that's true." I reached for a fiction book—any book—and held it up. The kids and I read the title. Then I said, "You know this is a fiction chapter book. Quick, with your partner, list five things you would be attending to if we were to start reading this book. Go!" I silently modeled counting out ideas on my hand to signal to students that they should collect their information in that same way.

Notice that I recall earlier teaching, using the same terminology used in Unit 1. You'll want to be consistent and repetitive in the terms you use, so that the language and the ideas they represent become a common vocabulary in your classroom.

Once children read your signals and start talking with each other, you'll probably want to shift into listening more so as to hear students as they talk. It's likely your students will suggest that they know it pays off to get to know characters, to notice the problems characters face, and to remain alert to how those problems are resolved and to how characters change.

I signaled for students to turn back around, and launched immediately into connecting the work students do with fiction texts to the work I wanted them to do with nonfiction texts. "Readers, you already approach fiction texts as experts, carrying with you tons of ideas for the kind of thinking work that will pay off. That's a big deal because as Mary found out, the more you know, the more you will see.

"Here's the thing." I paused dramatically and leaned in close. "It's no different for nonfiction."

❖ Name the teaching point.

"Today I want to teach you that readers don't see with their eyes alone, but with their minds. Reading *any* text well requires you to approach that text, knowing things that are apt to be important. That knowledge comes from knowing about the genre (in this case, nonfiction)."

TEACHING

Use an article to demonstrate that readers approach nonfiction with a short list of things that are apt to be important, reading with extra alertness because of that short list.

"When I asked you to brainstorm what matters in a fiction text, you rattled off an armload of things. I'm expecting you can do the same for nonfiction; let's try." I held up the article, "An Animal Like No Other," and said, "This will be one of our read-aloud texts for this unit. Let's get ready to read it. What kinds of things will we pay attention to in this text? And what *won't* we focus on? Turn and talk."

After just a moment, I continued, "So let's practice. Before we begin reading, let's brainstorm the kinds of things that you'll be looking for. Mary's son, Jack, knew things that happen in a baseball game that are worth paying attention to because they matter—what would you think might be worth paying attention to in this article?"

I asked the kids to brainstorm and I listened in. Then I convened the class. "I agree with you. We definitely want to notice the main ideas that the author seems to be putting forward. The author might well come straight out and say those ideas, and might even repeat them. What else will you want to notice?"

Children pitched out some more ideas and soon we had a short list.

It is unlikely that your students will quickly produce a tidy list containing all of the items on this list. As your students offer suggestions, be prepared to listen for the salient points, and if students do not offer those up themselves, you may wish to offer your own suggestions to round out this chart.

Nonfiction Readers
Know it Pays Off to
Think About...

• Main ideas and their supports

• Text structure
(notice signal words that suggest structure)

• Parts of the text and how they fit together

"Let's read the first part of 'Lessons from the Deep' together." I quickly distributed copies to students. "And as we do, be on the lookout for these things that we know it pays off to think about. When we come across one, and we probably will quickly, pop one finger up, signaling a piece of information you want to talk about."

I read aloud just the title and the first paragraph:

> "'Lessons of the Deep'
>
> "Of all the strange and wonderful creatures that live in the ocean, one unique creature stands out above the rest. It is the amazing octopus. There are over 300 different types of octopus, and they can be found in every ocean in the world."

I popped a finger up in the air and noticed a few students did the same.

After pausing, draw students' attention to cues you noted that helped you notice main ideas and their supports.

"Well, I haven't heard any clues about text structure yet, have you? I'm wondering about the main idea, though. I don't know about you, but I'm thinking the main idea of this chunk might be about the octopus. Wait, wait, wait . . . I can't just say *the octopus*; I have to say what it's teaching about the octopus here." I looked carefully at the text.

"So, I'm thinking a main idea here is that the octopus is an unusual creature, because the author says the octopus is a 'unique creature' right at the start of the paragraph, in a pop-out sentence. And the author uses other specific words that support the idea that the octopus is truly unique: *strange*, *amazing*, and *found in every ocean*." I underlined each word or phrase.

"I know there are lots of things that are important for nonfiction readers to think about," I said, and I glanced back up at our chart. "Let me think, too, about the parts of the text and how they fit together. If the title is one part, I have to look at whether this first paragraph—and part—fits with it. The title is 'Lessons from the Deep,' and then most everything in that first paragraph supports the fact that the octopus is unique, like no other. I'm not seeing a connection now. Let's see what we notice as we keep reading."

Step back to recall what you've done in ways that are transferrable to another text and another day.

"Readers, did you notice that as we started reading, we kept in mind the things that we know are important to think about when reading nonfiction? This helped us to see more in the text and to make sure things didn't pass by us."

The work you are doing here is supporting students in moving from fourth- to fifth-grade work on the "Orienting" strand of the Informational Reading Learning Progression. You are teaching students that readers carry their knowledge of genre with them to each new text they read, and they allow that knowledge of genre to shape their expectations for how the text will go and what they will learn.

Your think-aloud here supports students in differentiating between main topics and main ideas in a text. A student who describes the main topic of this part might say "the octopus," using a word or short phrase to describe what the selection is about. The main idea of this section could be "The octopus is a unique creature," capturing the point the writer is making about the topic.

Listen to A4

Channel students to listen alertly as you continue reading the text, then to engage in partner conversation about the things it pays off for nonfiction readers to think about.

"Let's read on this way, keeping in mind the things that pay off to think about when reading nonfiction." I tapped the list of things nonfiction readers know to attend to, and asked students to signal if something else came up in the text that merited attention. To make best use of the limited time in a minilesson, I jumped ahead to the fourth paragraph and began reading.

> One of the most striking characteristics of the octopus is the wide array of techniques it uses to avoid or thwart its attackers. When an octopus wants to move quickly to escape a predator, it can expel water from its siphon and push itself backwards. This is called jet propulsion. Using this technique, octopuses can travel many miles. An octopus can also protect itself by squirting ink at a predator, obscuring its view and causing it to lose its sense of smell temporarily. This makes the fleeing octopus difficult to track for the predator. Using a network of pigment cells and specialized muscles in its skin, the octopus can also instantaneously match the colors, patterns, and even textures of its surroundings.

"I see fingers popping up everywhere. Tell each other what you are noticing."

Listening to the students, I noted that nearly all had noticed a main idea being taught, while far fewer noticed that the section was written to show cause and effect. Picking up my marker, I said, "I heard a number of you wondering if this showed causes and effects. The octopus was being attacked, which caused lots of other things to happen. Remember that a cause is *why* something happens and an effect is *what* happens as a result.

"Will all of you look at this chunk again, and this time, see if you agree with the kids who suggested this is a cause-and-effect text? On your own copies of this article, mark the parts that tell about a cause, if there is one, and that tell about how that cause initiates a lot of effects, a lot of things that happen as a result."

As partners jumped into action, I passed my marker to two nearby readers, and soon they were marking up the enlarged paragraph on my chart paper. A moment later, it looked like this:

> One of the most striking characteristics of the octopus is the wide array of techniques it uses to (avoid) (or thwart) its attackers. (When an octopus wants to move quickly to escape) a predator, it can expel water from its siphon and push itself backwards. This is called jet propulsion. Using this technique, octopuses can travel many miles. An octopus (can also protect itself) by squirting ink at a predator, (obscuring) its view and causing it to lose its sense of smell temporarily. (This makes the fleeing octopus difficult to track) for the predator. Using a network of pigment cells and specialized muscles in its skin, the octopus (can also instantaneously match) the colors, patterns, and even textures of its surroundings.

cause *effects* *effect* *effect* *cause*

Notice that the section of text chosen for this active engagement is very short, yet presents a variety of possible challenges—a main idea that is taught explicitly using difficult language; unfamiliar, domain-specific vocabulary; a text structure signaled with less familiar transitions. I deliberately kept the chunk of text short and to the point to provide students with plenty of practice time during their independent reading.

Be sure you listen in as your readers talk. If they neglect to discuss text structure, as the students here did, then continuing on to discuss cause-and-effect text structures will make sense. However, you might find that students need support considering how parts of texts function together, in which case you might coach them to think about how the chunk of text they just read fits with the title and first paragraph.

Text Structure — — Cause / Effect

LINK

(handwritten margin left: Rdg Xpert)

Name what you've taught as a transferrable skill. Send students off to read, reminding them that great writers merit this kind of expert reading. Stir them up!

"Readers, you're ready to dive into your nonfiction books today, approaching them like the experts you are, carrying all the thinking work you already know how to do with you. Pull out the book you're starting with today." Students pulled out the high-interest nonfiction books they had selected just before the minilesson began.

(handwritten margin left: Make Plan)

"Right now, will you look over our 'Nonfiction Readers Know It Pays Off to Think About . . .' chart, and, with your partner, will you make a plan for your work today? What will you think about when you read nonfiction?" Quickly, students talked and generated plans with their partners.

"You'll notice there are no Post-it notes at your tables today—just some flags. For today, note things and plan to talk about them, but channel your time toward reading. Writing about reading can come later. You will, however, want to log the amount of reading you do today. Off you go!"

(handwritten: "Off you go to Rders Workshop ")

(handwritten: 10:35)

(handwritten: 13 min)

(handwritten top right: Tools for Rders Backpack)

You'll notice we are recommending that for the first several days of the unit students do not pause to write about their reading during their independent reading time. Instead, we suggest you provision students with flags they can use to mark key parts in their texts. While lifting the level of students' writing about nonfiction reading will be a thread across this unit, it's likely many of your students read nonfiction with a pencil constantly in hand, stopping to jot down every single fact they read. Your directions here help to break this habit, getting students used to reading large chunks of text before they stop and jot.

Launching the Unit

YOU'LL BE BUSY TODAY! You'll likely divide your time between helping students select books and helping them transfer everything they know about reading nonfiction from previous years over to this new unit of study.

Support readers in selecting texts within reach.

Presumably you will have already leveled the nonfiction texts in your classroom library. You may have done this using Fountas and Pinnell's leveling system for nonfiction texts, which is as good a system as any, or you may have relied on published Lexile levels. Know that most teachers find nonfiction more difficult to pin down by level than fiction, in part because prior knowledge plays such a big role in comprehension of a nonfiction text.

This doesn't mean that levels of nonfiction texts are inconsequential—they are not. If you encounter a child who is struggling with a too-hard text you will certainly need to channel that child to an easier text. As mentioned earlier, the child's comfort level with a text will vary depending on prior knowledge. A nonfiction book on excavating dinosaur fossils will be accessible to a reader steeped in that topic but not to a similar reader whose knowledge on the topic is thin. Then, too, the photographs and other text features can make the text look more accessible than it is. Because of this, matching readers to nonfiction books is often more complicated than matching readers to fiction books.

Today your students will choose texts that are within reach for them, and the way in which you have organized the classroom library will help. For example, you may decide to cluster information books that address the same topics. You can remind students that it pays off to read the easiest book on a topic first to build background knowledge before tackling trickier books on the same subject. These easier texts tend to more explicitly teach the concepts and vocabulary students need to know to access more complex texts.

Text and topic introductions will also channel students toward texts. Your crafty salesmanship as you describe the complexities of desert life and the staggering number of weeks cacti can go without water can convince any reader to give a set of texts on life in the desert a try. Carefully designed text introductions can also signal readers to pay attention to major concepts that will stretch across a set of texts.

Same-book partnerships will be incredibly supportive for your less experienced readers, and they simply require you to group paired copies of texts together in the library. Then, two readers can move through the same book in sync with each other. These readers can be encouraged to pause along the way and discuss their thinking, just as you paused and prompted students to think and talk while reading "Lessons from the Deep."

MID-WORKSHOP TEACHING
Reminding Readers to See More

Standing in the middle of the room, I said, "Readers, can I have your eyes and ears? Will you take a minute to look over the chart we created during our minilesson and, with your partner, name out the kinds of thinking work you're already doing as you read? Talk a bit about how that thinking work is helping you.

"Remember that readers are constantly working to outgrow themselves. That means they not only do the thinking work that's easy for them, they *also* push themselves to do work that's not as automatic. Look back at the chart, and set a quick goal for what you'll pay particular attention to as you keep reading. Then, get right back into your books!"

Rally students to the work of this new unit.

During your minilesson, you reminded students of previous learning you expected them to transfer over, and now is your chance to get this new unit off the ground. Like a hummingbird, you'll flutter from table to table, rallying everyone to the work of this new unit. As you did in the first unit of study, use table compliments, quick small groups, and voiceovers to highlight behaviors you hope all readers will emulate. For example, in the next session you'll teach more about how to preview complex nonfiction texts, but today you could be on the lookout for children who linger on the front or back covers of a book or on the table of contents. Name what the child is doing and compliment the behavior loudly enough for students nearby to hear. "I love how you're setting up expectations for how this text will go by looking closely at the table of contents. That gives you a sense of what the book will teach and how the book might teach it. Keep it up!"

Draw on the Informational Reading Learning Progression.

Throughout this unit, and all of your units that support nonfiction reading, you'll want to keep a copy of the Informational Reading Learning Progression on hand as you observe readers and begin making plans for them.

Today, at the start of your nonfiction work, you'll probably be most interested in students' literal comprehension. As you move around the room conferring, ask children to read bits of texts aloud to you. Listen with the "Fluency" strand of the progression in hand, noting whether their fluency fits the descriptions for fifth-grade work. For example, are students already using their voice to add meaning to the texts they are reading? Since the progression details end-of-grade goals, and since this is likely your first nonfiction reading unit of the year, expect to see students demonstrate the fourth-grade expectations. If not, give students a quick tip and coach them to improve their fluency right then and there.

Or, you might use the progression to study students' work monitoring for sense. Pull up next to a student reading a particularly dense page, and ask the student to talk a bit about what he is reading. Listen, learning progression in hand, to see if the reader talks about different parts of the page or anticipates that unexplained parts will be elaborated on later. If you notice a reader talking about parts of the text in isolation, use the fourth-grade expectations for "Monitoring for Sense" on the learning progression to suggest a next step. You might say, "When you read a new part, you have to ask, 'How does that part fit with my overall picture of the topic?'"

Rallying Students to Increase Their Reading Volume

Convene students in the meeting area, rallying partners to summarize the information they read today.

"Readers, we don't usually gather for share sessions at the end of our reading workshop, but we're starting a new unit, so let's come together today." Once students had gathered on the rug, I said, "Before we talk about anything else, will you get ready to summarize for your partner what the text you read today taught you, to teach your partner just the important points of what you read?

"Count out your main ideas on your fingers. Think, 'First the text taught . . . and then it taught . . .' Look back in the book to help you. Turn and teach." I listened in to students' summaries, noting where students' responses fell on the "Main Idea(s) and Supporting Details/Summary" strand of the Informational Reading Learning Progression. I wanted to determine to what extent they recalled teaching from fourth grade.

Coach readers to study, then to increase their volume of reading.

"Readers, remember that in your first unit, you paid attention to your volume, your sheer amount of reading, and you set goals to increase your volume? I told you about the research that shows that in forty minutes of nose-to-book reading time, kids should be reading about thirty pages. Take a minute to study your log from today. Did you read close to thirty pages in your forty minutes of reading?" I paused for a moment as students studied their data. "Tell your partner what your research revealed."

Scores of "Eeek! I was nowhere close to that!" rang out across the meeting area. I glanced quickly at pages logged: 8, 25, 12, 14, 23, 7.

"Sometimes when we read nonfiction, our pace slows, and it feels like we're inching our way through a book. That is not okay. You might not make it to three quarters of a page per minute, but you can certainly make it to half a page per minute. You'll have to push yourself to keep reading down the page, not pausing after every tiny fact, so you can hold onto the important ideas you're reading about. Try this as you're reading tonight and whenever you read nonfiction from now on."

INCREASING YOUR READING VOLUME

Readers, today in school you reflected on the volume of reading you could do in 40 minutes. Researchers suggest you should read three quarters of a page a minute. Many of you realized that you weren't close to reading at that rate.

For tonight, you have a choice. You could take home your nonfiction book to read. Or you could do some reading about one of your favorite nonfiction topics. You might read sports scores in the newspaper or online or do some research for a fantasy football team. Maybe you want to research a special product you want to buy on the Consumer Reports website. Try to read a variety of nonfiction texts on that topic—some longer, some shorter, some in one format, some in another.

Try to increase your reading pace without decreasing your comprehension too much. Aim to read three quarters of a page a minute. Notice how it feels to push yourself a bit. Are you still able to attend to the content?

Keep track of your reading, and devote at least 40 minutes (and probably much more) time to it.

How can I use text features & knowledge of the topic to help w/ comprehension?

Orienting to More Complex Texts

IN THIS SESSION, you'll teach students that readers orient themselves to complex nonfiction texts and then hold their initial ideas loosely as they read forward, remaining open to revision as they encounter new information.

GETTING READY

✔ Choose a complex nonfiction text to demonstrate how you orient yourself to a text. We recommend *When Lunch Fights Back: Wickedly Clever Animal Defenses* by Rebecca L. Johnson, which is woven throughout lessons in this bend and the next (see Teaching and Active Engagement).

✔ Be sure students have a new high-interest nonfiction text with them to orient themselves and use to practice reading fluently (see Link and Share).

✔ Encourage students to read examples of a speech, such as Malala Yousafzai's speech to the United Nations, President Barack Obama's "You Make Your Own Future" speech, or Lou Gehrig's farewell speech. Links to these speeches are available on the online resources or you may choose your own (see Homework). 👆

✔ Give each student a copy of the "Fluency" strand of the Informational Reading Learning Progression for grades 4 and 5 (see Homework). 👆

I N THE PREVIOUS SESSION, you reminded students to draw on all they know as they approach nonfiction, and today you hone in more on the topic of text orientation and teach students ways to prepare themselves for the new demands that the texts they read this year are apt to pose. Above all, you teach kids that when reading complex nonfiction, they need to anticipate that the main ideas and dominant structure may not be immediately evident. Often, complex nonfiction texts begin with a long lead that is slightly tangential to the main work of the text, and readers will frequently find themselves a bit mystified for a while, unclear how all the parts will fit together.

When students were younger, teachers taught them that if they started reading a text and it made no sense to them, they should abandon it as too hard. Now you revise that message. "Often texts are deliberately written to puzzle you, to make you curious. You'll need to tolerate some ambiguity, to postpone closure."

Of course, you also need students to yearn for clarity and to keep expectations in mind that they will soon figure out the main ideas the text is forwarding and the primary text structures the text relies upon. But even once they feel in command of a text, it is apt to morph midway, and readers need to be agile, able to adjust in response to whatever new cues the text puts forward. This is new work expected of your fifth-graders as they orient themselves to texts and anticipate what is to come. Look to the fifth-grade expectations in the "Orienting" strand of the Informational Reading Learning Progression to see how expectations for orienting to texts grow over time.

That agility and responsiveness to text cues won't be easy for students to develop and will only come with practice. So you can talk about it now, but you can't expect that naming the importance of this will mean that all of a sudden kids will be able to adjust their tone, inflection, and interpretations on the run as they digest complex text. To start giving them practice doing this, the share of this session invites kids to work for a while to read and reread just a few sentences from *When Lunch Fights Back* and from nonfiction books chosen by the kids themselves. The homework assignment continues the emphasis on reading complex texts (even complex sentences) with fluency. You invite students to read aloud a portion of a famous speech multiple times, rereading it until they can perform it well. Research shows that doing this work transfers, affecting kids' work not only with the one text but with other texts as well. Students will work to make each new performance better than the last by self-assessing their work against the "Fluency" strand and then trying, right then and there, to lift the level of their work.

"The agility and responsiveness to text cues won't be easy for students to develop and will only come with practice."

Note that this session highlights a particular book: *When Lunch Fights Back: Wickedly Clever Animal Defenses* by Rebecca L. Johnson. This book will comb through these sessions, and it is also a terrific book for students to read themselves. We hope you get yourself a copy and enjoy it. If you decide to substitute a different book, however, choose one that is organized into chapters with misleading headings and that includes long chunks of text containing multiple main ideas. It will also help if the book you select to showcase teaches main ideas both explicitly and implicitly, incorporates multiple text structures, and can be used for your teacher inquiry project in Bend II.

Orienting to More Complex Texts

CONNECTION

Tell students a story about how you wrote thank-you notes to their previous teachers. Highlight specific strategies students transferred over from fourth grade.

When you read NF you must consider

"Readers, I just couldn't resist writing long thank-you letters to all of your fourth-grade teachers last night. You know why? Because they taught you so well! Yesterday, I actually heard some of you talk about how you get ready to read nonfiction by looking over the text and thinking about the parts of it, about the way it seems to be structured. You weren't born knowing that—it had to come from your last year's teachers.

"The other thing I heard yesterday was that you thought about whether the text you were reading is structured as a problem-solution text or a compare-and-contrast text—in fact, you had a whole list of options. I even think you knew to set yourself up differently based on the text's structure. I mean: Holy moly!

"That's why I had to write your teachers from last year. Their great teaching set us to reach new heights this year."

Recruit students to join in a study of what makes nonfiction texts complex. Use a video game analogy to connect this challenging work to a familiar context.

Video game

"So, are you ready to rise to new heights? I want to make a proposal for a project we could work on together over the next few weeks. I have been thinking that maybe you'd be game to do a giant investigation with me into how nonfiction texts get harder and harder, more and more complex, *and* into how your reading needs to change as texts get harder. You see, I have a feeling that getting better as a nonfiction reader is a bit like getting better at video games. You need to be able to master the higher levels—and those higher levels have harder challenges and require different strategies.

"I think what you will find is that when you read *complex* nonfiction, every part of the reading process is a little different than it is when you read simple straightforward texts—starting even with the way you orient yourself to the text."

Across this unit and the series, we provide students with reminders of previous reading instruction. If your students are new to the Units of Study in Reading, you will want to modify these connections to fit their experiences.

Notice that you are bringing kids in on the focus of a bend of teaching. It's helpful for kids to get the main drift of instruction so they can help to construct a coherent message from all the instruction they receive.

Name your teaching point.

"Readers, today I want to teach you that when readers orient themselves to *complex* nonfiction texts, they use text features and their knowledge of the topic to help. But as you begin reading, you also need to live in the gray area for a while, to tolerate confusion, knowing the focus of the text may be revealed slowly."

TEACHING

Explain what will be challenging about this new work, suggesting that readers will need to live in a gray area, postponing closure as they read on in a text.

"I want to tell you, readers, that this work won't be easy. Remember those penguin texts you read in third grade? Remember how you could just *glance* at the table of contents and know *exactly* what the text was teaching you?" I continued, "You've heard that saying: 'things are rarely black and white'?" The kids nodded. "Well, when people say that, they usually mean that things are rarely clear. They're not usually either this way, black, or that way, white. That's how those penguin texts were—they were black and white (and I'm not talking about penguin colors!).

"The books you're reading now are not usually going to have crystal clear tables of contents that spell out what you will find in each chapter. And the introductory paragraphs in these books might not spell out the subtopics to follow. The complex texts you will read will often require you to live in a gray area where things aren't totally clear. This means you'll have to postpone closure, to do some hard work before you can form definite ideas about your texts. Are you up for it?"

Demonstrate how you preview the overall text, to generate a tentative hypothesis for how the text will go. Highlight that the topic is not always immediately obvious.

I projected the cover of *When Lunch Fights Back: Wickedly Clever Animal Defenses*, the nonfiction book that I planned on returning to often throughout the unit. "Let's figure out how this text seems to go." I read the title. "I don't know about you, but my lunch has never fought back (and, man, am I glad about that!). And really, I don't understand what the title means. That often happens when reading more complex nonfiction texts. Help me with this," and I rallied the kids to reread it with me: *When Lunch Fights Back: Wickedly Clever Animal Defenses*.

"We're lucky in this instance, however, because there is a subtitle. That second part—*Wickedly Clever Animal Defenses*—seems to suggest that this book *might* teach how animals protect themselves from predators. That could relate to the title. Maybe the animals are lunch, so this is about when the animals, the lunch, fight against becoming lunch. Does that make sense?" Students nodded.

The language you use here is intentionally tentative. It's important to convey that at the start of nonfiction texts, your goal is generate initial ideas about what the text is teaching, knowing you will learn more and possibly revise your thinking as you read on. Today's brief mid-workshop teaching point also supports students in developing this mindset, so you'll want to be sure to fit it in.

For this minilesson, it's important that the table of contents of your demonstration text has confusing or creative titles and sections of text that allow readers to revise their understandings as they read. The text we recommend now will resurface in Bend II to play a prominent role in the teacher's research project, so you may want to get hold of it rather than choosing a substitute text.

"In addition to the title and the cover, it can help to read the blurb on the back to piece together the book's topic and anticipate some of the sections." I projected the blurb and read it aloud.

"So it definitely seems like this book will teach about animal defenses, and I'm thinking it will teach about the *best* animal defenses since it says that *some* animals are good but '*these* animals are amazing.' I'm not certain yet who the animals are defending themselves from—is the 'Watch out!' a warning for us or for other predators?'"

Demonstrate a second way to orient yourself to a complex text, highlighting that a table of contents can be confusing (or nonexistent). Support muddling through ambiguity.

"Let's see if we can use what we know about the topic, animal defenses, and the blurb to predict the sections this book will have," I said. I gave students time to think, and meanwhile did the same, silently ticking possible sections off on my fingers. After a moment or two, I continued. "I'm expecting sections on different ways animals defend themselves: from poison, shooting blood, popping out bones. I'm also expecting a section on who animals are defending themselves from, aren't you?"

I flipped to the table of contents, displaying an enlarged copy on the document camera. "Let's see if the sections we predicted are in the table of contents or if we need to revise what we were thinking."

I read the table of contents aloud to students. "Ooh, these chapter titles are tricky too! Remember when the chapter titles used to tell us clearly what each section would be about? I don't think these do that, do they? I mean, Chapter 1 is clear: 'The Challenge of Survival.' That section might teach how difficult it is for animals to survive, about all the problems they face." I looked up at students, puzzled. "But the rest of these . . . : 'Slip-Sliming Away'? 'Concealed Weapons'? 'Toxic Bubbles'? What could the author be teaching here?"

I left time for students to think, and then continued. "Maybe they're about the different ways animals defend themselves, and they could teach all the solutions to the problems animals face. The 'Slip-Sliming Away' chapter could teach about how one animal uses slime to slip away from its prey, for example. So the book could give a problem first, and then all kinds of defenses that are solutions could come next."

Step back to recall what you have just done in ways that are transferable to another text and another day.

"Readers, do you see how even before we read our text together, we spent time orienting ourselves to the text? It is the same work as you did last year when you read nonfiction, and the year before, only the texts are becoming more complex (and more confusing). This means that the orienting you'll need to do this year won't be as straightforward as the orienting you did in the past. Since your texts are getting more complex—with titles and headings that aren't as clear—you'll need to tolerate ambiguity and to develop more tentative, open-to-revision ideas."

Note that in this teaching portion of the mini-lesson, you demonstrate how to orient yourself to a complex text. Your demonstration, however, is far from a performance in which kids are idle. Instead, you recruit kids to do this work alongside you, shifting often so that you are one step ahead of them to show how you'd do the work.

ACTIVE ENGAGEMENT

Channel partners to preview a chapter together to orient themselves to it. Help them revise hypotheses as needed as they begin reading, based on clues in the structure and content of the text.

"Now it's your turn." I asked students to look at pages 4 and 5, and I projected the pages from the text so students could see the author's use of color. "Will you carry those ideas with you as you and your partner get started previewing this chapter? You'll have to orient yourself to this section, just like we oriented ourselves to the whole book, looking at text features and the topic to get a sense of what this chapter might teach before you start reading." Partners immediately got to work previewing—and not yet reading—the text.

Looking at the barrage of text features on this first page, students in one way or another voiced "Huh?" Many conversations centered around the dramatic photo on page 4. I offered a tip. "This is a complex text. When you read complex texts, you should expect to think, 'Huh?' and 'Could this be about . . . ?' and to look at more text before settling anything. Keep questions in mind. Take in all the features on the page—the title, the illustration and pictures, the bold font—and think, 'What does this *whole* part seem to be about?' Tell your partner!"

Working with individuals, I asked, "What is going on with that line in yellow: 'The prey, of course, is you'?" I reread the line. "'The prey, of course, is *you*.' What does this part seem to be about? Tell your partner! Look at the picture and caption on page 5, too," I coached over.

Using the document camera, I zoomed in on page 4. "After you preview, dive in! Read a bit of the text with your partner. As you begin reading, work to figure out the focus, but be willing to live in that gray area for a while."

The room erupted into conversation.

I pulled up close to a couple of partnerships—kids I knew could use more support—and with great excitement, said, "Just listen. It's so cool," and then I read a bit of the text aloud to that huddle of listeners.

Introduction: The Challenge of Survival

No one said living on planet Xenon would be easy. Hungry aliens are everywhere. A new group just slithered into view. The aliens are well-armed with lasers and a contraption that shoots out nets for capturing prey.

The prey, of course, is you.

The active engagement is meant to be assisted practice, not a time for you to hand the reins completely over to your students. Whether they are reading, jotting, or thinking, be sure to voice-over to the class with coaching prompts and kneel down to coach into the work of individuals and partnerships.

INTRODUCTION
THE CHALLENGE OF SURVIVAL

No one said living on planet Xenon would be easy. Hungry aliens are everywhere. A new group just slithered into view. The aliens are well-armed with lasers and a contraption that shoots out nets for capturing prey.

THE PREY, OF COURSE, IS YOU.

You should stop here, with students on the edge of their seats, solidly in the gray area and full of misconceptions. Don't worry. You'll return to the text in read-aloud and in upcoming lessons, so students will have time to revise their current ideas about the planet Xenon.

LINK

Name what you've taught as a transferrable skill. Channel students to preview their texts in the same way and then to dive into reading with their tentative ideas in mind.

"Readers, it's time for you to get started reading the texts *you* brought with you. Can you pull out your books? Sitting right here, get started orienting yourself to your own texts. Just looking at the front and back covers, see if you can anticipate how this book will go. Think about what the author might teach you and how the author might teach. Try to name out the sections.

"Remember to orient yourself to the inside of the text too, and as you do so, expect that this text will be complex. You might ask yourself, 'Do the chapters in the table of contents help, or are they misleading?' You'll likely be in a gray area, and, don't just tolerate that confusion, celebrate it!"

After students worked for a bit, I said, "Partners, share what you found with each other. What initial ideas do you have for how your text might go?"

The children talked and I listened, then I said, "Readers, remember your first ideas are drafts. They'll keep you in that gray area. Hold them loosely as you begin orienting yourself to the first part of your text and then reading, and be ready to revise them. Off you go!"

As students turn and talk about their initial ideas, listen for them to support their thinking with specific evidence. If your students discuss how they anticipate the text will go without grounding their discussions in textual evidence, you might voice-over to the class, saying, "What in the text made you think that? Discuss the specific parts in the text that led you to your idea."

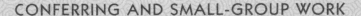

Helping Readers Construct Meaning Out of the Many Parts of Their Text

THE TEXTS STUDENTS ARE HOLDING are becoming increasingly complex, and the text features that draw readers in—the infographics and startling images, the popped-out facts and catchy subheadings—sometimes present major challenges to some readers. That is, while some students seem to seamlessly integrate the print on the page and the text features, other readers seem to view each part of the page in isolation. You'll notice this because when these readers talk to you or with partners, they may talk about a text box, recalling its content, but when you ask how that information relates to the main thrust of the text, they seem caught off-guard by the question.

You may decide to take ten minutes or so of the reading workshop and work with a small group of readers who could profit from instruction that aims to help them synthesize across text features. You might provide these youngsters with a text to read that contains lots of confusing, even contradictory text features. A later chapter in *When Lunch Fights Back* might be an option.

"Readers," you may say after you have convened the small group. "I want to let you in on a secret. When you read this text, it will probably be somewhat confusing. But here's the thing: the sections that are confusing to you are almost surely confusing to any reader who picks up that book because they are *meant* to be confusing.

"One of the complicated things is that there will sometimes be lots of text features, and these might not at first seem to go together. It is as if you have a puzzle piece that doesn't yet fit into the puzzle you've constructed, and so you put that tricky puzzle piece to the side, and keep going. As you read on, you think, '*Now* does that piece fit? *Now*?' Sometimes, it will take many pages before the puzzling piece clicks into place and you understand how the features fit with the text.

"Try reading this text, seeing if you can put the text features together with the text." As students get to work, you will want to move quickly around the circle, coaching them one-on-one as they try the work. "Does this fit with the main text on the page? Or could it fit with other text features?"

After a few minutes, you'll want to remind the group members that they could do this work anytime they read. "Readers, remember that authors embed confusing parts intentionally. When you encounter a part like this, it's wise to first ask, 'Is this a place where I need to reread, or is this an intentionally confusing part?' Then, you'll want to think, 'How might this fit into the rest of the text?'"

MID-WORKSHOP TEACHING **Revising Your Expectations Based on How the Text Is Unfolding**

"Readers, I need your attention. Right now, will you recall what you anticipated your book would be about at the start of reading today?" I paused while students did this.

"Here's my question: were your expectations for how the text would go correct? Or, have your expectations changed as you've read on? Talk with your partner about whether or not your book has met your expectations and, if it hasn't, what signals led you to revise your thinking." I gave students a minute or two to talk before giving a tip.

"I'm asking you this because, with the texts you're reading now, it's likely you'll want to read with a pencil in hand, not a pen. Now, I'm joking, mostly, but I do mean you'll need to be prepared to regularly revise your expectations as you read, almost as if you had a pencil in hand and could erase and then rewrite your ideas. As your texts become increasingly complex, this revision work will become even more important."

Reading and Rereading to Understand the Author's Meaning

Teach students to make use of the conventions of written texts and the text itself to read fluently and make meaning.

Standing in the middle of the classroom, I called for students' attention. Then I said, "Readers, remember when you were in kindergarten and the sentences in your books went like this: 'I see the dog.'" I used my hands to imagine an enlarged version of that sentence, hanging in front of my face, and I spelled out the simple line of four words. "Remember how short those sentences were? But you know what? When you were five, those four-word sentences were hard for you to read. Today they're a piece of cake.

"But now the sentences in the books you are reading are *no piece of cake*, are they? Earlier today, we previewed the introduction to *When Lunch Fights Back*. Will you get that out and look at the sentences in the paragraph at the start of page 5?" Students pulled out the text, and as they did, I said, "Read those first two sentences to your partner."

The room filled with a hubbub and then I said, "Eyes back here." Once I had their attention, I said, "When you are reading complex nonfiction, there will be a lot of information tucked into sentences (you have to expect authors will use parentheses or dashes or commas, as I am doing, to tuck in that extra information), which can make sentences harder to read. But also, it is often hard to read a sentence correctly until you know the tone the author wants to convey. Sometimes, the texts will have a hyped-up feeling, and you don't know if it is meant to be serious or if it is a spoof. Sometimes you have to read a passage two or three times to grasp the meaning.

"Will you go back to those same sentences and try reading them in different ways until you think you have them right? And if you have time, go to your own books, too, and find tricky sentences and try reading *those* sentences aloud to each other too."

The kids worked at this for a while. "Readers, there's one more way your texts are becoming more complex to read. Sometimes it's tricky to determine how your reading should sound. What is the mood of a passage—is it scary, for example, or ironic? Become accustomed to sometimes needing a few tries, making sure the voice in your mind conveys the tone and meaning the author intends."

READING SPEECHES ALOUD FOR FLUENCY

Readers, continue to read nonfiction at home tonight. You'll do two kinds of reading. First, continue to read free-choice texts that relate to things that really interest you. That reading may come from books you carry between home and school or from texts you find on your own.

The second kind of reading you'll do tonight is a speech. Read one of these three speeches: Malala Yousafzai's speech to the United Nations, President Barack Obama's "You Make Your Own Future" speech, or Lou Gehrig's farewell speech. These are some of the most famous speeches ever. Read them aloud. Read them many times until you read them really well (even if you only have time to do this for the start of the speech).

Use the "Fluency" strand of the Informational Reading Learning Progression as you read. Try to lift the level of your fluency from one level to the next. After you have read the speech many times, try reading your own nonfiction text in the same ways.

In life, you don't usually read nonfiction aloud. But if you work on your reading aloud voice, you work on your internal reading voice. Your internal reading voice is a huge part of reading nonfiction well.

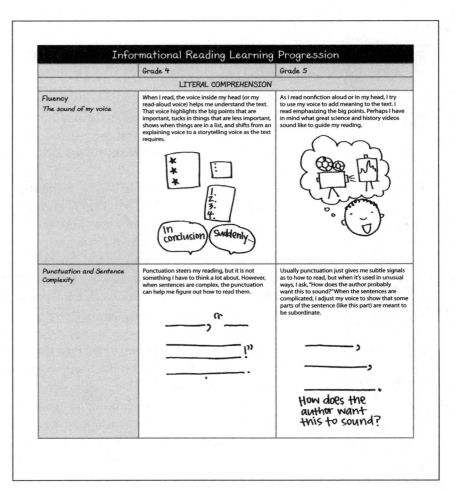

◆ A DAY FOR ASSESSMENT ◆

Dig into the rubric?

Dear Teachers,

We hope that today is the day for you to return your students' performance assessments to them and to recruit them to look with great earnestness at their work, noting ways in which they can improve their work, both on the spot and across the unit.

Too often, children come to you believing their abilities as readers are fixed and beyond their control. "I'm a bad reader," a child will say. "My brother is the good reader in my family." "I can get the words," a child will say, "but I can't get those questions." Through this assessment, you help challenge the notion that success in reading is hardwired into a child's DNA. Your goal will be to rally kids to take their own learning in hand, and to have the courage and strength to say, "I'm the kind of person who wants honest feedback so I can learn, learn, learn." To do this, you will make it crystal clear to kids that when they apply strategies, work hard, revise their first understandings, and get help, their reading will get visibly and dramatically better, right before their eyes.

In our Online Resources, we detail how this important day might go. You'll need to make decisions in conjunction with your colleagues, and we encourage you to draw on your students' experiences working with rubrics and learning progressions in Unit 1, and in previous years, as you plan. For now, let us share two pieces of advice. Don't postpone today—it is a big deal that kids get access to the rubrics and learning progressions now, noting areas of strength and setting goals worth working toward. Their work with these tools, early in the unit, will give shape and energy to their work moving forward. And secondly, don't let today swamp your schedule and drag on and on. Confine the important work of today into one period, and then return to the unit.

Thanks,

Katie and TCRWP Colleague

— copy chart p31
— Stnd dissect text then create subheadings to establish main idea

Uncovering What Makes a Main Idea Complex

(?) In what ways does the main idea become more complex? What are strategies to determine main idea?

TODAY'S SESSION launches a sequence of work that will thread through this unit, aiming to help students read increasingly complex nonfiction texts in ways that allow them to learn from those texts by grasping their main ideas. Your students' self-assessments of these skills with the "Main Idea(s) and Supporting Details/Summary" strand of the learning progression should help recruit their full attention for today's session, which is an inquiry. You will invite kids to inquire together about what makes complex nonfiction texts challenging, and to look, for today, specifically at the challenges that revolve around the work of determining the main idea. In the Share from the previous session, you contrasted the simple sentences kids read when they were in kindergarten with the complex sentences they are now asked to read, and again today, you will pop out the novel features of complex texts by juxtaposing the way simpler texts broadcast the main idea in titles and subtitles with the much subtler ways in which complex texts convey main ideas. You also help kids to discover the fact that the texts they are reading now will often have multiple main ideas.

It is important for you to know that this session is followed by more instruction that helps students determine main ideas as they read. You needn't worry that today's teaching isn't sufficient—look ahead and you'll see the next session addresses this topic again.

While you teach students to read, gleaning the main ideas from texts, they'll continue to read high-interest nonfiction texts during the reading workshop. Remember that you have asked them to not take notes—to simply read. Many students are accustomed to reading nonfiction with pen in hand and stopping every other sentence to record facts, definitions, dates. Your instruction aims to counter that. Your goal is for readers to read challenging texts with a laserlike focus on grasping the main ideas of those texts.

IN THIS SESSION, you'll engage students in an inquiry to determine how complex nonfiction gets challenging when it comes to determining the main idea.

GETTING READY

✔ Select an easier nonfiction book in which the main idea is clearly stated in the heading or the topic sentence. We use *Bats!* from *TIME for Kids*, but you may use any simple nonfiction book to demonstrate (see Connection, Teaching and Active Engagement).

✔ Prepare to read aloud page 8 from *When Lunch Fights Back* (see Teaching and Active Engagement).

✔ Have the inquiry question ready to post for students: *In what ways does main idea become more complex?* (see Teaching, Active Engagement, and Share).

✔ Begin a new anchor chart, "Ways Complex Nonfiction Gets Hard," and prepare to add to it (see Teaching and Active Engagement). 👏

✔ Provide Post-it notes for students to add to the anchor chart (see Link).

✔ Have the level 3 version of "The Amazing Octopus" ready to show the students (see Conferring and Small-Group Work). 👏

✔ Be sure students have their copy of the level 5 "Lessons from the Deep" text that you distributed in Session 1, so they can study how main idea is complex in this text (see Share). 👏

Uncovering What Makes a Main Idea Complex

CONNECTION

Share with students an example of how main ideas work in the simpler nonfiction books they used to read.

Once kids settled on the rug, I began. "Readers, do you know that feeling when you're playing a game—it might be a video game or a board game or a basketball game—and you win *too* easily? It's like you could win even if you were playing with your eyes closed." I acted that out, and giggles erupted.

"Well, that's exactly how determining the main idea would be in the books you used to read. Like, I bet if I opened up this book *Bats!* to any page, right away you'd know what the main idea is." I projected page 26.

"Well, what do you think? What's the main idea here?"

"It's right there," Marcus giggled, "Humans are the biggest threat to bats."

"How did you know that was the main idea?" I asked.

Kids piped in with a variety of comments: "It's there in the first sentence," "It's super obvious. The author put it in big, bold red letters."

Tell students that main idea works differently in higher-level nonfiction texts, and rally students to investigate this.

"I agree. Main idea *used to* work this way. The author would just *tell* you what the main idea was, right there, often in the first sentence!

"Nonfiction doesn't work that way anymore, at least not usually. The complex nonfiction texts you're reading now are just that; they're complex. And you can't just say, 'Sure, these texts are complex,' and keep reading the ways you used to. Instead, you'll have to figure out just what challenges the nonfiction texts in these harder levels pose, so that you can tackle them. It's serious work to figure out just what makes these texts complex, but I have confidence that you can handle it. You up for the challenge?"

There's no magic to the book we choose to model with here: Bats! *by the Editors of* Time for Kids. *We simply selected a book with one main idea on a page, and made sure the main idea was explicitly stated in a pop-out sentence. This page even has a bonus—the main idea is bold and red! Choose any text you have on hand that hits the kids over the head with the main idea.*

Name the question that will guide your inquiry.

"Today, let's explore one way nonfiction texts get complex: main idea. Let's study a text to figure out answers to the question: In what ways does main idea become more complex?"

TEACHING AND ACTIVE ENGAGEMENT

Engage students in a guided inquiry to determine different ways in which main idea becomes increasingly complex, coaching along the way to lift the level of the inquiry.

I posted the inquiry question for students on the white board.

"Yesterday, we noticed that orienting to a complex text such as *When Lunch Fights Back* was getting more challenging. Let's dive back into that same text today, this time, thinking: In what ways does main idea become more complex? Let's study page 8 together.

"Let's read through this text. I'll read it aloud, and will you follow along? And, as I read, will you ask yourself, 'In what ways does main idea become more complex?' You'll likely have to determine the main idea to answer this question. Mark up the text in ways that help you." I began reading.

> *The Science Behind the Story*
>
> *Hagfish aren't fish, despite their name. They are primitive eel-like animals that have been roaming the ocean for millions of years. Hagfish have no jaws and no backbones. What they do have, however, is slime. Douglas Fudge should know.*

"Whew, it already feels like main idea is becoming more complex here. This is so much tougher than *Bats!* As soon as you notice ways the main idea is getting trickier, jot them down."

> *Fudge is a biologist at the University of Guelph in Ontario, Canada. He has been studying hagfish and their slimy defenses since 1997. "The slime is amazingly effective at preventing hagfish from being eaten by fish predators, including sharks," said Fudge. Hagfish release slime the moment something tries to bite them—or even just bothers them. Fudge has been "slimed" many times while gently handling hagfish in his laboratory.*

Pause in the middle of reading, coaching students to notice the ways the author is teaching about the main idea and giving them time to discuss their thoughts about what they are seeing.

"What are you already noticing? In what ways does main idea become more complex?" Partners broke into conversation.

This minilesson is an inquiry lesson, so it follows a different structure. Inquiry minilessons don't have a teaching point that captures the entire lesson. Instead, they have a key question that guides the inquiry. You'll also note that the teaching and active engagement portions of the lesson are combined.

It's likely that many of your students are watching you, pencil down by their side, as you read through the first part of this text, while you notice numerous ways finding a main idea is becoming more complex. If this is the case, you will not want to read any further before pausing to think aloud. Your embedded think-aloud will remind students of the work they need to do, and it's likely you'll see students pick up their pencils after your gentle reminder. If you find your students are jotting furiously and not in need of this scaffold, simply remove it.

While partners talked, I voiced over, "It might help to compare how the main idea works in this text to how the main idea worked in *Bats!* What's more complex now than before?" I projected this page again so students could compare across the two texts.

Name the big ideas partnerships discovered, and add those ideas to the anchor chart.

Soon, I called students back. I unveiled a new anchor chart, "Ways Complex Nonfiction Gets Hard." Gesturing to it, I said, "I heard you saying that one way that determining the main idea is becoming hard is that the heading doesn't help. Like here, the heading is 'The Science behind the Story,' and it's the same heading in each chapter, which isn't helpful at all." I added "The headings and subheadings don't help or are misleading" Post-it to the chart.

"A ton of you said that main idea was easier in the *Bats!* text because there used to be only one main idea on the page. How's that different in this text?" Students turned and talked briefly, and I shared out what they found. "That's right, now there are often several main ideas in a section of a text, and you have to figure out what they all are." I added that Post-it note to the chart.

ANCHOR CHART

Ways Complex Nonfiction Gets Hard

- The headings and subheadings don't help or are misleading.
- There are several main ideas.

Continue reading aloud the text, setting students up to identify additional ways main idea becomes complex.

"Let's finish this section of the text, looking out for additional ways main idea gets complex." I read aloud the rest of page 8.

> The slime comes from special glands in the hagfish's skin. The glands actually release two ingredients that combine to make the slime. One ingredient is slippery mucus. The other is threadlike fibers. "Hagfish slime is the only slime we know of [in nature] that has such fibers," Fudge explained.

"What else are you noticing about the ways main idea gets complex? Work with your partner to add to our list."

After a few moments for partner conversation, I continued. "I heard you saying that unlike in *Bats!*, Rebecca Johnson doesn't come right out and tell you what the main ideas are. You have to do a lot of work to figure them out. Reading researchers say that means the ideas are *implicit*. They're hidden in the text, and to figure out what they are, you have to dig through all the facts and details and quotes." I added the relevant Post-it note to our chart.

This inquiry minilesson could easily run long, eating into the valuable chunk of time your students spend each day reading. To avoid that, we suggest you listen in as partners share their ideas and study the notes they jot down, on the lookout for ideas you could share out with the whole class. Then, too, we suggest that you be the one to share those ideas with the whole class, saying, "I heard you say . . ." and "In this corner, students suggested . . ." and then naming out the ideas you heard being generated. This will help you move quickly through your minilesson and ensure productive ideas are shared with the class.

You may think, "My students aren't coming up with these ideas—what do I add to the chart?" You can help a partnership notice one of the ways the main idea becomes complex and then broadcast the noticing as if it was that partnership's own invention. Then, too, you needn't report on what partnerships have discovered. You could instead say, "I'm wondering if some of you are thinking of. . . ."

Ways Complex Nonfiction Gets Hard

- The headings and subheadings don't help or are misleading.
- There are several main ideas.
- **The central ideas and main ideas are implicit (hidden).**

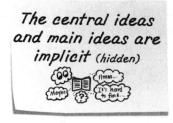

The central ideas and main ideas are implicit (hidden)

LINK

Set students up to read while thinking about how main idea works in their text, and challenge them to determine additional ways nonfiction texts become complex.

"Readers, our quick inquiry turned up so many ways that it becomes more complicated to determine the main idea now that texts are more complex. As you read today, you'll be armed with new knowledge about ways it can be hard to determine the main idea. That knowledge will help you figure out how main idea works in the text you read today.

"There's a chance you'll notice other ways main idea gets complex, and if you do, will you jot them down on a Post-it and add them to the chart? Be on the lookout, also, for other ways complex nonfiction gets hard, because it's likely you'll want to add those ways to our chart as well, since those would be great for us to investigate together later on!

"Log your reading, and then get started reading and flagging parts worth talking about."

By inviting students to add their own ideas about how complex nonfiction gets hard to the class's anchor chart, you are in a sense inviting students to coauthor upcoming minilessons. Wouldn't it be grand if a student added "There are tons of tricky words" to the chart, and then when you prepared to teach minilessons on determining the meaning of complex vocabulary, you could make it sound as if the inquiry into vocabulary came from that student's suggestion? You might alter the connection of that session, saying, "The other day, Josh noticed that there are tons of tricky words popping up in his nonfiction books now, and it got me thinking this would be important for us all to investigate."

Supporting Foundational Work Around Main Idea

TODAY'S LESSON spotlights students finding multiple main ideas including implicit ones. You will want to carry the "Main Idea(s) and Supporting Details/Summary" strand of the learning progression with you as you confer today. During your research, take note of where students' work on main idea falls on the progression. While some of your students may be ready to tackle the work you highlighted in today's minilesson, others will ready more foundational work. When asked to state the main ideas of a text, some of them, for example, will instead name topics, saying, "This was about the octopus body and this was about food." If so, you'll want to gather these students together for some small-group work that can thread across a few days.

Find one main idea.

You might teach students who struggle with main idea (and are presumably reading texts where the main idea tends to be explicitly stated) that it's often helpful to look for the "pop-out sentence" as they read, the one sentence that seems to summarize the content of each part. Suggest that the pop-out sentence is often the first or last sentence—but not always! As students identify a potential pop-out sentence that seems to summarize the other sentences in the section, teach them to ask, "How does this fit with what's been said so far?" Then, coach them as they check each sentence to ensure the pop-out sentence they identified holds true for the entire section.

These students are apt to be reading texts that do have helpful headings, and so you can teach them to look at all the facts within a section and ask, "What is the main thing this author is teaching me about the subtopic that the heading has named?" Show students how you might try this work, pulling out the level 3 text, "The Amazing Octopus," demonstrating how you move from the heading "Talents Like No Other" to a main idea, "Octopuses use their talents to escape their prey." This will support students in moving from main topics to main ideas.

If students easily notice facts, capitalize on what they do naturally. You might teach these students that one way to find a main idea of a text is to start with the key details.

You'll likely teach students to list out the important details they are learning and then ask, "What are the big ideas that these details are trying to show or support?"

MID-WORKSHOP TEACHING
Asking the Question, "What *Else* Is This Text About?'

"Readers, can I stop you? As you're reading today, you're probably noticing many ways in which it is getting challenging to determine the main ideas in your texts. But, here's the thing, it's not enough to *notice* ways texts get complex. You'll need strategies to help you deal with that complexity.

"I have two tips that will be useful to you. First, when you come across headings and subheadings that don't help or are misleading, it can help to reword them so they match the content of the part you just read. So instead of titling this part of *When Lunch Fights Back* with the current subtitle ('The Science behind the Story'), you could add a new subheading. Perhaps your subheading would say 'Hagfish Slime Is Really Great at Protecting the Hagfish from Predators.' Rewriting the heading can help you hold onto what a chunk of text is mostly about.

"And here's my second tip. The learning progressions can remind you that the texts you're reading now will be about more than one thing. That is, when you read, you should always be asking, 'What *else* is this text teaching?'

"Can you try this out right now with whatever section of text you just read? Will you think, 'What's this mostly about?' and then, when you have an answer, will you think, 'What *else* is this text teaching?' See if you can identify more than one main idea for that section of text.

"Keep these two tips in mind as you dive back into your books!"

Students can do this work within one paragraph, noticing how the details add up (__ + ___ + ___ = ?).

Notice when texts teach new main ideas.

Once students become more proficient at identifying a main idea with a section of text, you'll likely support students in noticing when the text shifts. As readers move from one paragraph to another, they have to determine whether the second paragraph builds on one main idea or whether the second paragraph lays out a new idea. You'll teach readers to ask, "Does this new part go with the idea I was just reading about,

or is this a new idea?" Often, this change is invisible, so you'll teach readers to be vigilant.

Sometimes students' difficulties with main idea come from misunderstandings about what they are being asked to do. To demonstrate, you might cut a photocopy of one page of a book into paragraph-sized chunks and ask students to group the paragraphs into larger categories of information, perhaps grouping two paragraphs that teach about the octopus's body into one pile and paragraphs that teach about how the octopus protects itself from predators into another pile. Readers can look across the paragraphs asking, "Is this a new idea? Or is this the same idea?"

FIG. 3–1 A teacher created a mini-chart to support a small group in determining multiple main ideas in a text.

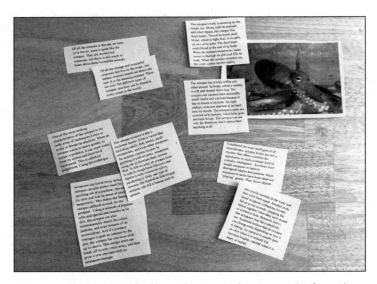

FIG. 3–2 Students worked together to study paragraphs from the level 5 text, "Lessons from the Deep," and grouped paragraphs that taught the same idea together.

Comparing How Main Idea Works in Different Texts

Ask students to examine the read-aloud text to determine how main idea works with the text.

"Readers, complex texts are kind of like snowflakes. Did you know that each snowflake is unique, that you'll never find two that are identical? The same is true for complex nonfiction texts. They're each challenging in their own way. Let's study the level 5 text, 'Lessons from the Deep,' asking, 'How does the main idea work in this text?' Pull your copy out of your folder, and as soon as you get your copy, start studying!"

I voiced over to lift the level of student work. "We already found *three* ways that determining the main idea of a text can be challenging. Our chart can remind you of those ways. Do those hold true for what you are reading? Are there other sorts of challenges?"

> **ANCHOR CHART**
>
> **Ways Complex Nonfiction Gets Hard**
>
> - The headings and subheadings don't help or are misleading.
> - There are several main ideas.
> - The central ideas and main ideas are implicit (hidden).

After a bit I added, "Look across both pages to determine how main idea works. Come to some conclusions."

Ask partnerships to compare what they found about how main idea works across pages of the read-aloud text.

Once many students had read the text, I said, "Will you and your partner talk with another partnership? Teach each other what you found around our big question: 'How does main idea work in this text?' Figure out whether you think the main idea works in the same way across all the parts of this text, or do different parts of the text advance the main ideas differently?"

NOTICING HOW YOU DETERMINE MAIN IDEAS

Readers, today in school, you all did a shared inquiry. You investigated how *When Lunch Fights Back* conveyed main ideas in one small passage of that text. You only read a tiny portion of the text so you were looking for the main ideas of a few paragraphs, not of a larger text. In real life, however, you won't have that support. Nor will I be at your elbow. In real life, you need to read texts on your own. The real job is to read large swatches of text—maybe ten pages, twenty pages—*and then* determine the main ideas of that whole swatch of text. To do that, you almost need to look at the text as if you are in an airplane, flying over the terrain. See how the larger chunks of text fit together. Then you can figure out what the whole text is mostly about.

Tonight, continue your research into ways that readers determine the main idea(s) of complex nonfiction texts. But this time, study two things. First, study a much longer text. Read something that is at least ten pages long. And second, study *yourself*. Notice what you do to determine the main ideas of the text.

Remember we have a chart started. That chart is going to shape what fifth-graders across this class do to determine the main things that authors are teaching. Decide if the items on our chart actually work for you. Decide if you think there are other bullets to add to that chart. And bring your research into school tomorrow.

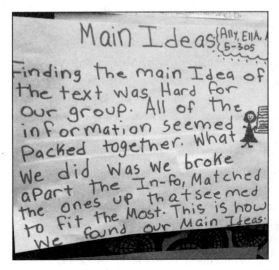 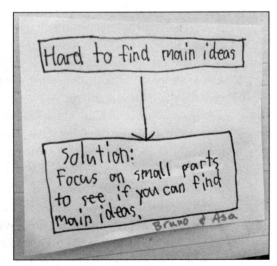

FIG. 3–3 Students develop their own strategies for determining main ideas.

[handwritten notes:] main Idea · Support details

Strategies for Determining Implicit Main Ideas

[handwritten note:] ? How can I organize my thinking to determine Implicit (Not Obvious) Main Ideas? How can I teach others about my findings? (chart p. 41)

IN THIS SESSION, you'll teach students specific strategies that readers use when they encounter texts that teach main ideas implicitly.

GETTING READY

✔ Prepare to show the "Ready New York: NYC in an Emergency" video to the class (www.youtube.com/watch?v=ZJd-DMPmFzQ) (search terms: ready New York emergency nyc youtube). A link is available on the online resources (see Teaching).

✔ Both you and your students should bring your reading notebooks to the meeting area to jot down notes during the video (see Teaching).

✔ Have chart paper and a marker ready to jot down main ideas from the video (see Teaching).

✔ Students should bring their nonfiction text with them to the meeting area (see Active Engagement).

✔ Prepare a chart titled "To Teach Well . . ." (see Mid-Workshop Teaching and Share).

I N THIS SESSION, you'll revisit the idea that when reading complex nonfiction texts, fifth-graders need to be able to glean main ideas that the author is advancing, and to do this even if the text doesn't include headings or topic sentences that explicitly name those ideas. You'll also continue to help students approach nonfiction texts expecting to learn more than one big idea.

From the start, you should know that there is not one way to teach this skill to youngsters. Over the past few years, students have often been taught to scan a text and to determine the main chunks of the text, noticing how each of those chunks is structured, and then to use that text structure (say, problem and solution, or cause and effect) to help them crystallize almost a miniature version of the text. Readers, then, might come from a book about hurricanes saying, "This book begins by comparing hurricanes with other kinds of storms, suggesting that one big difference is the warning signals for hurricanes are less, and then the text lists and describes a bunch of those signals, ending with stories of the disasters that happen if you ignore them."

This session does not approach the job of teaching kids to learn the main ideas in a text by suggesting that kids think first about text structures—although they may. Instead, the session simply helps kids know that a goal of reading complex nonfiction is to determine what the main ideas are in the text—and to be able to talk about not just those main ideas, but also supporting details. The lesson emphasizes the fact that readers are apt to encounter more than two or three big ideas when reading, and part of the challenge is to choose among those candidate ideas just two (or three) that, when taken together, represent the bulk of the text, and then to be able to talk about them using a few supporting examples to buttress each of the main ideas. The reader of that same hurricane book might, for example, say that the book stresses that hurricanes are uniquely dangerous because of this or that, and that preparation for them is especially important.

The session helps readers get a sense for what it means to read for several main ideas by using a one-minute video clip as the text. The clip is a fast-paced one, and a lot of information comes at the viewer quickly (as it does when reading many nonfiction texts).

Students will find that the video clip has at least half a dozen possible main ideas (and they can be articulated in a host of ways) with a bunch of supportive details that could buttress any one of those main ideas. Be sure that you validate the fact that readers won't all see the same thing in a text, and there are many ways to talk about the ideas a text sets forth.

"A goal of reading complex nonfiction is to determine what the main ideas are and also supporting details."

You may find that students have difficulty discerning main ideas the first time they view the video. It's natural to watch an engaging text and first respond in awe, distracted by the flashing images and statistics. Because of this, you might decide to show the video twice, suggesting that students first watch the video and share their thinking more generally before they view the video with a more focused lens. If you do choose to show the video clip an additional time, look carefully at the remainder of the lesson and consider places where you can make cuts to preserve reading time.

The session ends by inviting kids to begin taking notes—this time, a sort of boxes and bullets, with main ideas and supporting details.

Strategies for Determining Implicit Main Ideas

CONNECTION

Suggest students pool their insights, gleaned from last night's research on the challenges they encountered and the strategies they used to tackle those challenges.

"Readers, I'm already hearing that you came to some interesting realizations as part of your homework last night. Will you share what you learned from your research with your partner? I'm going to race around and try to hear what you are saying too." Students launched into conversations.

Draw parallels between reading increasingly hard texts and moving up levels in video games, suggesting that in both endeavors, strategies for tackling trouble help.

After listening a bit, I convened the class. "What you are saying has me thinking. It seems like you not only observed what was tricky in your texts, you also observed yourself inventing little strategies for tackling those difficulties. Am I right? That is super important because just think—if we share those strategies, everyone in this room will have a toolkit of ways to discern the main ideas in complex texts.

"You are getting me to think about how, when I was a kid, my favorite video game was Mario Kart. Have you ever played it?" I began an animated description, acting things out as I described them. "We raced these tiny cars around tracks, dodging enemy racers, trying not to take turns too tightly, and, of course, avoiding the dreaded bananas that would make a car lose total control.

"My brother and I would study the racetracks for hours to figure out the hard parts—especially Rainbow Road. The name sounds friendly, but it wasn't. It was this flashy track in the middle of outer space, and what made it so tough was that there were a ton of places where you could fall off the edge.

"My brother and I thought that if we could just figure out where the tough parts were to Rainbow Road, we'd be able to beat that track. But, it turned out, just knowing what made it tough wasn't enough. We had to develop strategies—like eventually we learned to stay a foot away from the edge and to go slower on the third turn.

"It seems like you are saying that you need to do the same thing with nonfiction texts. You need to not just know the hard parts, but also come up with strategies to help you with them."

◆ COACHING

By now, your students are well aware that the texts they are holding are becoming increasingly complex. It's likely they are also finding that the strategies they relied on in past years to determine the main idea of a text, such as looking for a pop-out sentence where the main idea is explicitly stated, are no longer sufficient. To help them feel energized and ready to tackle this change, rather than discouraged, we suggest you share a real-life story of how you developed strategies that helped you to be successful (in this case, while playing a video game, something it's likely that many of your students can relate to), and then rally students to do the same work with their nonfiction reading.

❖ Name your teaching point.

"Readers, today I want to teach you that once readers know how a nonfiction text is complex when it comes to main ideas, they can develop and draw on a toolkit of strategies to support them in determining the main ideas."

TEACHING

Suggest that many students reported that they invented a strategy for discerning the main idea when none is stated explicitly. Detail that strategy.

"As you were talking, I heard some of you say that when the main ideas in your texts aren't stated straight out, when they are instead implicit, it helps to chunk the text into parts and then to pause after each part to say, 'What does this chunk seem to be about?' After that, you read on through another chunk, and do that same pausing. After a bit you think about how the chunks fit together."

Recruit students to study a video clip. Set them up to note the multiple main ideas forwarded in the video and then to determine which main ideas are most supported by the text.

"You game to practice this? I'm going to show you a video clip of a public service warning that New York City shows its citizens. As you watch this, think, 'What is one main idea that is being put forward in this text?' Just like you discovered last night, you'll have to chunk the text to do this, noticing what different chunks seem to be about and then seeing how those chunks fit together."

"But here is the challenge. Think also, 'And what else? What is another main idea that is being put forward?' You will probably find yourself jotting four or five possible ideas, but in the end, for these to be *main ideas*, you will want to choose just a few—say, just two. You ready to watch? This lasts less than two minutes, so get ready to watch with some intensity." I showed the clip, which explains how New York City is vulnerable to emergencies because of its geography and densely populated area. The video asks New York residents to consider if they are prepared to respond to natural or man-made disasters.

After the clip was over, I said, "So what are the two main ideas you felt were most advanced in this video? Try to decide on two *main ideas*." Students began talking with their partners to hone in on the main ideas they'd found. I noticed there was overwhelming consensus about one main idea and some disagreement about the second. I decided to name two that had the least overlap with each other.

Record two main ideas the video forwards. Ask students to record the main ideas they found and to find the strongest details that support those main ideas. Show the video clip again.

"Let's come back. When we come to a text expecting it to be about more than one thing, a lot jumps out, right? For the first main idea, you were pretty much all saying the same thing—you need to be prepared for disaster to strike at any time. For the second main idea, many of you said it was that cities are dangerous places (or that NYC is a dangerous place)." I quickly jotted those main ideas down on chart paper.

It may not be the case that many students actually did tell each other about this strategy—probably some did, and you may or may not have been listening in at the exact moment to overhear this. You'll still get extra leverage by suggesting that the strategy you'll demonstrate is one that some kids have devised.

A special nod of thanks to Mary Ehrenworth, Deputy Director of TCRWP, who first used this video to help students learn to discern main ideas and supportive details in a text and weigh their importance. How lucky we are when teaching (and curriculum) grows out of a fusion of many minds!

Video: Public Service Warning

—Intro Boxes & Bullets Strategy

You need to be prepared for disaster to strike at any time.

Cities are dangerous places to live.

Then I said, "Record your two boxes. They might be the same as mine or you might have your own—maybe that New York's aging infrastructure makes it especially vulnerable, or that weather extremes can have devastating effects on a city. We're going to watch the video again, and this time, will you find supportive details for your two main ideas? These details might come in any order, so sort them as they come! Again, you will probably notice a bunch of them. Jot them all down. And in the end, I'm going to ask you to rank them and choose the most important supportive details—just two for each main point." Again I showed the clip, modeling how I jotted notes furiously in my reading notebook as I watched.

"Yikes! I've got a ton of details!" I said, holding up a filled page in my notebook. "I've got to prioritize, make sure these details actually fit with this idea. Will you do the same?" I hunched over my notebook, crossed out some details and starred others.

"Turn and talk with each other. What were your strongest supportive details?"

ACTIVE ENGAGEMENT

Name the transferrable reading work students just engaged in with the video clip, and set students up to try similar work with the texts they've been reading.

"Readers, I'm thinking it will pay off for you to try this work in the texts you're reading now. With longer texts like yours, we can't just say back every little thing the text is teaching in every chunk and all the teeny, tiny supportive details. Instead, we've got to notice individual chunks and then put them together, thinking, 'How do these chunks fit together? What are the *main ideas*? And what are the strongest supportive details?'

"Right now, will you find a familiar part in your nonfiction text where you could try this work? Make it a part you've read before so you can reread it thinking about what the *main ideas* are that the author's trying to teach. As soon as you find that part, get started reading and jotting those main ideas and supportive details down."

Coach in to support individual readers as they work to find the main ideas taught in their texts. Voice over with feedback to support the entire class based on your students' needs.

As students read, I knelt alongside one cluster, then another, offering tips to individual readers. Giovanni had found a main idea that was explicitly stated in the text. "You've got the explicit main idea, the one that was popped out in a sentence," I said. "Look again and ask, 'What other less explicit main ideas are advanced in this text? What else is this text teaching?'"

We suggest here that you take notes in a format we refer to as boxes and bullets, jotting down the author's main ideas in a box and recording the supporting details as bullets underneath. Most of your students will be familiar with this note-taking tool from fourth grade.

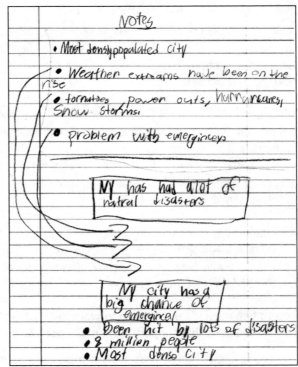

FIG. 4–1 This student jotted notes quickly while viewing the video, then identified main ideas by considering how supporting details fit together.

I saw several students writing all the details the text taught in order, so I offered a tip to all the students. "Jot critically. Really study the supportive details and think about which are strongest before you start writing."

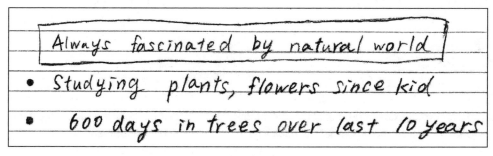

FIG. 4–2 Omnia quickly jots a main idea and supporting details.

LINK

Remind students to pull flexibly from their repertoire of main idea strategies and to begin taking notes that mirror the main ideas and supportive details in the text.

"Readers, as you head off to read today, draw on (and invent) strategies that will help you determine the main ideas your text is teaching. Keep in mind that often the main ideas won't be stated clearly. They'll be implicit, and often there will be multiple main ideas across a text. Prioritize as you read on, pushing yourself to identify the main ideas and supportive details that are most dominant in the text.

"As you do this, will you keep in mind those big goals you set a few days ago? Many of you set a goal around 'Main Idea(s) and Supporting Details/Summary.' Work toward that goal as you read today.

"I still don't want to see you reading with pencil in hand and pausing to take notes every fourth line. Instead, pause only when you reach the end of a meaningful chunk. Please pause and do as we did when watching the video. Take notes on the main idea—or ideas—in that chunk of text and on the most important supportive details. You'll probably work in a boxes-and-bullets structure, but remember that if your text is structured in a compare-and-contrast way or in some other structure, you may want to mirror that. Do anything that helps you find and capture the main ideas and most important supportive details."

Since my big focus today is on helping students draw on strategies for determining implicit main ideas, I chose not to have students share out with the class here or to share what details different partnerships found. I wanted to ensure students had a good chunk of time to dive into their texts during the active engagement.

If time is short, you can bypass this part of the minilesson, moving forward to the link. Students will have a chance to transfer the work with the video clip to written texts during reading time. It is always helpful for you to look at any minilesson and imagine ways you can revise it—especially noting ways you can shorten it.

We have for the first time in this unit advised students to take notes on what they are reading. Notice that the emphasis here is on students reading large portions of text before pausing to take notes. Be alert for any readers who disregard this suggestion and instead revert to inching their way through a text, constantly stopping to jot facts. You might use the first few minutes of reading time today to move from table to table, briefly coaching students to read a large chunk of text before note-taking.

Pushing a Student's Thinking about Main Ideas

AS USUAL, you'll divide your time between small-group work and conferring. Your conferring, as always, will begin with an effort to try to understand the work that particular students have been doing—and are ready to do next. Sometimes you'll find that your whole-class instruction sets children up to do one thing, and that in your conferences, you adapt those whole-class instructions so they are more helpful to individual students.

When I sat down next to Fallon, she started telling me about Charlotte Wilcox's book, *Mummies, Bones, and Body Parts*, speaking in her usual rush of words. She'd read a big portion of the book when she was younger and had thought it was boring. "But when I started to read it again last night, it was like—'Whoa! How did I ever think this was boring?'"

As I scanned the book, Fallon showed me her notes, which resembled an abbreviated timeline. "There's a murder mystery part. These workers, in 1983, found a human head. They thought it was from a missing woman from the 1960s whose murderer was never found. They called her husband and said they found her head, and he confessed that he had killed her. Then one of the detectives didn't believe it, so he had the head radiocarbon dated, and it turned out the head was around 2,000 years old, so it wasn't the man's wife. They named the head Linda 1."

Fallon was all set to continue retelling the book in all its detail, but I jumped in to celebrate the fact that she had returned to a book that she'd previously abandoned. "Many readers are unwilling to reread, and they miss so much!" I said. "I'm totally pleased that you realize how much there is to find on a second trip through the same book!"

Hoping that I'd earned the right to now push her, I said, "Fallon, as I listen to you retelling all the details about this book, I'm thinking that I need to revise the instruction I gave to you and the rest of the class. I know I suggested that you read a big chunk, then capture the main ideas on the page, and I can see from your timeline that you've done that. But Fallon—my thought is that it would help you even more if you recorded not just what the book says, but also your ideas about that."

I tapped her book and pointed out, "I can tell by the way that you're bubbling over that your mind is on fire. But your notes don't really show that . . ."

Fallon looked at me, a bit annoyed. "I remember *everything* I've read. I can list all the facts for you. Like mummies . . ."

I quickly reassured her. "Oh, Fallon, first of all—I *told* you to record the main ideas in the book. Plus, I can see you can remember the *facts*. I'm actually suggesting this because your fact-gathering muscles are so strong that I thought you might devote more attention to the opposite muscles, the 'thinking about the facts' muscles. It isn't something I've taught yet this year—but I'm suggesting that when you pause in your reading to think, 'What are the main ideas this book has taught?' you also think, 'What are *my* ideas about that?'"

I pressed on. "You told me a lot about what Charlotte Wilcox has to say about mummies. But I'm wondering what you, Fallon, were thinking as you read?" I wanted to support Fallon in meeting fifth-grade expectations for "Critical Reading" on the learning progression, which pushes fifth graders to develop their own ideas based on their readings and to use the text to think in new ways.

"Oh," she said. "Well, on this page, I was thinking I want to be an archeologist, to discover things no one knows anything about. And on this other page, I thought that it's so cool but weird that the skull falls off while the rest of the body stays together. Maybe heads aren't attached as well as, like arms, are, or they are attached with muscles not bones, and muscles can rot. Gross and weird because isn't your brain the most important thing? You'd think it would be attached better." Fallon excitedly started flipping through the book, looking for a particular picture.

"Readers, can I have your attention?" I waited until the class was looking at me. "I feel so lucky because I've been able to go from one of you to another, hearing about your books. I had no idea we had such interesting books in our shelves! I mean— you are learning *amazing* things. Fallon has read about a head named Linda 1 that is 2,000 years old! Sasha has been learning about how there are 100,000 stray dogs in a city in Romania, and every day those wild dogs bite about fifty people.

Partner work

"So listen—I'm thinking that in our share today, you should have a chance to teach each other what you are learning. I know you are reading for the main ideas and the supportive details. As you do that, set yourself up to be teaching some of your classmates about those ideas and those details."

I gestured toward the "To Teach Well ..." chart, which students had seen in fourth grade and said, "You'll be teaching, as always, by thinking about how you want to structure your teaching, by communicating the main ideas and supporting details, and by pointing to charts and pictures, role-playing or otherwise using gestures . . . the works! So as you read, be readying yourself for your teaching."

To Teach Well...

- Use the text structure to organize your teaching

- Know the main ideas and supporting details

- Use an explaining voice

- Use gestures

- Use a teaching finger to point to charts, illustrations, and diagrams to help explain

"Wow, Fallon! These ideas are fascinating. I definitely think you should spend a little time jotting down your thoughts—after all, writing is the most powerful way human beings have to think, to push our own thinking."

"Okay, I'll try!" Fallon said, picking up her pencil as I pointed to it.

"Fallon, what you are helping me to realize is that archeologists and readers are a lot alike. Both make discoveries by excavating, by finding treasures. And my hunch is that both find things that others don't realize are treasures—and it's their work, their thinking, that makes other people see their discoveries for what they are."

Teaching as a Way to Learn

Set readers up to plan how they will teach their partners what they've been learning.

"Readers, you've seen the lesson plans that I carry around. Before I teach all of you, I plan out the main ideas I'll teach and how I'll teach them. You'll need to do the same. Will you take a few minutes to get ready to teach your partner? Think again about the main and central ideas your text taught, and plan for how you'll teach them. Will you use gestures? Are there visuals that will help you? And, importantly, how will you organize your teaching? Use our 'To Teach Well ...' chart to help you." I gave students a few months to plan.

Move from partnership to partnership, coaching to lift up the teaching work that each student does.

Then I continued. "Will you get with your partner and decide who's teaching first? And if you're listening first, you've got two jobs. First, you have to listen in a way where you can learn. And second, get ready to compliment your partner on something specific they do well." The classroom erupted in eager conversation, and I moved around the classroom listening to partners teach each other what they had learned.

LEARNING FROM PRINT AND VIDEO TEXTS

Readers, continue reading up a storm tonight! Try to learn not just from print texts, but also from video texts. If you can, try to find videos about a topic that you have also been reading about. As you watch and read on the same topic, explore what it is like to try to take notes from several sources. You might find that both the book and the article teach about the same subject. And so your notes may end up being smashed together.

Take notes in any way that allows you to be the most powerful learner you can be on the topic.

Chart stand-
Vocab hard & technical

CA Notebook
* Chart of p47

Session 5

Using Context to Determine the Meaning of Vocabulary in Complex Texts

(?) How can I make sense of unfamiliar words?

TODAY'S SESSION BEGINS a two-day exploration on vocabulary. As students read increasingly complex texts, it is vital that you support students' progress toward the fifth-grade expectations on the learning progression for "Word Work," a key skill for this unit and for life. Your students will encounter challenging academic vocabulary that is often essential to a passage's meaning, and the miscues students make can completely alter the meaning of a passage. Even when students can sound out a word, that word may not be familiar to them, so sounding it out won't trigger recognition and lead the reader to ascertain the word's meaning. More complex texts also tend to provide less vocabulary support. Even if there is a glossary or a text box that includes the definition of key words, authors often use tricky academic vocabulary in those definitions. Chances are great that your students will need support navigating these complexities.

In this session, you'll help your students determine the meaning of unfamiliar words from the context in the passage. In *When Kids Can't Read: What Teachers Can Do* (Heinemann, 2002), Kylene Beers points out that although teachers often talk up the importance of context clues, "we must recognize that using context as a clue is something that requires lots of practice, something that separates dependent from independent readers, something that is much harder than we may have realized" (186).

To do this, you'll remind students that in fourth grade they learned to *look around* words, reading beyond the sentence that contains the word, so as to take into account several sentences before and after the tricky vocabulary word. You'll also encourage students to think about the type of word that's being used, to note whether the word is positive or negative, and to envision what's happening in the text based on the clues the author provides. Students will try this work with an accessible word—*predator*—noticing how the word is taught across several levels of "The Amazing Octopus" texts. Students will see that as texts become more complex, the vocabulary help embedded into easier versions of a text is peeled away, leaving readers to make more textual inferences. You'll help your students learn how to make those inferences, supporting students in meeting fifth-grade expectations for word solving on the learning progression.

IN THIS SESSION, you'll teach students that readers rely on a host of strategies to help them make sense of the increasingly complex vocabulary used by authors of nonfiction texts.

GETTING READY

- ✔ Before this session, use read-aloud time to preview with your students several levels of "The Amazing Octopus," a nonfiction article that we have rewritten "up the ladder" as a series of progressively challenging texts (see Teaching and Active Engagement).
- ✔ Display the "Ways Complex Nonfiction Gets Hard" anchor chart (see Teaching and Active Engagement).
- ✔ Prepare to display the fourth paragraph of "The Amazing Octopus" at levels 2, 4, and 6, and provide students with copies to mark up (see Teaching and Active Engagement).
- ✔ Create a chart titled "Figuring Out the Meaning of Unknown Words" from Grade 4 Unit 2 *Reading the Weather, Reading the World.* Today you'll display the "Look around" section (see Teaching and Active Engagement).

Later, in the mid-workshop teaching and share, you'll work toward developing readers who are word conscious and willing to use the new words they're learning. Just as you delight in watching toddlers take risks with their vocabulary, trying out the new words they've heard grown-ups use, you'll want to encourage your students to be risk takers as well. Too often, fifth-graders are worried about making mistakes and don't attempt to use words they've just encountered in texts. Today's lesson confronts this head on, addressing the "Building Vocabulary" thread on the learning progression.

"Too often, fifth-graders are worried about making mistakes, and don't attempt to use words they've just encountered in texts."

Be sure to continue to support an interest in vocabulary as you read aloud sections of *When Lunch Fights Back*. Model your own word consciousness. You might slow down around unfamiliar words, model your own confusion, and then project a section of the text, inviting students to study the passage closely to determine all the clues the author gives that help them know what the unfamiliar words mean. Then, too, you might keep a running list of words the class is learning from the read-aloud, posting the words prominently during whole-class conversations and when students are writing in response to the read aloud. You'll model looking at the chart and using the new words, showing students how they can do the same.

Using Context to Determine the Meaning of Vocabulary in Complex Texts

CONNECTION

Connect students' experiences dealing with complexity in their lives to their experiences with text complexity in their nonfiction reading.

"Have you ever noticed that when you're playing video games, or any game really, that as you go up the levels, things just get tougher? It got me thinking about those kids who get to the Little League World Series. I was watching it on TV a few months ago. I bet when they're in their hometown, playing against other kids their age, things feel pretty manageable. But, as they climb up the levels, moving from playing teams in their town to teams in their state to teams from all different states, things probably get a ton more challenging.

"Right now, can you think about a situation like that you've encountered, a time where things started out easy and got more and more complex as you went along? Thumb up when you've got a story."

I waited until many students had a thumb up. "Tell your partner the story of that time!"

Kids broke into stories about battling opponents in chess tournaments, beating bosses in Super Smash Brothers, even climbing to the top of a mountain on a hike with the family. "It's like swim school," Nina said. "At first the levels were super simple but then moving up the levels got way harder, and I got stuck at dolphin for a while."

"Readers, this is just like the nonfiction texts we're reading. They started out much easier, and now they're getting harder. And, what's tricky is that they're not just getting harder in one way, but in a lot of ways. Today let's study a new way texts get tricky: through their vocabulary."

❖ **Name the teaching point.**

"Readers, today I want to teach you that as nonfiction texts become more complex, the vocabulary the author uses becomes hard and technical, and the clues that help readers figure out what the words mean are often hidden. When this happens, you have to search for clues all *around* the word to determine what it might mean."

◆ COACHING

In his book Opening Minds: Using Language to Change Lives, *Peter Johnston discusses the need, in order for students to have agency, to believe that things are changeable, both "aspects of the world outside them, but also aspects of themselves—their learning, their identities, their intellect, their personal attributes, and their ways of relating to others" (2012, 27). The examples you give here support students in developing this disposition.*

This turn-and-talk is meant to give students a sense of voice by asking them to recall times they faced difficulties, similar to the difficulties they now face with their nonfiction texts, and then share those stories with a partner. That said, because it does not actually teach anything, you won't want to drag it on by allowing students to share their stories one by one. Instead, give them a quick minute to share with their partners and then call them back together.

TEACHING AND ACTIVE ENGAGEMENT

Explain to students how the day's work will go, setting them up to read a text across several levels.

"Here's how our work will go. Let's look at a section of 'The Amazing Octopus' text at a bunch of different levels—levels 2, 4, and 6. I thought we could zoom in on just a small part, studying how the author teaches us what a *predator* is."

Engage students in studying an excerpt of a text written at a level 2, noticing how the text teaches the meaning of unfamiliar vocabulary words and what strategies are helpful.

I displayed a paragraph from the level 2 text, "The Amazing Octopus," on the document camera. "Let's dive into the level 2 text first. How does this author teach you what a *predator* is? Look carefully, and mark up what you find." Partnerships quickly noted the definition tucked in after the word *predator*.

> *The amazing octopus has many ways to defend itself. When an octopus wants to move fast, it can shoot out water to push itself backwards. An octopus can travel many miles that way. An octopus can also protect itself by squirting ink. The ink makes the predator, or animal hunting the octopus, become blind and lose its sense of smell for a little while. That gives the octopus a chance to escape!*

I listened and then said, "Readers, many of you said the author teaches you what a predator is by coming right out and saying it. You noticed the phrase 'or animal hunting the octopus.' So sometimes, the definition will be right there, and we can look *around* the word, maybe right before or right after, to figure it out."

Have students read a level 4 version of the same text, and ask them to study how vocabulary demands become increasingly complex.

Now I displayed the same paragraph from the level 4 text, "An Animal Like No Other," for comparison. "That's how vocabulary used to work in our texts. Now, look up two levels to the level 4 text. How does the author teach you what a *predator* is in this text?"

> *The octopus has many amazing ways to defend itself from predators. When an octopus wants to move quickly to escape a predator, it can shoot out water out of its siphon and push itself backwards. This is called jet propulsion. Using this technique, octopuses can travel many miles. An octopus can also protect itself by squirting ink at a predator, causing it to become blind and lose its sense of smell temporarily. This makes it difficult for the predator to track the octopus once it has darted away. The octopus can also escape predators by changing its colors like a chameleon to blend into its surroundings. But, if a predator does manage to grab an octopus by the arm, the octopus has one more trick up its sleeve. It can break off its arm, swim away, and then grow a new one later!*

You might be thinking that predator *is not the most challenging word to choose, and you're certainly correct. However, I chose* predator *because I wanted to emphasize that authors draw on a variety of clues to make sense of unfamiliar words, and I know students will be more successful at this work on their first try if they work with a somewhat familiar word. There will be time to tackle totally new words later.*

Vocabulary becomes increasingly complex in the level 4 text, "The Amazing Octopus." Look for students to notice that the definition of the term predator *is absent and the reader has to rely on context as a clue to determine the word's meaning. Then, too, you'll want students to notice that the density of academic vocabulary is increasing. That is, the author is using harder, more technical terms to discuss the octopus. See Chapter 5 in* Reading Pathways *for more information about how vocabulary demands increase and suggestions of how to support students with tackling these demands.*

Kids dove back in. Some circled the word *predator* every time it came up.

Remind students of previous learning by revisiting a familiar chart. Ask them to use these strategies to notice an author's embedded clues.

"Remember from fourth grade, how sometimes the author didn't come right out and tell the meaning of the word, but instead tucked in all these clues? You learned that if you looked *around* a word, you could often figure out what the word meant, just by noticing the clues the author included. Here's a chart you may remember from fourth grade." I made sure only the "Look around . . ." section of the chart was showing.

"Look back at the text, and this time, push yourself to look *around* the word. Can you use some of these strategies you know from last year to help you?" Students glanced up at the chart, chose a strategy, and got started trying it while I coached and listened.

"Wow! The clues are just flying in. Some of you studied whether *predator* was positive or negative. I heard you saying the word *predator* seemed really negative, because the author wrote you have to *defend* yourself from it, and you only have to defend yourself from something bad, not your best friend! So thinking about whether the word is positive or negative could help us get the gist of the word.

"And picturing the word helped a few of you. You saw this amazing, gentle octopus with this big creature, the predator, maybe a shark, chasing after it with this open mouth filled with sharp teeth."

Ask students to transfer the strategies they just practiced to a new section of a text, written at a level 6.

I posted the same paragraph from the level 6 text, "Lessons from the Deep," on the document camera. "Carry those strategies with you to this new text," I said, "and see if there are any you need to add. How does this author teach you what a *predator* is?"

Figuring Out the Meaning of Unknown Words

Look around...

- *What do you picture?*

- *What's happening?*

- *Is it positive or negative?*

- *What type of word is it?*

  object   action   describing word

One of the most striking characteristics of the octopus is the wide array of techniques it uses to avoid or thwart its attackers. When an octopus wants to move quickly to escape a predator, it can expel water from its siphon and push itself backwards, a process called jet propulsion. Using this technique, octopuses can travel many miles. An octopus can also protect itself by squirting ink at a predator, obscuring its view and causing it to lose its sense of smell temporarily. This makes the fleeing octopus difficult to track. And if a predator manages to grab an octopus by the arm, the octopus has one more trick up its sleeve. This escape artist can break off its arm, swim away, and then grow a new one later with no permanent damage.

Partners worked together, while I coached in. Adjua decided that the level 6 text supported the word *predator* in exactly the same way as the level 4 version of the text. "Really?" Dimitri asked. "I'm not sure, 'cause it seems like the author uses different words. Like here, in the level 4 text, she said it *defends itself from predators* and now she's saying *the wide array of techniques it uses to avoid or thwart its attackers*."

"I think I see what you're saying," Adjua replied. "It felt like the same thing was happening that happened before, but the author just used much fancier words to describe it."

I called students back together and I added to our anchor chart:

As I listened to partners, I noticed a few either seemed to have no strategies or listed "sounding it out" as the main strategy for determining the meaning of unfamiliar vocabulary. I made plans to work with these children in a small group.

ANCHOR CHART

Ways Complex Nonfiction Gets Hard

- The headings and subheadings don't help or are misleading.
- There are several main ideas.
- The central ideas and main ideas are implicit (hidden).
- **The vocabulary is hard and technical.**

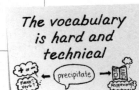

LINK

Connect the work students did today determining the meaning of unfamiliar vocabulary words with the work they should do when they read, today and every day.

"Readers, you're really noticing and taking on the challenges of your texts! Today, we noticed that as vocabulary gets more complex, there's often more work determining the meaning of those tricky words. Sometimes, the author might just come out and tell you the definition, but, more often, you'll have to do some real work to determine the meaning, looking all around the word to get a sense of what it might mean.

"As you read today, I'm sure you'll encounter unfamiliar vocabulary words in your text. If the author doesn't tell you what the word means, you'll need to do some work to figure it out. Use the strategies you know from fourth grade, and new strategies you develop, to help you.

"But here's the thing. As you read today, you can't just think about *unfamiliar vocabulary*. Instead, you have to read, thinking about *all* the ways texts are complex, using your strategies to help you when you hit those complex parts. Look over our charts and make a plan for your work today. Share your plan with your partner and then get started reading."

As students shared their work plans, I circulated, encouraging them to remember that they should be reading at a good pace (something close to three quarters of a page a minute) and that they should pause at intervals to take notes. Those two instructions can contradict each other unless note-taking is quick—which it should be.

Keeping the Work of the Unit Going, While Also Supporting Vocabulary Development

YOU'LL WANT TO CONFER and lead small groups to support your students in doing all that they know how to do as nonfiction readers. High on your list will be making sure that students are monitoring for meaning, noticing when texts are *too* complex for them—too hard—and putting those texts aside until they are able to read them. You might encourage those readers to read texts on the same topic that are considerably easier and, in that way, to develop their prior knowledge of the topic in the hopes that once they are more knowledgeable of the topic, they might have more success with those texts.

You'll also want to remind readers to keep track of the pace at which they are reading, aiming to read at something like three quarters a page a minute. Their note-taking will slow them down a bit, but if you see that note-taking consumes too much time, you may need to encourage students to write briefer notes and to pause less often to take notes.

You'll also help students with the topic of today—tackling challenging vocabulary words. Students need to be able to read the sentence that contains an unfamiliar word and to substitute a word that is the same part of speech as the tricky word. You probably don't want to teach this strategy by talking about parts of speech, as that is an elusive concept for children even if they have been taught it repeatedly, but you can help them think about the "kind of word" they are replacing with a synonym.

If, during the minilesson, you noticed readers listing "sounding it out" as their main strategy for determining the meaning of unfamiliar vocabulary words, you may want to lead a small group to support students in noticing clues in the text and using those clues to determine the meaning of tricky words. You may find it useful to carry the "Word Solving" thread of the Informational Reading Learning Progression with you as you support this group, noting where each individual's work falls on the progression and varying coaching in response.

When I did this, I began by saying, "Readers, we know that as texts get more complex, authors use more and more tricky words. Luckily, authors often include clues along the way to help us determine what a tricky word means. Sometimes the clues will be obvious—the author might come out and tell a definition—and other times, the clues will be more subtle. We put these clues together to come up with a definition.

MID-WORKSHOP TEACHING **Celebrating Risk Taking and Creating Readers Who Are Word Conscious**

"Readers, can I stop you? I want to congratulate you. It takes a lot of bravery to admit that there are words you don't know, words you really need to figure out. Congratulations!

"Right now, let's fill the room with the sounds of these new words you're learning. I'm going to be the conductor, and when I signal to you, say one of the new words you've encountered loud and proud, so the sound travels across the world."

I pointed my imaginary baton toward individual students, and the sound of the new words we were learning filled the room.

"*Precipitate.*"

"*Indivisible.*"

"*Phalanges.*"

"Wow, readers. I'm blown away. Keep up this brave work, honestly admitting when you find words you don't know and working hard to figure out what they might mean."

"Let's read through this text on the lookout for unfamiliar words. When you find a word that's unfamiliar to you, or a word you think would be tricky for other kids, will you make a stop sign?" I started reading from the level 5 text, 'Lessons from the Deep,' jumping right down to the fourth paragraph because there were several tricky words we could study. I was planning to use this same chunk of text with students in tomorrow's minilesson, studying it with a different lens, and I knew these students would benefit from first working with the text in a small group. By the time I hit *jet propulsion*, hands were flying up!

"That's definitely a tricky phrase, right? *Jet propulsion*? We know authors often give us clues about what the word means. I'll reread and read on a bit, and, as I do, will you and your partner hunt for clues?" I reread and read on, and then asked students to turn and talk, naming out all the clues they found.

"I see you all circling that phrase *this is called*. Why did that phrase seem important? What did it help you know?" Students talked with partners about how that phrase was signaling that the name for something was coming, and they said usually that meant a definition had come before.

I nudged them to read on past the phrase, and they did, deciding *this technique* referred to jet propulsion and that jet propulsion must have to do with moving many miles.

"Readers, did you see how once you noticed a tricky word, you relied on the clues the author gave you to determine what the word might mean? You noticed the author gave us a *ton* of clues. You had to look all around the page to really figure out its meaning.

"Return to your book and give this a try. Read, on the lookout for tricky words. When you find one, make a stop sign and start searching for clues to the meaning of the word. When you've found all the clues that are there, see if you can make use of them." Students worked for several minutes in their texts, while I coached in with quick questions and prompts.

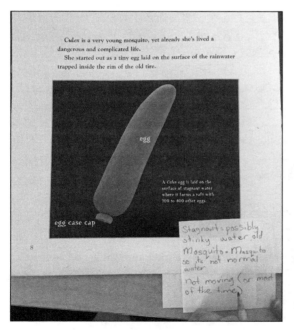

FIG. 5–1 Omala marks unfamiliar words and works to figure out the meaning of one.

> Stagnant = possibly stinky water, old
> Mosquito = Mosquito so its not normal water
>
> not moving (or most of the time)

FIG. 5–2 Omala's Post-it note captures how she used context as a clue to determine the meaning of *stagnant*.

Using the Lingo of Experts (as You Take Notes, as You Talk)

Introduce students to the fifth-grade expectations for Building Vocabulary. Rally students to incorporate vocabulary into their notes and talk.

"Readers, noticing these snazzy new vocabulary words will only take you so far if you just notice them and then read on, flipping the page and forgetting your new learning. Reading researchers say it's really important for kids to *build* their vocabulary. To do fifth-grade work building vocabulary, you have to not just accumulate, or collect, vocabulary, you also have to use it. The only way to really learn these new words in your books is to use them!

"One place where you can use the language of experts is in your note-taking, incorporating the expert words you're learning across your notes. Right now, scan the notes you took today. Are the expert words you learned today included in your notes? In a flash, revise your notes to include more of the expert words you've learned." Students quickly revised.

"A second place where you can use your new vocabulary is in your talk. As you prepare to teach your partner today, pay special attention to the vocabulary you'll teach. What new words will you use? How will you help your partner know what exactly those words mean? Will you come right out and define them? Use gestures? Point to pictures to help you define the words?

"When you're ready, start teaching!"

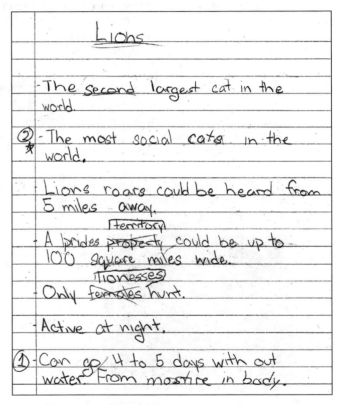

FIG. 5–3 Marcus revised his earlier note-taking on lions to include additional expert words.

LEARNING AND USING NEW WORDS

Readers, continue reading across texts tonight. Jot down notes in ways that help you capture what you're learning. While you read, pay special attention to the new words you're encountering in your reading. When you come across an unknown word, try different strategies to determine its meaning. When is it helpful to look around the word? Be sure you use the new words you're learning in your writing and in your talk. I'm including a copy of our chart from earlier for your reference.

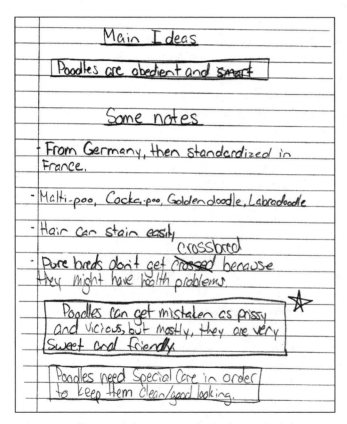

FIG. 5–4 Adjua used the new words she learned while jotting notes on poodles.

Figuring Out the Meaning of Unknown Words

Look around...

- What do you picture?

- What's happening?

- Is it positive or negative?

- What type of word is it?

object   action   describing word

P-Chart 58 & example

Session 6

Inquiry into Using Morphology of Words to Tackle Tricky Vocabulary

(?) How can I look inside words when they are unfamiliar?

IN THIS SESSION, you'll teach students that readers can use word morphology to tackle tricky vocabulary.

GETTING READY

✔ Prepare a quote from "Vocabulary: Five Common Misconceptions" to share research with students about word morphology (see Connection).

✔ Today, students will need the fourth paragraph from the level 5 text, "Lessons from the Deep" (see Teaching and Active Engagement).

✔ Prepare to reveal more of the "Figuring Out the Meaning of Unknown Words" chart from Session 5 (see Teaching and Active Engagement).

✔ Students will need copies of the grades 4 and 5 "Word Solving" thread of the learning progression (see Share).

I N THE PREVIOUS SESSION, your students began considering the way that challenging vocabulary adds to text complexity. Today's session will deepen that work. By the time kids are in fifth grade, the hard part about challenging vocabulary is not *saying* the word, it is not decoding—it is *understanding* the word. And the prompt to use context clues is less apt to work as kids move into more complex texts, because if a definition is tucked into the text, the terms used in that definition are often hard to understand.

In our work with CBAL (Cognitively Based Assessment *of*, *for*, and *as* Learning), the research arm of Educational Testing Service (ETS), we found that one of the most important indicators that a student is able to handle more complex texts is that student's ability to use word morphology to figure out what a word might mean.

Today's session will let students in on some of the research behind vocabulary, in particular around word morphology. In the connection to today's session, you read a small snippet of an article about vocabulary, a snippet that clearly states that being able to break words up into meaning units is important. We use the article "Vocabulary: Five Common Misconceptions" by Nancy Padak, Karen Bromley, Tim Rasinski, and Evangeline Newton, but there is a plethora of research on vocabulary instruction. You could also share excerpts from texts such *Bringing Words to Life* by Isabel Beck, Margaret G. McKeown, and Linda Kucan or *What Research Has to Say about Vocabulary Instruction*, edited by Alan E. Farstrup and S. Jay Samuels, or others.

Today's session is designed as an inquiry. You ask students to consider what research says and then to think about that research in relation to the octopus texts they have been studying. It will be especially important for all your students to be able to work with the level 5 text today—it is a level at which students can see that studying word morphology will pay off. By the end of the session, students will also be reminded that risk-taking is important in determining the meaning of vocabulary words.

Inquiry into Using Morphology of Words to Tackle Tricky Vocabulary

CONNECTION

Convene readers at the meeting area. Let them know that you have been doing some research around vocabulary instruction. Tell them how you have read that morphology is a big deal.

"Readers, we started thinking about vocabulary yesterday, noticing ways that vocabulary is part of how texts get harder. Last evening, I started to do more research on learning vocabulary, because I was interested in what others have said about the topic. I came across some *extremely* interesting things that I wanted to share with you. The first is a quote from an article called 'Vocabulary: Five Common Misconceptions.' I want you to listen to this quote, and then we'll think together about how it relates with what we have seen in the octopus texts, in our class read-aloud, and in our own texts." I read the quote, omitting the citations.

> *More than 60 percent of academic words have word parts (also called morphemes or roots) that always carry the same meaning (Nagy, Anderson, Schommer, Scott, & Stallman, 1989). Knowing that words can be broken down into meaning units is a powerful strategy for vocabulary development (Ayers, 1986; Baumann, Kameenui, & Ash, 2003; Harmon, Hedrick, & Wood, 2005).*

I sat back. "Readers, do you realize what this means? What these researchers are saying is that *more than half* the words you come across as your texts get harder have parts that always mean the same, in every word they appear. So when you find a difficult word, it will pay off to look *in* the word, not just around it. These researchers call the word parts 'meaning units' because each part of the word has a meaning. The fancy research word for studying the parts of words is *morphology*."

Offer a quick example of what it means to study word morphology, and break a word down into its meaning units.

"Let me give you a quick example of what studying word morphology means. Let's say I'm trying to figure out the word *indestructible*." I jotted it on the white board. "I'm sure many of you have seen this word before or know it, but I want you to look *in* the word with me for a minute to practice this word morphology work. If I look in the word, I can see parts that I know."

As this lesson progresses, you'll note the continued emphasis on the word in *(looking in words). This is not accidental. Stressing some words over others can help students to grasp the most important parts of the lesson. And in this case, you are really pointing out that looking in the word and looking around the word are different sorts of strategies. And they have different roots—one relies on word morphology; the other on context clues. Both are important, but today you will really be addressing word morphology.*

I quickly drew slashes within the word so it looked like this: *in/destruct/ible*. "Think about these parts with me. So, *destruct*..." I pointed to the middle part. "Well, I know that *destruct* is like to *destroy*, like to destroy a building—like destruction, right? And *-ible*," I pointed, "is sort of like *able*. And *in-*, well, that usually means *not*. We know that prefix, right? So, if I put those three meaning units together, I have ... not able to be destroyed. So I think *indestructible* means not able to be destroyed. Do you all see that? Do you all see how I looked in the word and broke it into meaning units?

"And these researchers are saying that that kind of work will pay off more than half the time. Interesting. I wonder if that is the case for the texts we are reading in here? I thought today we could do an inquiry and delve even deeper into thinking about vocabulary."

❖ **Name the question that will guide the inquiry.**

"Today we will do an inquiry and ask, 'How often does it really pay off to push ourselves to look *inside* words when they are tricky?'"

TEACHING AND ACTIVE ENGAGEMENT

Explain how the inquiry will go. Let students know that just for today, they will be focused on looking in words.

"Let me explain how our inquiry will go today. In the last session, you looked at just the fourth paragraph of a couple of different levels of the octopus texts, and you circled words you thought were tricky. In a minute I'm going to ask each of you to focus on that fourth paragraph again, but just look at the level 5 text. You'll circle any hard words that you see.

"But this time, you are really going to push yourself to look *in* the words. That is, you are going to study the circled words and see how much you can figure out about their meanings just from looking *in* them—at their parts. See if you can break them up into meaning units the way I broke up the word *indestructible*.

"Even if you can't break a whole word up and figure out all of its parts, you may be able to figure out just a part of the word and use that to help you to take a guess at what the whole word means. I want to be clear that looking *in* words is one thing to do, and you can also still look *around* words. But for today, let's first practice looking only *in* words, and see how often that pays off.

"So, study the words you circled and push yourselves to look *in* the words, asking, 'How often does it really pay off to push ourselves to look *inside* words when they are tricky?' Get to it."

Notice how I shift briefly into a demonstration, making clear the process I'm using to break down a word. That is, I don't just say, "There are three parts in this word. The first part is. . . ." I actually spell out what I'm thinking about the different parts of the word in a way that will transfer to any book.

Keep the word study work you've done recently with students in mind. You might choose to modify the directions you give to students so they take that recent work into account. For example, if your class has recently studied prefixes, remind students of that work.

Listen in and coach as students practice looking in words. Especially be prepared to push them to try looking in words that they don't at first think they can.

Dexter and Lily were studying the word *obscure*. "I don't think we can look inside of it," Dexter said. "I don't know any of those parts."

"Hang on," I interrupted. "Try pushing yourself to see if you can. The word starts with *ob-*. Do you know any other words that start with *ob-*?

Dexter and Lily were quiet for a minute, then Lily looked up, "*Obstacle*!"

"Okay," I encouraged. "Any others?"

They both shook their heads slowly. "Okay," I said. "So *obstacle*. Does that help you at all? Does it give you hints about whether this other tricky word is a positive or negative word? Push yourselves."

"Well," Dexter said. "*Obstacle* is a bad thing, so maybe *obscure* is bad, too."

I moved off to listen to others.

Convene readers and share a few examples of what they noticed when they pushed themselves to look in words.

"Readers, you're doing powerful work. You noted this strategy helps with a lot of words. Many partnerships tried it with *instantaneously*, and they looked inside and saw the word *instant*, so it gave them the idea that something was happening right now, right this instant. This word morphology is powerful stuff."

Caution students that it is equally important to look around words, and channel them to return to the same words they have studied, this time looking at context clues.

"Now, I want to tell you something very, very important. Remember the researchers said that knowing a word could be broken down into meaning units is *a* powerful strategy." I emphasized the *a*. "They didn't say this is the *only* strategy. In fact, I actually think that if you now tried to go back and look *around* the words, now bringing all you know from looking *inside* the words, you'll probably find that can really tackle them so much better. Do that now. Bring all you know about figuring out words and all you just did to look in the words and see if you can determine what they mean."

When fifth-graders word solve, they are expected to use their knowledge of prefixes, suffixes, and root words to determine a word's meaning. Your coaching here supports students in reaching these expectations on the "Word Solving" thread of the learning progression.

Be sure to keep this share brief. Your goal is to highlight the work of partnerships who tried a strategy you know other students would benefit from. This is not a time to hear the word-solving strategies the class used.

The meeting area erupted into buzzing.

Convene readers and emphasize that looking in words can be an underutilized strategy, one that is powerful.

"Readers, do you see how much more power you have in tackling these tricky words when you bring all you know from looking *inside* the word and all you know from looking *around* the word? Looking inside the word and breaking it up into meaning units is a strategy that I don't think you all use all of the time, and as you saw today, it can pay off big time. This is a strategy that should always be one of the ones you have in your toolbox for dealing with tricky vocabulary, because as you heard from the researchers, it's a big deal." I revealed this strategy on the chart.

LINK

Send readers off to continue to read, paying special attention today to how they figure out tricky vocabulary.

"Readers, I'm going to send you off to read, and I'd like you to pay special attention to tricky vocabulary as you read today. What strategies are most helpful for you today? What kinds of words were tricky? Be sure to mark some tricky words so you can study them with a partner later and talk about helpful strategies. I also want to tell you before you go off that vocabulary directly relates to reading comprehension. That means the stronger you are at figuring out vocabulary and the more words you know, the stronger you'll become as a reader, too. So take this vocabulary work very seriously. It is a big deal. Okay, readers, head off."

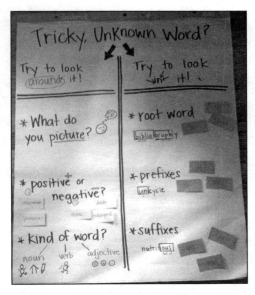

FIG. 6–1   Students add words and word parts to an interactive version of the chart.

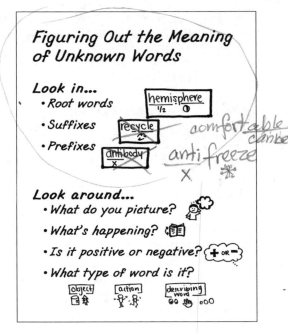

Supporting Today's Learning and Previous Learning

AS YOU CONFER and lead small groups today, remember that your emphasis needs to keep the work of the entire unit alive, while also helping students put the day's new instruction into action. You will definitely want to overview the class's work and to think about what needs your support especially.

Ensure that students are reading accessible nonfiction texts.

Chances are good that some students are bogged down with nonfiction texts that are too difficult for them. All your talk about the strategies for tackling complex texts may well lead students to think you want them reading texts that are well beyond their reach. If you think this is a problem, you may want these children to self-identify. You could stand in the middle of the room and say, "A number of you are reading texts that feel a bit like black diamond ski trails. They may not look that hard at first glance, but nonfiction texts are often deceptive. They have pretty pictures and look like no big deal, but actually they are hard. If your text seems that way—like it is black diamond—will you bring the text to the meeting area and let's talk."

Once kids gather, you can remind them that they should mostly be reading books they can read with 96% accuracy. Most people would suggest that students stick with texts in which their accuracy is 94% or above. Help kids realize what that means in terms of the number of tricky words they're going to encounter in a chunk of text, and point out that probably every student in that group is holding a text that is just too hard. "You need to basically understand the text and to read it like you are talking, like your regular speech, for the text to be working for you." Get the kids to work together to decide if the text is hard, and then be ready to give book introductions on one or two super high-interest, easy texts. Ideally you have multiple copies of a few of those texts so you can get this group of readers onto an accessible one you have introduced, reading in sync with a partner. Plan on gathering this group every day for the next sequence of days. It might help to lead guided reading groups with them.

Coach readers to lift the level of their work.

Meanwhile, you will also want to coach readers in ways that lift the level of their work. For example, you'll decide that some of them, like Fallon, should be taking notes in which not only do they record the main ideas and supportive details of the text but they also think in response to the text. If you recruited one youngster to begin this work before others do, you could empower that one child—in this instance, Fallon—to show others what she has been doing and to tell them about the strategies she has used. Then other students, as well, could begin taking notes in which they record their own thinking about a text.

You might help other readers to get onto lines of inquiry. As they finish one text and begin another, are they thinking about how they can continue to learn more about the first text? The next bend of this unit will highlight the importance of this work, and so if you do teach students to make their own text sets, you can look ahead into that bend for ideas on ways to lift the level of students' work once they are reading several related texts.

Boost students knowledge of prefixes, suffixes, and root words.

Some of your teaching today might boost your students' knowledge of prefixes, suffixes, and root words. You might pull together some students to help them notice prefixes. For example, you might teach them the prefixes that mean *not*: *a-*, *un-*, *im-*, *in-*, *dis-*, *anti-*, *il-*, *mis-*, and *ir-*. You could teach this directly, but it might be more memorable for students to form an inquiry group and collect examples of these prefixes (with words to accompany).

You might say, "There are many prefixes that mean *not*. One of those is *a-*," as you jot that down on a Post-it or index card, "Let's look at the word *typical*. That means normal, or average, for a person or place. When you add the *a-* it becomes *atypical*, or not typical. It means that someone or something is not its usual self." Then you could ask students to add to the list of words, saying, "Do you know others that fit this

(continues)

"Readers, I know you are reading up a storm and don't want to stop, but I just have to tell you two really cool things. First, there are some members of this class who have decided, all on their own, to make word walls of the words they are discovering. Better yet, some of you have invented totally amazing things to do on those word walls. Ryan is drawing little pictures of each word he figures out (and some of those words aren't easily illustrated!). Sasha is using every word she learns in a teeny entry about our cafeteria food!

"I'm pretty sure others of you have other ways you are working to own your vocabulary, and whatever you are deciding to do is great as long as you don't just see a word, skip past it, and read on, leaving that word behind you. Skilled readers are people who learn from their reading, and one of the ways to learn about an octopus is to learn about *jet propulsion*, and one of the ways to learn about whatever topic you are studying is to learn the topic's key words.

"Back to your reading, and your word work!"

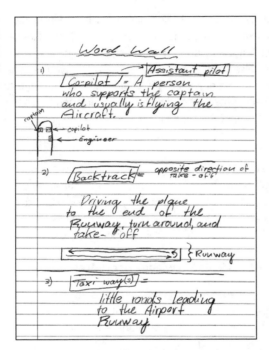 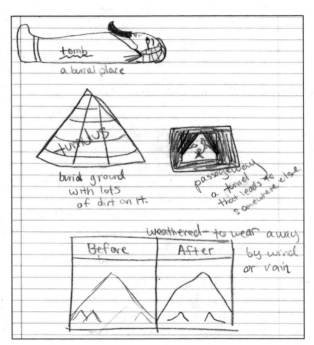

FIG. 6–2 Samples of students' innovative word walls.

pattern as well?" They might be able to think of a few, or you might drive them back to their books to see if they can find words to add to this.

As they go off, anticipate that some students will find words that begin with those letters but do not fit the pattern. For example, one or two will find *important* and say,

"It's got *im*-! Let's add it to the list. Like *important* means *not portant*." You will need to say something like, "Here's the tricky part. Some words start with those letters but don't fit the patterns. In those instances, the letters are part of their root word, not a prefix."

Sharing Tricky Words and Strategies

Convene readers with their texts, the hard words they have marked, and their notebooks. Coach students as they share word-solving strategies.

"Readers, in a minute, I'm going to ask you to talk to a partner about some of the tricky words that you found and the strategies that you used to figure out those words. Be sure to let your partner know about your process. You might say, 'I started off by looking *inside* the word and that gave me some ideas . . . because I noticed . . . and that made me think of . . . . Then I looked *around* the word and I thought that some of the clues in the text were . . . so I thought maybe the word could mean . . . .'

"Take some time to get ready to share," I said. After a bit I said, "Okay, turn and share."

Channel partnerships to self-assess their work using the "Word Solving" thread of the learning progression.

"Here's a copy of the 'Word Solving' thread of the learning progression. You haven't studied this one yet, but you know a lot about how to use this tool. With your partner, will you take an honest look at the work you've been doing in Word Solving? Think about the strategies you just shared—where do you see those strategies on the strand? Mark up the strand in a way that shows the strategies you've been using." I gave students a few minutes to self-assess their work in partnerships.

"Don't just circle a whole paragraph," I voiced over. "Only circle the parts you've really been doing, the parts you and your partner can cite evidence of. Look at each part of the strand closely."

After students worked a bit, I voiced over again. "Will you also notice what you're not yet doing? With your partner, make a plan for how you can lift your word-solving work.

"So it does seem, readers, that as books get trickier, it does pay off more and more to look in the word. That's something we should definitely all keep in mind. Tonight, you can put your plan into action and really strengthen your practice."

CAPTURING THE MEANINGS OF NEW WORDS

Readers, today we continued our study of tricky words. We learned when it paid off to look *inside* a word to determine exactly what the word meant. You even developed your own plan to strengthen your word-solving work.

Tonight, begin putting your plan into action. Continue to look for the multiple main ideas in your texts. Also, make sure you're learning multiple words. Use a variety of strategies to help you figure out what tricky words mean. And make sure you have a system to capture the meanings of these new words. If you created your own system today in class, keep adding new words you're learning. Create a system if you don't have one yet. You might make your own personal word wall with little pictures and definitions. Or you can come up with your own unique system.

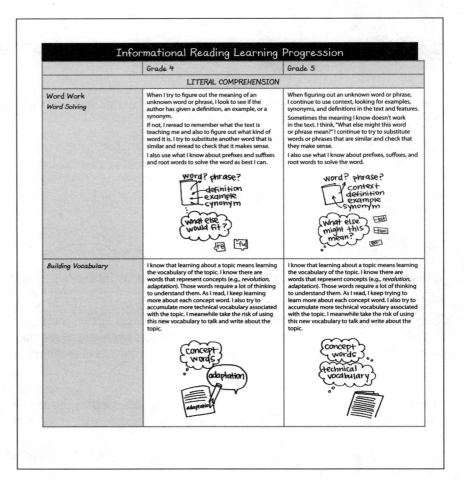

Handwritten note at top left:
③ How can I consider the structure of longer texts—noticing OVERALL structure & how chunks of texts are built?

Complex Thinking about Structure
From Sentence Level to Text Level

THIS SESSION RETURNS to the concept that complex texts are structured in complex ways. Instead of an emphasis on naming the structures (compare and contrast, problem-solution, and so forth), this session has another way to approach the challenge of constructing meaning from fragmented texts. You point out that a reader always needs to integrate information. Sometimes readers of nonfiction texts integrate information that comes from text boxes, diagrams, and charts, as well as from the main text, and other times those bits and pieces are actually all part of the main text. That is, the page can look monolithic—presenting itself as just one page of paragraphs—but that text may actually consist of a collage of bits. Whether the text has text boxes, charts, diagrams, and the like or is comprised of one page of print, either way the reader is asked to create an overarching understanding of what the text is saying.

During this session, you remind students that even if a text appears at first glance to be a single, coherent text, it may well be a patchwork of pieces—containing, for example, passages that are written as narratives and passages that are clearly expository. Students dig deeply into one section of the read-aloud text, noticing how structures change within parts, chunking how subtopics may be broken into smaller parts, which each deliver additional information on the topic. They'll explore how those parts sometimes shift in structure. Later in the session, you'll look with students at structural challenges at the sentence level, noting that as texts become more complex, sentences carry additional information.

Today's share supports students in inferring within texts and provides an opportunity to support students in using academic and domain-specific vocabulary, including those that signal contrast, addition, and other logical relationships. As students analyze phrases within a text, coach students to use phrases such as *nevertheless, however, in addition,* and *similarly.*

IN THIS SESSION, you'll teach readers that they can study and consider the structure of texts at many levels. They can think about how texts are built at the smallest level—the sentence level—to how part of a text is built to how the entire text is built.

GETTING READY

✔ Prepare to project an article with many related text features on the same page for students to figure out how they connect to the whole. The example we use is "Earthquake Alert" from *Super Science Magazine* (September 2014) but you could use any article that has many text features (see Connection).

✔ Prepare to add to the "Ways Complex Nonfiction Gets Hard" anchor chart (see Teaching and Active Engagement and Mid-Workshop Teaching).

✔ Enlarge a class copy of pages 42 and 43 of *When Lunch Fights Back* (Teaching and Active Engagement).

✔ Display the "Common Nonfiction Text Structures" chart from Grade 4 Unit 2 *Reading the Weather, Reading the World*, highlighting familiar text structures and transition words (see Teaching and Active Engagement).

✔ Have chart paper and markers handy to use to develop complex sentences (see Mid-Workshop Teaching).

✔ Remind students to bring their copies of the level 5 text, "Lessons from the Deep" (see Share).

✔ Create a "Lenses to Carry When Reading History" chart (see Share).

Complex Thinking about Structure
From Sentence Level to Text Level

CONNECTION

Show readers an article with lots of different text features on a page. State the obvious: reading texts like this involves building something coherent from the fragments.

"Readers, I want to show you an article from a magazine I was just reading." On the document camera, I showed a page or two from the magazine.

"As I am showing this article to you, I want you to notice how much is on a page. I mean look at this! In addition to the columns of main text, there's also a map and a labeled diagram." I peered more closely at the article. "And the diagram seems to be showing a process. Plus, there are illustrations, as well as a whole separate text box at the end, which seems to be how to do a procedure. Whew! That's a ton on the page, right? To really read and understand this article, we need to carefully consider every single part of the article, asking how all the parts fit together. So, one of the things that makes this article so tricky is its structure, right?"

Point out that when texts look monolithic—all print—they may in fact be structured as a mosaic of pieces. Suggest that tackling text complexity involves constructing meaning from fragments.

"Readers, here is the point I want to make. When you look at a text like this—with text boxes and maps and charts and so forth—it is really clear to you that reading involves building a coherent meaning out of all these pieces of text. But there are other texts that don't have so many obvious parts," I picked up *When Lunch Fights Back* and leafed through a few pages, "but which actually are written in similar ways, just without all the boxes that make the parts so obvious.

"As we continue tackling complex nonfiction, then, I think it's a good idea for us to figure out how one reads texts that look like this," and I again showed the first text, "and also texts that don't at first glance *look* like that, but which actually have a very similarly complex structure.

"I think it might help if we consider the word structure. In the spirit of yesterday's work of looking *in* words," I smiled at the class and winked, "let's look inside the word structure." I jotted the word down on the white board. "*Struct* is a root word that means to build. So *structure* is about building. It's about how texts are built. And just like you can connect and build a single row of Legos, or a part of a Lego building or an entire Lego building, the same is true of texts."

◆ COACHING

Teachers, it doesn't really matter what article you choose to show here. Any article from Junior Scholastic *or* Super Science *or another magazine with lots of text features would work well. The point is to show students how many different text features are on the page. Another choice would be a higher-level text from the* Time Nonfiction Kids *series. Those often have many text features on a page as well. In order to keep this connection concrete, know that I am actually referring to the article "Earthquake Alert" from* Super Science Magazine *(September 2014) but the points made here are transferable to lots of other texts.*

Suggest jotting text structure for chunks in margins

Name the teaching point.

"Today I want to teach you that as texts get more complex, readers must study and consider the structure of those texts, noticing the *overall* structure and how chunks of texts are built."

TEACHING AND ACTIVE ENGAGEMENT

Set readers up to discuss the overall structure of a nonfiction text, in this case the class read-aloud. Coach in as readers discuss the text.

"Let's try discussing the structure of a pretty complex text—our class read-aloud, *When Lunch Fights Back*—talking about it at the whole-text level. This would be like talking about the kind of building we're making out of Legos—an apartment building, a fort, a castle."

I opened up to Chapter 8, "Meet My Bodyguards," and started flipping through the pages. "Hmm, . . . structure at the text level? Well, one of the things we've noticed is that each chapter goes a predictable way, that the structure kind of repeats. With your partner, talk through how each chapter goes."

Partners turned and talked, discussing how the first section of each chapter tended to tell a story about an animal and its incredible defenses. However, when they discussed the second part, they only discussed the content of the section, not how it was structured. I decided to stop students and give some tips to lift the level of their work.

Share out what students noticed and what was hard. Ask them to listen as you read aloud a chunk of text from a tricky section and to name its overall structure.

"I heard you say that the structure of the text is really interesting, that it's a hybrid made up of these two different parts. You noticed that each chapter taught about a different kind of animal defense, and then inside the chapter, the author started by telling the story of an animal. You said it felt like a narrative, about a tiny chunk of time in the animal's life. Then, you noticed that the second part was trickier to describe. You knew what it was teaching, but it was harder to talk about the overall structure. Let's try it again, looking at evidence in the text that helps us notice how the text is structured.

"Let me read you a bit of the 'The Science behind the Story.' As I do, will you think about how this chunk is structured and if the structure always works this way for this section?" I read aloud the section on pages 42 and 43 and then gave students a chance to turn and talk.

> *Plants can't hide from predators. They can't fly or run away. Even so, plants are far from defenseless. Black mustard plants produce substances that make their leaves taste bad to most plant eaters. But cabbage white caterpillars actually like the taste of mustard leaves. So when cabbage white butterflies mount an egg-laying attack, mustard plants fight back by getting wasps to defend them.*

When students were in fourth grade, they learned that some texts are hybrids, texts that contain distinct parts. For example, a text might include a narrative part that sounds like a story and an expository part that reads like it's teaching a lot of information. Students learned to notice the signals authors use to let readers know when to read with a narrative lens and when to read with an expository lens, and then to read those sections differently. Your discussion here of a text's overall structure draws on this earlier work.

I called on Spencer to share out what he and Matthew discussed. "The follow-up section seems trickier. Sometimes it sounds like a report like it did here, but not always, 'cause sometimes it feels a bit like a story, with the scientists as the characters."

Debrief the replicable moves the class made and add a bullet to the anchor chart.

I sat back. "Okay, readers, do you see how when we talked about the structure of our read-aloud, we talked about the big ways it was organized, noticing a complex, hybrid structure, and read small snippets of text as examples?" I added to the "Ways Complex Nonfiction Gets Hard" anchor chart.

> **ANCHOR CHART**
>
> ### Ways Complex Nonfiction Gets Hard
>
> - The headings and subheadings don't help or are misleading.
> - There are several main ideas.
> - The central ideas and main ideas are implicit (hidden).
> - The vocabulary is hard and technical.
> - **There are many complex/hybrid structures.**

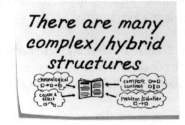

"What's tricky about this work is that it can look, at first glance, like *When Lunch Fights Back* just has these big overall text structures. There aren't all those captions and headings and diagrams that let us know that the section, obviously, is made up of a ton of parts. But we know that texts like this are still made up of all kinds of parts, even if you can't obviously see them. It's likely our subtopic here—about how scientists studied black mustard plants—is going to contain a lot of parts. These smaller parts might contain different text structures, and the author will include signals—though they may not be obvious ones—to help us identify the structure of a chunk."

Set students up to study structure at the part level, noticing parts contained within a subtopic and then labeling those parts to describe their structure. Remind students of common text structures.

"Remember this chart from fourth grade? Last year, it helped you remember common structures in texts and transition words that signaled each text structure. With this chart in mind, will you and your partner read pages 42 and 43 from *When Lunch Fights Back*, noticing and noting the different parts of the text?" Partnerships sprang into action.

Your tone and pacing is critical here. You want to make it clear that the work you are asking students to do identifying common structures in texts is nothing new. You know they've done this work before, and now you're simply asking them to apply what they already know in a new context. This work should be familiar to students, so you will want to move through it quickly, posting the chart and resisting the urge to read it aloud and teach students what each text structure is.

Common Nonfiction Text Structures

Structure	Transition words
Chronological	first, then, next, after that, finally, before, after
Problem/solution	a problem is, a solution is, if . . . then . . . , so that
Cause and effect	because, since, reasons, then, therefore, so, in order
Compare/contrast	different, same, alike, similar, although, but, yet, or

Coach into partnerships to raise the level of their work, and voice over relevant tips for the whole class.

I handed markers to two partners, saying, "Will you try this work marking up what you find?"

As partnerships worked, I coached in and voiced over with tips. "Don't just label the text structure! Look for signal words that clued you into the text structure and mark those words somehow." Students leapt into action.

A bit later, I added, "Remember that one paragraph might have multiple parts in it, and multiple paragraphs might be one part. With complex texts like this, you have to be flexible."

Debrief, naming what students noticed while studying the text in transferrable ways.

Soon, the text was marked up with parts boxed out, text structures labeled, and key words that signaled text structure circled.

"Readers, you're noticing something complex about the paragraphs in your text. You found that each part of the paragraph, too, can carry more information and that is a big way in which paragraphs become more complex. A famous researcher once called this 'writing in paragraphs of thought, not sentences of thought,' because a single sentence gets elaborated upon, so it is now a paragraph. And as a result, readers, for example, learn about the research that German biologist Nina Fatouros did in not just one paragraph but across several.

"And I heard you saying it felt like the author Rebecca Johnson was kinda sneaky, because sometimes she changed structures on you right in the middle of a chunk. Like at first, you thought the text was organized into a problem and solution, and then boom, she switched to cause and effect, without hardly any warning.

"That's definitely another way texts get complex, by shifting in structure unexpectedly." I added to our "Ways Complex Nonfiction Gets Hard" chart.

As you support partnerships, note the way students talk about the structure of the text. Do students identify signal words that indicate the structure of the text is changing? Do they note an overall text structure but fail to notice that paragraphs (and even chunks of sentences within paragraphs) can have their own text structure? Jot down any needs you notice, and use them to inform your small-group work later.

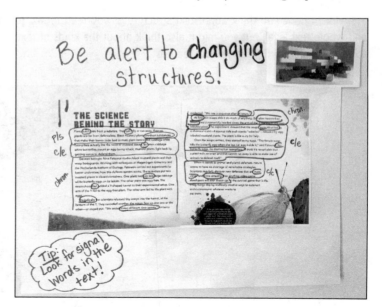

FIG. 7–1　This chart captures what one class noticed about shifting text structures.

Ways Complex Nonfiction Gets Hard

- The headings and subheadings don't help or are misleading.
- There are several main ideas.
- The central ideas and main ideas are implicit (hidden).
- The vocabulary is hard and technical.
- There are many complex/hybrid structures.
- **Subtopics may each be broken into multiple parts.**
- **Parts can shift in structure.**

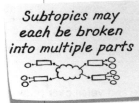

Subtopics may each be broken into multiple parts

Parts can shift in structure

LINK

Send readers off to continue to read and to notice anything interesting or unusual related to structure as they read today.

"Readers, I hope you think about text structure as you read today. You might think about the challenges at the part and whole-text level, but you might also think about the kinds of text structures you see (compare/contrast, problem/solution, and so forth). Off you go, readers!"

Watching and Listening Carefully to What Students Are Doing around Text Complexity

AS YOUR STUDENTS MOVE OFF to read today, you might decide to devote some time to really listening to what they are thinking and doing around text complexity. They have had a series of lessons on what makes nonfiction get harder, and so you'll ask questions such as, "What are you thinking are the challenges in your book? How are you working to address them?"

As students begin talking about what they have been trying to do, look for opportunities to say, "Show me how you've been doing that." You are looking for a student to show you a part of the text, perhaps reading that to you, and then show you what he or she did to make sense of that part. You might see a series of Post-its or a notebook entry, or you might hear about rereading and perhaps going to other texts on the same topic.

There are some general principles of conferring that you will want to remember as you work with students. One of these is the idea that when conducting research at the start of a conference, it is really important to explore more than one line of inquiry. So if your first question is, "What have you been working on in your reading?" and the reader talks about, say, pace, you will want to learn about that work but to not necessarily feel bound to teach into that. Instead, you can then say, "So one thing you are working on is your pace. What else have you been trying to do to get better as a nonfiction reader?" Of course, there are a million other possible questions you could ask, but my point is that you won't want to simply jump onto whatever the reader first mentions. You will, instead, want to draw on more sources of information about the reader before deciding what you could teach that would make the biggest difference.

You'll want to note patterns as you confer with your students, realizing that what you see reflects not only them, but also your teaching. If, for example, you notice that most of them are not taking notes after all, you will need to think, "What did I do to signal that note-taking is entirely optional?" If students seem to start and abandon books rather than committing to one, you again will need to see that as a reflection on your

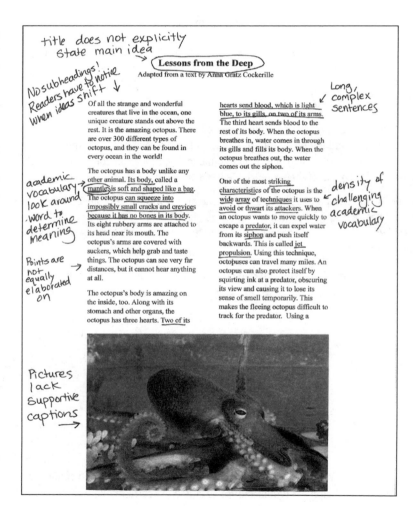

FIG. 7–2   A teacher uses a marked-up copy of "Lessons from the Deep" in his conferences.

Longer/complex sent.

"Earlier, we looked at how the structures of parts and overall texts were complex. In the texts we're reading now, sentences are getting more complex too. Instead of saying, 'The octopus can be found in every ocean in the world!' the texts now say, 'There are over 300 different types of octopus, and they can be found in every ocean in the world.' That information about the 300 different types of octopus is just tucked in!

"As texts get harder, one sentence can hold much more information. There are different parts to the sentence—the front part of it, the back part of it, the middle of it—and each part can hold more or less information. Let's take this sentence," I said as I wrote it on chart paper.

> I went to the park.

"Will those sitting over here," and I pointed to one side of the classroom, "think about how to add information to the front end of the sentence, those here (in the middle) think about adding information to the middle of the sentence, and those on the right, to the end of the sentence? Talk to each other."

After listening to partners speak for a moment, I rewrote the sentence based on what I heard: first, when and under what conditions the person did the action, then to tell what the action was like, and finally to develop the ending of the sentence by telling more about it.

> Late in the morning, after the rain stopped, I went quickly down the road and to the park, the one at the far end of my street where there is a giant baseball field.

"Right now, will you dive into your text? Can you find a sentence like this in your text, a sentence that carries a lot of information? Share it with your partner, naming out some of the different parts and what those parts include. Then, continue reading, paying careful attention to all the information carried in each part of these complex sentences."

I added to our anchor chart.

ANCHOR CHART

Ways Complex Nonfiction Gets Hard

- The headings and subheadings don't help or are misleading.
- There are several main ideas.
- The central ideas and main ideas are implicit (hidden).
- The vocabulary is hard and technical.
- There are many complex/hybrid structures.
- Subtopics may each be broken into multiple parts.
- Parts can shift in structure.
- **Sentences are longer and may deliver more information.**

> *Sentences are longer & may deliver more information*
>

teaching. And, of course, whatever patterns you notice will influence your mid-workshop teaching and your shares as well as your conferring and small-group instruction.

You might prepare for your conferences and small-group work by bringing some tools with you. Think how helpful it would be, for example, to carry marked-up copies of the octopus texts with you, as well as clean copies that you can use to either help you demonstrate something or as texts for the students to practice on. In addition, you'll want to carry your read-aloud with you. Some teachers also create toolkit pages designed to support students in practicing predictable specific strategies and carry these with them as well.

Carrying Familiar Lenses to Scientific Texts

Share

Remind students of familiar lenses from fourth grade that readers carry when reading historical texts. Suggest that these can also be used when reading scientific texts.

"Readers, let's gather together in the meeting area. Do you remember how last year when you were studying the American Revolution you learned that people read differently based on the discipline in which they are reading? In particular, you learned that readers of history pay attention to *who*, *where*, and *when*." I posted the "Lenses to Carry When Reading History" chart students had studied in the previous grade.

Channel students to investigate whether these lenses hold true for scientific texts by first studying one lens as a class.

"I thought we could investigate this together and see if those lenses also apply to scientific texts. Are you up for it? Let's try carrying the first lens together, *people and relationships*. We'll read a chunk from "Lessons from the Deep," and ask ourselves, 'Who are the players? What are their relationships? Who holds power? Who doesn't?'" I projected the text, skipped down to the fourth and fifth paragraphs, and started reading aloud.

> One of the most striking characteristics of the octopus is the wide array of techniques it uses to avoid or thwart its attackers. When an octopus wants to move quickly to escape a predator, it can expel water from its siphon and push itself backwards. This is called jet propulsion. Using this technique, octopuses can travel many miles. An octopus can also protect itself by squirting ink at a predator, obscuring its view and losing its sense of smell temporarily. This makes the fleeing octopus difficult to track for the predator. Using a network of pigment cells and specialized muscles in its skin, the octopus can also instantaneously match the colors, patterns, and even textures of its surroundings. And if a predator manages to grab an octopus by the arm, the octopus has one more trick up its sleeve. This escape artist can break off its arm, swim away, and then grow a new one later with no permanent damage.

> This unique creature is also a nocturnal hunter. It has a varied diet, including snails, fish, turtles, small crustaceans, and even other octopuses. An octopus catches its prey by grabbing it with its arms, sometimes using ink to disorient their victims first. To kill its prey, an octopus bites it with its tough beak-like jaws and injects it with venomous saliva, paralyzing it. Only one type of octopus, the Australian blue-ringed octopus, can kill a human with its poison.

Lenses to Carry When Reading History

Who: people, relationships
- *Who are the players?*
- *What are their relationships?*
- *Who holds power? Who doesn't?*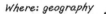

Where: geography
- *How does the geography affect big events?*
- *How does the geography affect people's lives?*

When: timeline
- *What is the sequence of big events?*
- *Are there cause and effect links?*

"With your partner, think about the *who*, the people (or creatures!) and relationships in the text. Ask yourself the questions on our chart if you need them." I gave students a minute to talk and then called them back.

"I heard you saying that the octopus is one player, and the predators and prey, like snails and turtles, are the other players. You said it's a predator–prey relationship, that one of the creatures is always trying to eat the other one. I heard some of you say that who holds power changes, that sometimes it seems like the octopus holds power over its prey, grabbing it and disorienting it and then paralyzing it! And other times, it seems like the prey almost always holds power over the octopus, and they make it flee to escape them! So, carrying the lens of people and relationships can definitely pay off in scientific texts."

Rally students to study how the remaining lenses apply to scientific texts. Coach students as they work.

"What about those other lenses? This half of the rug, will you think about *where* the text is taking place, the geography, and see if you can figure out how the geography influences what happens? And this half of the rug, will you pay attention to the timeline, to *when* things happened, and see if you can figure out what led up to big events and what resulted from them?" Students launched into their work.

I knelt down next to the side of the rug studying geography. "Think about the place where the octopus lives and what that place is like. How does where the octopus lives, the deep ocean, affect the events in the octopus' life? Consider how the octopus uses its environment to help it and how it changes its environment."

To the side of the rug paying careful attention to the timeline, I said, "Use your knowledge of text structure to help you. Where do you see events happening in order? Where do you see cause-and-effects links? Study those parts closely."

SESSION 7 HOMEWORK

 # NOTICING TEXT STRUCTURES

Readers, tonight as you read, keep an eye on structure. What else do you notice? Also, you might try looking at the structure of other nonfiction texts, such as an article in the paper. Does that article's structure fit with what we were talking about today? How about your manual for playing a video game? Does that fit? Come in with some new thoughts and ideas about structure. Be sure to write these in your notebook so you don't forget!

Handwritten notes at top of page:

? What tools & strategies do I have when the text get confusing?

T-Chart: Ways NF gets / Strategies hard / I use

Midlesson: Working w/ text @ their level. Not too hard.

Share: 3 things interested in researching

Session 8

Rising to the Challenges of Nonfiction

OVER THE PAST SEVERAL LESSONS, you've engaged students in an exploration of text complexity. Your students are alert to ways their texts are complex, and probably could give a mini course on text complexity to anyone visiting your classroom.

Today's session seeks to extend this work. You'll introduce students to a tool that the Teachers College Reading and Writing Project community has developed to remind students of the ways nonfiction texts are complex and of the strategies they know for dealing with those complexities.

In a sense, you've been building this tool with students since Session 4 when you began the "Ways Complex Nonfiction Gets Hard" chart. For us, this kind of tool is used almost like yarn on the finger to remind students of concepts and strategies that they've already studied. This is not a substitute for the work that your students have done over the past two weeks, but rather a reminder of that work.

You'll see that the tool consists of two charts—one listing ways that nonfiction texts tend to become more complex and the other listing matching strategies for tackling those sorts of text complexity. Because the chart has lovely artwork accompanying it, it has a bit of grandeur. Don't let that convince you that there is something sacrosanct about it. There are lots of other ways that texts become complex and other ways to deal with text complexity. Think of this as one approach, and feel welcome to alter it as you wish.

We have found that when a student is daunted by the complexity of a text, it helps the student to name the kinds of challenges the text poses, to mark those challenges, and to note strategies that he or she can use to tackle them. This work is reasonable for students to do for a little while. It allows the reader who might otherwise feel paralyzed to at least have one way to proceed: he or she can find the right card, place it in the right spot on the text, and feel productive just because that job is done. Then the reader can begin reading and use the self-identified card as a whispered cue suggesting the strategy the reader might use.

IN THIS SESSION, you'll teach students that readers monitor their own comprehension, and when they notice their comprehension breaking down, they rely on a toolkit of strategies to help get themselves unstuck.

GETTING READY

✔ For each student, print out a set of text complexity cards, double-sided with the challenges on one side and the strategies on the other. Cut them apart and place them in a baggie (see Connection, Teaching, and Active Engagement).

✔ Prepare to project "Lessons from the Deep," the level 6 version of the "Amazing Octopus" text, for the class (see Teaching and Active Engagement).

✔ Be ready to rally students to select topics for the inquiry projects they'll pursue in Bend II (see Share).

✔ Take a close look at the homework section for tonight, as it launches important research that students will draw on in Session 11 (see Homework).

This could, of course, make reading feel more like playing cards than reading. Avoid that! Keep in mind that if a reader doesn't experience difficulty, then that reader doesn't need to reach for strategies. The conscious decision to try one strategy or another is a reader's response to difficulty. You and I read nonfiction texts without thinking about needing to pause to chunk what we have just read, nor needing to think about looking around a new term to ascertain its meaning. Hopefully many of your readers function on autopilot a good deal of the time as well, and those readers won't need to think about text complexity and strategies until they encounter a text that raises the bar.

"When a student is daunted by the complexity of a text, it helps to name, mark, and strategize about those challenges."

Notice that you will tell students that this tool is just temporary, something to scaffold them as they try this new and challenging work. You name the tool as something they'll use only until the work becomes automatic, internalized in their minds, at which time you'll remove it.

Remember, finally, that this tool can be adapted and extended. Students in one class that piloted this unit rose to the challenge of creating their own text complexity cards,

personalizing their set with the strategies that worked best for them. You might choose to separate and color-code the cards, with one color for complexities and one color for strategies, and then ask students to sort and match the complexities and strategies themselves.

The possibilities are endless. Enjoy! Remember Don Murray's advice, "The learner's energy should go up, not down." Make sure this tool increases energy.

In addition to introducing the text complexity cards, today's session also launches the personal inquiry projects students will devote themselves to in Bend II. During today's share, you'll demonstrate how you think over the research you've already done, consider other topics you're interested in, and then determine what you'd like your inquiry project focus to be. As part of this, you'll highlight a few topics that would pay off for students to study—most likely topics for which you already have resources in the classroom. Then, you'll channel students to select inquiry topics they're dying to study. Today's homework builds off of this, as does the homework for the next few days. Students will begin researching their topics, not only gathering and studying print sources, but also conducting primary research, interviewing people knowledgeable about their topic, conducting surveys, and making observations.

We recommend you look ahead to the first session in Bend II, reading at least the prelude of that session so you can orient your students toward their upcoming research. Note that this research will be most potent if it truly does revolve around topics of personal interest. Allow for video games, music groups, sports teams, origami, and the like even if these aren't subjects that will have a lot of academic currency. In this particular instance, passion for the topic will be important.

MINILESSON

Rising to the Challenges of Nonfiction

CONNECTION

◆ COACHING

Remind students of the journey they have taken into text complexity, and introduce students to a new tool that will help them tackle those challenges.

"Readers, we've been doing a lot of thinking about what makes informational texts get harder, and I think you guys have really unlocked some big secrets. I have a tool for you that shows some of those discoveries you have been making.

"Before I give you your own copies of this tool, let me just tell you a little bit about it. You know how we began talking at the beginning of the unit about how we needed to figure out what makes texts get harder and devise strategies for what to do to tackle those challenges? Well, this tool captures some of the challenges you found in your texts, and it conveys some of the strategies that you have developed for tackling those challenges." I fanned a small deck of text complexity cards (available in the online resources), which I had printed on cardstock. Each card named and visually showed a challenge posed by complex informational texts on one side and a strategy to tackle that challenge on the other side.

Explain to readers how they might use the new tool to monitor their own comprehension.

"Readers, if you are reading along and the text feels fine—if you can make a mental model of what you are learning and you feel like your mind is on fire—then that is not a time to use this tool. But if, on the other hand, you are not sure what you just read, or you are feeling a bit daunted by the text, then you might use this tool to think about the part of the text that feels hard, asking, 'What's making this so hard?' Then you can use these cards to help you think about the sources of text complexity.

"Perhaps, for example, you think, 'There are no headings or obvious chunks.' You can stick that card onto that part of your text, and if you flip it over, it suggests one strategy—and you all helped to develop these strategies for how you might deal with that challenge. You can try out that strategy, using it on the part of text that was just tricky, then read on until you perhaps encounter another challenging part."

❖ Name the teaching point.

"Today I want to teach you that as nonfiction readers monitor their own comprehension, they notice when they're confused or feeling stuck, and they turn to tools and strategies for help."

Here you communicate to students that while the text complexity cards provide reminders of complexities in the text and the strategies students can use to tackle those complexities, students should only turn to the text complexity cards when they face difficulty and need support. That is, the goal of today's work is not that students will turn to their text complexity cards at the end of each section of the text. Instead, you want to emphasize that this is a temporary support students should only draw on as needed.

SESSION 8: RISING TO THE CHALLENGES OF NONFICTION

75

TEACHING

Read an excerpt from a text aloud. Model how you notice ways that the text gets complex and how you determine whether you can keep reading or need to turn to a strategy for support.

I distributed baggies to students with their text complexity cards inside and asked one student from each partnership to lay out their cards. "Readers, let's put this tool to use. Will you help me read through the sixth-grade version of the octopus text, 'Lessons from the Deep'?

"Let's read this passage as we would read any nonfiction texts. I'll read it aloud, and you try to grasp what it says, trying to learn as much as you can. When this is working, we'll just keep going. But chances are good that we'll come to parts of the text where things feel confusing, and it's really important to notice that confusion and stop reading. For now, accentuate the act of stopping by holding up a stop sign," and I gestured with my hand to show the signal I imagined kids using.

I projected the level 6 version of "Lessons from the Deep" and began reading aloud.

> *"Lessons from the Deep"*
>
> *Of all the strange and wonderful creatures that live in the ocean, one unique creature stands out above the rest. It is the amazing octopus.*

I glanced out at the readers. No stop signs. "So far, so good," I said, and continued reading.

> *"Mischief and craft are plainly seen to be the characteristics of this creature," Claudius Aelianus, a Roman natural historian, wrote at the turn of the third century A.D.*

Demonstrate how you use the new tool to identify a complexity in the text and find a strategy that will help you tackle that complexity.

"Huh?" I said, looking up and scratching my head. "I'm confused, aren't you?" Across the rug, students nodded enthusiastically. "Well, I know that when I'm reading along and start feeling stuck, I can turn to our tool to help me.

"I think what's feeling tricky about this text is that there are all these details layered in this tiny part." I scanned the cards in front of me. "So maybe the 'Text is dense, with lots of details' card will fit best.

"So, let's play this out." I flipped over the card. "The strategy suggested here is to 'summarize often, by talking or jotting; summarize as big ideas and supporting details.' So let's give this a try. I'll go back and reread, and will you listen to the big ideas and supports here?" I reread the first three lines.

> *Of all the strange and wonderful creatures that live in the ocean, one unique creature stands out above the rest. It is the amazing octopus. "Mischief and craft are plainly seen to be the characteristics of this creature," Claudius Aelianus, a Roman natural historian, wrote at the turn of the third century A.D.*

You'll want to pause early in the text, before the text feels confusing, so you can model how when the text makes sense, you continue reading along without turning to a tool to support. This helps students understand that they only need to turn to their text complexity cards when comprehension starts to break down.

"Let me try to summarize, to tell the main ideas and important supporting details. I think this is mostly about . . . maybe mostly about how the octopus is a unique ocean creature. The author says that clearly in the first two lines. So maybe the confusing quote is just a support to highlight a way the octopus is unique, that he's mischievous.

"Readers, do you see how using this tool is helping us think more deeply about what we're reading? We've even got some new ideas about the octopus that our previous articles didn't give us."

ACTIVE ENGAGEMENT

Set students up to continue reading, monitoring for their own comprehension. Coach students as they use the tool to tackle tricky parts.

"Now it's your turn to call the stops. I'm going to read on in the text, and as I do, notice when you stop really learning because you are confused or feeling stuck. In those moments, hold up a stop sign."

> *Humans have been catching and eating octopuses for hundreds of years, and yet their mystifying biology and intelligence continue to inspire and puzzle the researchers who study them.*

There were a few hands up, but I read on, on the lookout for more stop signs.

> *There are over 300 different types of octopus, and they can be found in every ocean in the world. This cephalopod's unique body, called a mantle, is soft and shaped like a bag.*

By now, nearly all hands were up and waving vigorously. "Readers, you know what to do. Turn to your tool, and work with your partner to identify the complexity you're finding here."

After looking through their text complexity cards, several students decided that the challenge was "There are several big/central ideas." Other students said the big challenge was that "There are no headings or obvious chunks." Still more thought the big idea was "The vocabulary is hard and technical, and it's explained by other hard, technical words."

This work moves students toward sixth-grade level work in 'Monitoring for Sense' on the learning progression. You teach students to come to texts expecting them to make sense, and then to monitor their own comprehension as they read, turning to strategies when comprehension breaks down.

FIG. 8–1 Allie turns to her text complexity cards when she encounters a tricky part.

"Whatever complexity you found, flip over the card. Look at the suggested strategy and give it a try on this text. You might need to reread or read on, or you might need to talk and jot." I coached in as students worked to apply the strategies they found to the text.

Debrief, and suggest that students utilize other strategies if the suggested one doesn't help.

"Readers, this is work you can do whenever you read. You can read on with your mind on fire, and, when you get confused, stop, notice what's challenging and try a strategy to address that challenge. Often, the strategies on your cards will help you, but sometimes you'll need to create your own strategy, turning to other resources in our room, like our charts, to help you."

LINK

Send students off to read, paying special attention to when their comprehension is strong and when their comprehension breaks down.

"Readers, I know you're eager to use this tool. Over time, though, I'm expecting that these kinds of challenges and strategies will be internalized in your mind, so that you won't need to go get the chart each time you are reading. For now, though, when things get a bit tricky and you've slowed down or stopped, you can think, 'What's tricky about this? What can I do?' and have a wide repertoire of ideas to help you answer that question. Off you go, readers!"

As you listen in, be on the lookout for a partnership who identified a challenge, used the strategy from the text complexity card, and found that the strategy suggested did not work. Coach in, and encourage this partnership to try another strategy, drawing on all the strategies they know from the unit to help them. Then, you might choose to highlight the work this partnership did so the other students in the class know what to do when they encounter a similar situation.

FIG. 8–2   Matthew uses the strategy suggested on the "there are several big/central ideas" card to help him navigate a dense chunk of text.

Using Text Complexity Cards in Your Conferences and Small Groups

YOU WILL PROBABLY WANT TO ENCOURAGE STUDENTS to use the text complexity cards. You are apt to find that before distributing the cards, many students had different feelings about texts being challenging. They may have been saying things like, "It's just boring, really. And crazy. It talks about all these random things that I've never even heard of." Or, "It started okay, but now I am sort of lost. I keep reading and hope it makes sense in the end." You'll find that the text complexity cards pinpoint challenges so that readers are now able to note, "The text expects an expert reader" or "The text demands prior knowledge," and this makes students feel less incapacitated by the level of challenge they encounter.

Of course, the text complexity cards can also make your conferences more concrete. You may say to one student, "I want to give you a tip that will help you whenever you come across pages filled with visuals, like these." Citing the strategy named on the card, you can say, "Some people find it helps to explain why a visual is here. You can ask yourself, 'Why is this here? What can I learn from it?'" After naming out a teaching point, you can quickly demonstrate the strategy or coach the student as he or she tries it.

In some schools, teachers worry that the full array of text complexity cards will overwhelm students, so they study the levels of text difficulty at different challenge levels of texts and then distribute the cards to the readers they believe will wrestle with those challenges the most. In other schools, teachers have decided that rather than giving the students the illustrated strategy cards, they believe their students will benefit from inventing the strategies and making their own set of cards. If you do distribute the cards, bear in mind that there are expectations of shared knowledge that may need to be explained. You might, for example, feel that the card that says, "There are several big/central ideas" and is illustrated with a light bulb going off in someone's brain may need an explanation. You may need to say, "Have you ever seen that in the cartoons? A character's walking along, and they start thinking about something and then, 'Bam!' an idea pops into their head and a light bulb pops on." The larger point is that always, tools like these need you to negotiate how they are brought into your classroom.

MID-WORKSHOP TEACHING   Holding Texts You Can Read

"Readers, some of you are using the text complexity cards to support you trying to read texts that are *way* too hard for you. Don't do that. We know that kids can zoom forward as readers and even do that in just one year, making huge dramatic strides. But for that to happen, you need to read books that you understand, that you can read as if you are talking, and that you can read almost all the words. Nonfiction texts will *still* be hard even if the text is within reach for you, so don't think there is somehow something good about holding texts you really can't understand. The thing is—those texts don't teach you to read, and what you really want is to get *so* much stronger. Have the courage to say, 'This book is still too hard for me. I'll come back to it in another month.'"

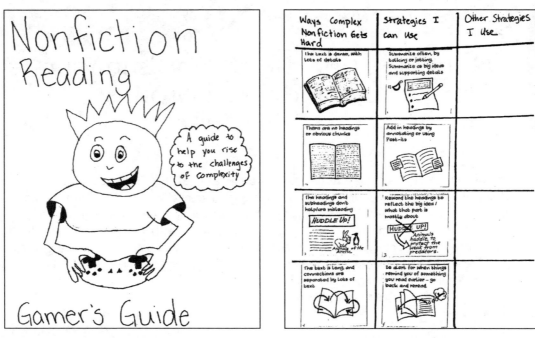

FIG. 8–3   One teacher made the cards into a text complexity packet—A Gamer's Guide to Nonfiction Reading.

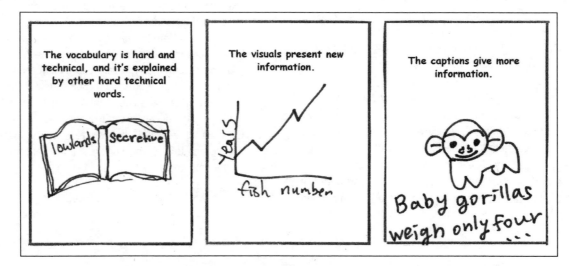

FIG. 8–4   Students in another class illustrated their cards as they encountered complexities in their texts.

Selecting Powerful Personal Inquiry Topics

Let students know that they have been doing all this text complexity work not only to get stronger at nonfiction reading, but also to read more about what they care about.

"Readers, I told you at the start of the unit that getting better as a nonfiction reader is a bit like getting better at video games. You need to be able to master the higher levels—and those higher levels have harder challenges and require different strategies. Well, I think you've certainly done a ton of work to master the higher levels. Well done!

"But . . ." I paused here, letting my voice trail off, letting students get curious. "Although I did tell you that getting better at nonfiction was a bit like getting better at playing video games, I need to point out that that isn't quite true. You haven't done all this work to understand text complexity just because you wanted to get better at a *game*. Instead, when you are able to read more complex nonfiction, that will actually open the world to you. It's a way for you to hang out with the big kids (the grown-ups) when you read. When you can tackle more complex texts as you read, it is like you are told that you don't need to be contained in the children's section of the library. You can go anywhere."

Channel students to think right away of at least three things they'd like to research to learn more about. Have them turn and tell a partner.

"I know you all have things you'd like to learn a ton more about. I've heard you talking about things you were really interested in. Sophia, I heard you telling Luna the other day that you're getting into soccer, and you've been learning everything you can about pro soccer teams. Lila was telling you, Marcus, about how she's totally curious about animal venom and how it works. And Spencer, I heard you telling Matthew that you're about to get a guinea pig, and you've never had a pet before, so there's a ton to learn there.

"I've been thinking about my interests, too. Our class read-aloud—*When Lunch Fights Back*—is getting me really interested in animal defenses and adaptations and it's making me wonder about scientists, who they are, what kind of research they do, and how they do it. Oh, and I'm also curious about the human brain. It does so much, and I know so little about it.

"Those are things I'd like to learn more about. Think of things you'd like to learn about," I said. "List at least three things across your fingers." I waited until I saw most of the class had three fingers extended and everyone had a least one. "Okay, tell your partner your three things you want to learn more about."

I listened, and then broadcast a few of the topics the class wanted to learn about.

"There are a lot of different interesting things that this class wants to know. Nina wants to know more about mummies, but she also wants to know more about the Loch Ness monster! Dexter wants to know more about being a singer and what that life's like. Iris wants to know more about video games. Fascinating!"

Let students know that they will have the chance to study a topic of their choosing. Set them up to choose a topic and begin researching as part of their homework tonight.

"In just a few days, you're going to launch head-on into inquiry projects on one of these topics, the one you're most interested in researching. For now, I'm going to ask you to choose the one topic you most want to investigate and then start thinking about and researching your topic, to get your feet wet, so that you're ready to hit the ground running when we start!"

SESSION 8 HOMEWORK

 # BEGINNING RESEARCH FOR YOUR INQUIRY

Readers, tonight begin researching your personal inquiry topic. First, make sure you select a topic for your inquiry project. It should be a topic you want to spend a few weeks studying. Choose a topic you can imagine researching in a lot of different ways: through books and articles, through Internet searches, through talking with people, doing surveys and more!

Once you've got your topic identified, start researching. You might:

- Look for books, articles, websites, and videos that will help you with your research.
- Start thinking about who you could interview to learn more about your topic. Do you have a friend who is an expert on your topic? A family member or neighbor who could help? Is there someone in the school you could turn to?
- Find places you could go to learn more about your topic. Is there a museum you could visit? An animal you could observe?

Jot down a plan for your research. You'll likely want to start a new section in your notebook that you can devote to the research you do on your topic.

Handwritten margin notes:
? How can I create in-depth summaries of complex NF text?
Mid-Lesson: Self-Assess Summaries & Revise
Share - Summary w/ Peer

Summarizing as Texts Get Harder

Y OU MAY BE SURPRISED to find summarizing reserved until the end of Bend I, but we've found that summarizing effectively is no simple task. Summarizing first requires students to read and comprehend a text. They have to determine main ideas the text teaches, condense similar points together, and then weigh the importance of the remaining points. To summarize, students are required to differentiate between information that's personally important and information that is significant to their summary. Then, too, they have to understand the text deeply enough to translate the information into their own words.

This is important work. In the March 2010 issue of *Educational Leadership*, Robert Marzano stated that "although the process of comprehension is complex, at its core, comprehension is based on summarizing—restating content in a succinct manner that highlights the most crucial information." Additionally, his research has found that teaching students summarizing strategies has a positive impact on students' understanding of the texts they read. Summarizing can help students understand the text they're reading, recognize when meaning breaks down, and remember the content they're reading. The ability to summarize a text down to its essential points and supports is a skill your students will draw on through college and beyond.

This lesson builds off the work your students did summarizing expository texts last year. However, as the texts they read become more complex, the work of summarizing those texts becomes increasingly complex. Likely, they'll be summarizing texts where the main ideas are unstated, and they'll have to draw on the strategies they learned earlier for determining main ideas stated implicitly. They may be summarizing texts where information is separated by large swatches of text, and they'll need to recognize and make sense of the chunks in the text before they begin to summarize. Or, they may be summarizing texts comprised of multiple text structures, and they'll need to craft summaries that take these structures into account.

IN THIS SESSION, you'll teach students that readers can summarize complex texts, drawing on previous learning about main idea to lift the level of their summaries.

GETTING READY

✓ Today students will study "The Science behind the Story," pages 18 and 19 from *When Lunch Fights Back* (see Teaching and Active Engagement).

✓ Have chart paper and markers ready to chart main ideas and parts of the class-generated summary (see Teaching and Active Engagement).

✓ Prepare a "Predictable Challenges with Summarizing" chart to record common problems that arise as you confer with students (see Conferring and Small-Group Work).

✓ Distribute the "To Acknowledge the Author In Our Summaries, We Might Write. . ." chart (see Conferring and Small-Group Work).

✓ Students will need their copies of the "Main Idea(s) and Supporting Details/ Summary" strand of the Informational Reading Learning Progression for Grades 4 and 5 (see Mid-Workshop Teaching and Share).

✓ Look carefully at tonight's homework. Students will need to draw on this work in Session 11 (see Homework).

We suggest that halfway through today's lesson, you remind students of the "Main Idea(s) and Supporting Details/ Summary" strand of the Informational Reading Learning Progression they studied earlier in the unit, and ask students to self-assess their summaries, noticing what they're doing well and setting goals for strengthening their summaries moving forward. It's likely you will see many predictable problems popping up at this point, and the Conferring and Small-Group Work section included in today's lesson lays out many of those predictable problems and ways to address them. Rest assured that, though this skill will be difficult for many students at first, students will have additional opportunities across this unit and across the upcoming *Argument and Advocacy* unit to hone their skills.

"The ability to summarize a text down to its essential points and supports is a skill your students will draw on through college and beyond."

The homework for today is essential to the start of the next bend, so be sure you rally your students to do that work, if not through homework then in school.

Summarizing as Texts Get Harder

CONNECTION

Using an anecdote, bring students into the idea that summarization is important. Suggest that as texts become more complex, summarizing becomes more challenging.

"The other day, I was talking with my younger brother. He had just gotten back from the amusement park, and he couldn't stop talking about how great it was. There was no stopping him. He kind of sounded like this. 'First, we went on the Corkscrew. It was this tall, blue, twisty slide with three turns. You sat in a seat and your legs dangled. The line was long, but we got to wait under this protective structure so we stayed dry. We kind of got hungry while we were waiting so then we . . . .

"He was telling me EVERY. SINGLE. DETAIL.

"Finally, I couldn't take it anymore, and I cried, '*Stop*! If I wanted to know everything, I would have gone with you. Can you just give me a summary of the important points so I can hear the highlights of your day?'

He said, "Oh, okay," and backed up, sharing the five big things he had done at the amusement park.

"That got me thinking about the work you did with summary last year, when you read a text and created a short version of the important points in a text. That work is still important—and here's the thing. As your texts get tougher, the work of summarizing becomes even more complex, and, even more necessary."

❖ **Name the teaching point.**

"Today I want to teach you that when readers summarize complex nonfiction texts, they craft short versions of a text. These summaries tend to include the author's main ideas, how those main ideas relate to each other, and the key supportive details."

There is nothing magical about the story we chose to tell here. We encourage you to substitute your own anecdote, because the stories you sometimes weave into your minilessons help your students connect with you. Think about a time when someone told you all the details of an event without emphasizing importance, and then lean in, and share that story with your students.

TEACHING AND ACTIVE ENGAGEMENT

Channel students to reread a text that the class will summarize today, asking them to look for multiple main ideas in the text and consider how those ideas relate to each other.

"Readers, earlier when we studied what makes it more challenging to determine the main ideas of a complex nonfiction text, we noticed that texts now have more than one main idea. There may be one main idea for one part, then another main idea for another part, or the main ideas might thread across the text. The really important thing is for a reader to be able to think about how those main ideas go together and relate to each other.

"Right now, can you and your partner try this with a chunk of *When Lunch Fights Back*, the part about the termites with the toxic bubbles on their backs that we studied for structure earlier? Will you reread asking, 'What main ideas is this text teaching? How do those ideas relate to each other or go together?' Note key sentences that provide evidence for the main ideas. We'll use what we find to craft a summary together." I projected pages 18 and 19 from *When Lunch Fights Back*.

Coach with lean prompts. Then convene the class, calling for suggestions as to the first part of the shared summary.

Partnerships sprang into action, and I moved among them, coaching into their work. To one partnership, I said, "Look for evidence across the text. Often a main idea is taught in multiple places, and you'll see threads all woven together."

Some partnerships were noticing explicit clues but were missing implicit clues embedded across the text. "Look beyond the obvious! Where does the author give you subtle clues to support that main idea?"

"Look across all those places where you think the author's teaching you a main idea," I said to another partnership, "and try to put the main ideas into your own words. What is the author teaching?"

After a few minutes, I called students back. "What do you think? What main ideas is this text teaching, and how do those ideas go together?"

I elicited main ideas from the class and charted them.

- Termites use defenses on their bodies for protection.
- Scientists ask questions and research to find answers.

"Now that we've identified two main ideas this section is teaching, let's think about how these ideas go together. Hmm, . . . With your partner, talk a bit about how these ideas fit together."

When students think about how main ideas go together and relate to each other, they are thinking about "central ideas." This is not part of fifth-grade expectations, but it is important work that you will want to move your students toward being able to do.

In this minilesson, the Teaching and Active Engagement are combined. Rather than demonstrating, you are providing students with guided practice. You'll alternate between providing students with a bit of coaching, handing the work off to the students, and pulling them back in as you coach again.

I gave the students a minute to talk while I listened in, and then I called the class back together. "I heard you say the two ideas are related because the scientists' research, the questions they asked and explored, are what led to the discovery about how the termites fend off their enemies."

I quickly jotted an introductory sentence on chart paper below the two main ideas: "In this section, Rebecca Johnson teaches that research led to discovering how termites fight off their enemies."

Channel partnerships to identify the key supportive details the author uses to support the main ideas, drawing on previous work with main idea.

"Our summary can't list every supportive detail, so we've got to prioritize which supportive details are the strongest. Take another look at the text. What are the strongest supportive ideas the author gives to illustrate the two main ideas?"

As students worked, I voiced over with a tip. "Remember from our earlier work that the supportive details are often threaded all throughout a section, rather than grouped all together. Try to sum them up using your own words."

Direct the class to take the shared main ideas and supportive details and to "write-in-the-air" their own iteration of a summary of the passage.

"Okay, let's write this thing! Now that we've identified the main ideas this section is teaching, how those main ideas fit together, and the key supportive details, let's get our summary down.

"Can you and your partner try writing this summary in the air? You can start with our first line, 'In this section, Rebecca Johnson teaches that research led to discovering how termites fight off their enemies,' or you can craft your own. Then, name the main ideas the author teaches and the details that support them."

Many of the students' initial summaries sounded like this:

> In this section, Rebecca Johnson teaches that research led to discovering how termites fight off their enemies. One main idea is that scientists ask questions and research to find answers. These scientists asked what the blue pouches were made of. Another main idea is that termites use their bodies to kill their enemies. They carry packs that burst open when they are attacked.

"Readers, let me give you a tip. When we summarize a text, it helps to keep our author, in this case, Rebecca Johnson, in mind. We might include her name, saying, *Johnson writes* or *Rebecca Johnson shows* or *Johnson gives evidence to support*, and then tell the main ideas and supportive details she taught us. We mention her because she's the one who made all these decisions, and she made them for a reason. Try out your summary again, this time keeping our author, Rebecca Johnson, in mind.

Fifth-graders are expected to sort and rank supporting details in a way that allows them to choose the best supporting details to make each point.

We use the term "writing in the air" to signify the thinking aloud you do when you say the way your writing would go were you to actually write the words on the page. By "writing in the air" rather than writing on paper, students can try out a few versions of a summary quickly.

I asked Leela to share her summary with the class. "Listen as Leela shares, and notice where she mentions our author, Johnson."

"Here goes," she began. "In the passage 'The Science behind the Story,' Rebecca Johnson teaches that scientists did research to find out how termites fight off their enemies. Rebecca Johnson teaches that scientists ask questions and research those questions. She gives evidence to support this when she tells how scientists observed the pouches the termites carried. Rebecca Johnson also explains that termites use defenses on their bodies to kill their enemies. She explains that termites carry blue protein packs on their backs."

Debrief, naming the work one reader just did that you hope all readers will do.

"Readers, did you see what Leela just did there? She started by explaining how the main ideas the author taught fit together. Then, she said more about each main idea the author taught, naming the main idea and the key supportive details. And, all throughout, she gave the author credit for doing that teaching, actually naming her as a person involved in the text."

LINK

Launch students into independent reading, reminding them about how the work they just tried can support them in holding onto the content they're reading.

"Readers, this work summarizing isn't just one-time work. This is work you'll do from now on when you read nonfiction. You'll read a chunk and then pause to say back the main ideas the author just taught you, how those main ideas fit together, and the key supportive details. This work is transformative! Try it, and I bet you'll find you start holding onto what the author's teaching you even more.

"Today, as you head off and start reading, will you try this work of writing out a summary at least once? Likely, you'll pause when your brain is feeling full, seeing if you can say back the main ideas and supportive details the author just taught. Off you go!"

Summary Formula:
- Title of text
- Author
- How main ideas fit together?
- Explain main idea
- Key supportive details
* Give author credit throughout

> Summary
>
> One main idea in the text is that although the immune system can help your body, it also can cause problems. According to KidsHealth.org, if you have lupus or rheumatoid arthritis, instead of fighting the germs, the immune system fights the good cells, which could cause problem. Another main idea in the text is that sometimes the immune system can overreact. For example, KidsHealth.org also states that the immune system can overreact and treat something harmless, like peanuts, as something really dangerous to the body.

FIG. 9–1   A student crafts a brief summary of her text during reading.

Predictable Challenges with Summarizing

TEACHING STUDENTS TO SUMMARIZE is no small feat, and it's likely you'll see predictable needs as you study your students' summaries. In the "Predictable Challenges with Summarizing" chart below (and available in the online resources) we've listed the most predictable needs we see in the summaries of students we work with around the world. You'll notice we've added a few blank spots to the chart, as you're certain to encounter additional challenges as you study your students' work. Carry this chart with you as you move around the classroom today, and use it as you study your students' written summaries in the future.

Predictable Challenges with Summarizing

Too many main ideas or main ideas overlap	Confused main ideas and details	No connection between main ideas	Details don't fit with main ideas
Too many supporting details	Author is absent from summary		

Once you notice patterns in student needs, you can then pull together clusters of students around predictable challenges and respond based on strategies you have at the ready. Here are some suggestions for predictable small-group work.

(continues)

BEFORE

> _Lost: Macedonian King_ is about the tomb of Philip II. One main idea is that he was a really good warrior. One detail is that even though he was shot with an arrow in his eye, he still lived. This shows how strong he is. Another detail is that his tomb is really fancy. Back then, only important people could have tombs built just for them.
>
> Aside from he was a good warrior, another main idea is that his tomb is hidden. When he was buried, his gold and silver objects were hidden inside plain marble boxes, sealed very tightly. Also, when he was buried, they closed the tomb's outer door and heaped a lot of dirt over it, to make it blend in with the earth.

AFTER

> _Lost: Macedonian King_ tells that Philip II was a well respected person. One main idea to support this is that his tomb was really fancy. For example, his gold and silver objects were hidden inside plain marble boxes. Another main idea is that he was a great warrior. An example of this is that even though he got shot in the eye with an arrow, he survived.

FIG. 9–2   This before-and-after sample shows how a student revised his summary to include only the most important main ideas and supporting details.

MID-WORKSHOP TEACHING
Teaching Students to Self-Assess Their Summaries

"Readers, can I have your eyes and ears? Will you get out the 'Main Idea(s) and Supporting Details/Summary' strand of the learning progression you studied earlier? Remember how, before this unit even started, you read those articles about scientists at work and you wrote a summary of one of them? Then, we had that day where you studied your work carefully against the rubrics and strands of the learning progression, and you self-assessed your work with summary? Since that point, you've learned so much—about identifying multiple main ideas, about making sense of complex text structures. What's more, many of you have been working toward big goals around this strand.

"I think you're ready to revisit this strand with your new and improved summaries in hand, noticing first where your work falls and naming ways your work now is already stronger than your work two weeks ago. Try this out with your partner now." Partners sprang into action. I voiced over, "You might say, 'I used to . . . and now I. . . .'"

After a few minutes I said, "And readers, right now, before you return to reading, will you revise your summary work to make it even stronger? Look for parts of the strand that you have not mastered yet, and try some fast-and-furious revision to incorporate them into your summary. Write a new draft if you need to.

"Back to reading, keeping the strand we just studied in mind."

There are too many main ideas, or main ideas overlap.

Gather a small group of readers and show them how, once they've identified main ideas for each section of a text, it is helpful to stop and look across the main ideas that have surfaced so far, and think about how to consolidate them. You might model this work with the level 5 "Lessons from the Deep" text, showing students a list of the main ideas you've generated:

- The octopus has a body unlike any other animal.
- The octopus's body is amazing on the inside as well.
- The octopus's body helps it defend itself from predators.
- The octopus's body helps it to be a skillful predator and hunter.
- The octopus is intelligent.
- The octopus, like people, has feelings, too.

You might say, "Readers, we know that as texts become more complex, there are going to be multiple main ideas. When this happens, it is helpful for readers to place the ideas next to each other, look across them and ask, 'How do these ideas fit together? Are there main ideas that are similar that I can group together?'" Then, recruit students to help you do this work using the main ideas you generated from "Lessons from the Deep." It's likely you'll end up with two main ideas, which might sound something like: The octopus has an amazing body, both inside and out, and the octopus is an intelligent creature with feelings like humans. End by coaching students as they try this work with their texts.

Students confuse main ideas and details.

You'll also find that readers have confused details as main ideas. If this is the case, it would be helpful for readers to reread what they've written, asking, "Does this fit with (or support) one of the other ideas I've found while reading?" If so, it is more than likely a detail than a main idea.

Students don't make the connection between main ideas.

Another common challenge we see when readers summarize is that students are able to pull out the main ideas, but don't explain the thread that connects them. In this situation, it can be helpful to provide language prompts to help students explore the connections between their main ideas. You might give a small group of students prompts. Support these students in using these prompts first in their talk, orally rehearsing what they could write in their summary, before they capture their thoughts in writing.

- These ideas fit together because . . .
- All in all, it seems like the author wants us to think that . . .
- Together, all of these ideas seem to add up to this bigger idea that . . .

Details don't fit with main ideas.

Share a metaphor with students to help them draw a connection between the abstract concept of connecting main ideas and details and something a bit more concrete. You might relate it to drawers inside a dresser. Just like it is important to make sure that shirts go with shirts and socks with socks, it's important to ensure details go inside the correct main idea drawers. After sharing this metaphor, coach students as they look across their details, asking, "Do each of these details *fit* with this idea? Does that detail belong in that drawer?"

There are too many supporting details.

Too many supporting details can swamp student summaries, leading them to drown in a sea of details. You might say to a small group, "When we are deluged with details, we need to train our brain to look across our details, asking, 'Out of all of these details, which *best* support the main idea of this section? Do some of these details feel repetitive, like the author is saying the same thing in a different way?' If so, we need to cut the details or collapse them—tucking them inside of each other." You might craft a summary of "Lessons from the Deep" that's filled with details and use it to demonstrate cutting extraneous details, and then ask students to reread and revise their summaries in the same way.

The author is absent from the summary.

Show readers how to craft more credible summaries by referencing the author of the text. Remind readers of how you tried this work during the minilesson. It might be helpful to provide readers with their own copies of a chart that lists prompts to support acknowledging the author and then to coach readers as they revise their writing with those prompts in mind.

> ## To Acknowledge the Author In Our Summaries, We Might Write...
>
> *(handwritten note: Include in Notebook)*
>
> - According to (author)...
>
> - (Author) goes on to explain / share / claim...
>
> - The author writes / shows / gives evidence to support / state...

Sharing Our Summaries

Invite students to share summaries in partnerships to celebrate their growth across this bend.

"Readers, I'm just blown away by all the work you've done so far this unit. You've faced challenges head-on, and you've developed ways to work through all the complexities authors are tucking into their texts. I feel like you're ready for anything, even middle school." I smiled. "So, let's spend our next few minutes really demonstrating for one another everything we've learned so far. To do this, let's share our summaries, since to make strong summaries you had to navigate all the ways your texts were tricky. Let's make sure our summaries are as strong as can be before we share them. Keep the 'Main Idea(s) and Supporting Details/Summary' strand from earlier in mind."

I gave students a few minutes to strengthen their summaries, and then I grouped pairs of partnerships together for their summary shares. "We'll share our summaries in small groups today, and, as your partner shares, listen for what they do in their summary that's particularly beautiful. Maybe it's the way they sum up the main ideas the author teaches into a clear sentence. Maybe it's the powerful vocabulary they use as they talk. Whatever it is, be ready to compliment your partners when they finish sharing, and, make your compliment feel big and important. Keep your copy of the strand nearby, because it can give you ideas of what to compliment. Get started!" Conversations erupted, as students shared their summaries with one another. I listened in, offering compliments as I toured the room.

SESSION 9 HOMEWORK

 ## STARTING YOUR RESEARCH

Readers, you've already developed a plan for the research for your inquiry project. Now it's time to dive into your research. Instead of picking up a book or article, do some hands-on research. You might jot down some interviewing questions. Then call or email an expert on your topic to learn more. You might design a survey related to your topic. Then survey other people to collect some results. Or, you might sit next to your fish tank and jot observations about fish behavior. Or you might watch your little sister play video games to see just how she does it. Add whatever you find to the new research section of your notebook.

Learning from Sources

How is the research we do as researchers of our topic similar & different fr the reading work we do in books?
Brainstorming ideas. for Primary Research
Mid-Lesson: Develop an Action plan
Share: plan

IN THIS SESSION, you'll teach students that researchers can learn from a variety of sources—videos, observations, interviews, and even field trips—using the same reading skills to make meaning from them that they do when they read their print nonfiction texts.

GETTING READY

✓ Before this session, you'll want to know the topics students have chosen to research, so that you can form groups around topics that are roughly similar to each other. When students come to the meeting area, have them sit with their group. Partner students within the groups, or have students select a partner (see Connection).

✓ Be sure students bring their reading notebooks to the minilesson, so they can study the research they've done on their inquiry projects (see Teaching and Active Engagement).

✓ Have chart paper and markers ready to create a chart with two parts: "Ways Our Primary Research Resembles Reading" and "Ways Our Primary Research Is Unlike Reading" to collect student responses (see Teaching and Active Engagement). 👆

✓ Select the topic you'll research for your inquiry topic. We suggest researching scientists, which is woven across the bend. Prepare a research plan, quickly jotted in your reading notebook, to share with students (see Share).

AT THE START OF THIS UNIT, you told students that getting stronger at non-fiction reading was a bit like getting better at video games. They need to be able to master the higher levels, you told them—and those higher levels have harder challenges and require different strategies. Your students have certainly been working to master those higher levels. Recently, you qualified, even debunked that idea a bit. Yes, sure, students do need to unlock the secrets of informational texts and get stronger at reading more complex texts—but not because they are trying to get better at a game. Rather, they need to get stronger at reading informational texts so that the world is more open to them.

For students to read about current events in the newspaper or digital magazines—or read academic research and compare it with what others have said, or read widely about topics that are hot or about topics about which they care deeply and personally—they need to be able to access informational texts at higher levels. If you have a student who is deeply interested in the Knights Templar, for example, and the only books about them are written above the level at which he can comprehend, he is denied the chance to learn more about his topic of personal interest and expertise. And so helping him (and all of the others) get stronger at reading nonfiction is vital. Reading nonfiction will offer students more reading selection, more of a reading life, and above all, more reading power.

That is why students have spent so much time studying how nonfiction gets more complex—so they can read to learn more about what *they* want to learn about.

Bend II will emphasize this to your students by getting them engaged in inquiry projects on topics of their own choosing. Your students selected topics as part of the Share during Session 9. As they begin to study things they truly love, you will help them draw upon what they learned in fourth grade about finding and evaluating sources so they can gather sources for their inquiry project.

Today you will help students engage in an inquiry about why it is important to learn from a wide variety of sources, including interviews, observations, and survey data. To do this, they'll spy on the work they've done for homework over the past few days. They'll study the work they've done as researchers, noticing the similarities between their real-life research and the work they've been doing reading print texts. Then, too, they'll reflect on what they've learned about their topic so far, noting the main ideas that are likely to come up across their study.

Reading nonfiction will offer students more reading selection, more of a reading life, and above all, more reading power.

You'll want to help students start gathering sources. You may want to schedule a trip to the school library or even the local library, if you can, to give students more opportunities to find sources. No matter what, you will also definitely want to let other teachers and the school's media specialist/librarian, if there is someone in that role, know about these projects!

The bend and the unit will end with seminars that students teach to others. To make sure that students do not simply regurgitate facts about their topic during these end-of-unit seminars, we suggest that they may eventually zoom in on a specific focus. So instead of just studying the Loch Ness monster in general, a student might eventually realize she wants to focus in on "The Loch Ness Monster Could Be Real." A project all about football might become "Playing Football Is Way More Than Knowing How to Tackle," and that student might teach a seminar with sections on intense training, developing and learning strategies, collaborating with teammates, and so on. The point is that students will need to approach texts with their own agenda, seeing how their research works in relation to their project, not just regurgitating that research. (For students who need more support, you'll want to keep the focus broader.) This work will come later. For now, you'll support students in reading and researching widely as they get to know their topic.

Prior to the start of today's lesson, consider whether you can form groups around topics that are roughly similar to each other. You might have a group of students studying animals, another group investigating pop culture topics, and a third grade studying famous people or teams. Students will work with these groups regularly across the bend.

Learning from Sources

CONNECTION

Share a story about a real-life experience in which you were actively taking in the world around you. Connect that story to the work students are constantly doing as readers.

I called students to the meeting area with their reading notebooks and asked them to find spots next to their new topic groups.

"Readers, yesterday after work, I went on a long walk through the park, and I ended up in this really heavily wooded part. At first, it just felt like the woods were silent and full of trees, almost the opposite of the busy streets by our school. But then, as I kept walking, I started hearing sounds. Chirps coming from nests of baby birds, leaves crunching under the footsteps of something, I'm not sure what—perhaps squirrels scurrying down from trees. I was surrounded by what seemed at first to be one kind of tree, but then all of a sudden turned out to be a ton of different kinds of trees, way more than I could even begin to name. And it felt colder as I walked, too. I noticed the tree cover was getting so dense that the sunlight couldn't make its way through.

Note that we deliberately use the term topic group *to differentiate this from a book club. In a book club, readers usually read the same texts and spend time discussing their shared reading. Members of a topic group are more apt to share their individual findings, analyze their research processes, and support each other in working toward goals.*

"I'm telling you this because as I continued on my walk, it almost—and this might sound strange to admit—well, it almost felt like I was *reading*. I know, sounds crazy, right? At first I thought this walk in the woods was the farthest possible thing from reading, but then I realized I was using a lot of the same skills I use when I read nonfiction texts. It was almost as if the way I was walking in the woods was really no different from the way I'd read about the woods.

"It got me thinking that we use a ton, maybe even *all*, the same skills when we're reading our nonfiction texts as we do when we're studying anything in real life. When we are watching a video, we're determining importance and synthesizing the new information with what we already know. And is it any different when we are observing a fish swimming in an aquarium or star gazing or visiting a museum exhibit? Now, this is just an idea I have, I'm not sure. I haven't had a chance to test it out yet, so I was thinking today, we could investigate this together. Are you up for it?"

Substitute a place where you walk regularly, someplace you go that your students are likely familiar with. You could weave in an open desert landscape or a busy city sidewalk. It can be anywhere you can describe in detail, showing how you saw more and more as you continued to survey the world around you.

❧ **Name the inquiry question.**

"Here's the question I want us to investigate today: how is the work we do as researchers of our topics (and of our world) similar to and different from the reading work we do in books?"

TEACHING AND ACTIVE ENGAGEMENT

Begin the inquiry by asking students to reflect on their experiences of conducting primary research, and compare that to researching in nonfiction books.

"To investigate this, I thought you could think about the work you have done learning about your topic from firsthand things—from interviews and observations and experiences. And you could think about whether the way you learn from those vehicles is similar to or different from the reading work you've been doing in books.

"Think about what you've done so far to learn about your inquiry topic, if you did follow my instructions to learn about the topic in some nonbookish way. Whether you observed your goldfish as he swam around his bowl or interviewed your karate teacher about the sport, my question is this: what thinking were you doing? How was it similar to (and different from) the thinking you do as you read a bunch of texts?

"Do some investigating by looking through your notebook and start studying!" Notebooks sprang open, and students began rereading their recent notes.

As students shared, I created their ideas, creating the chart shown in Fig. 10–1.

Call on students to report their key findings to the class. Alternate between asking students to share with the whole class and asking students to share with their topic groups.

"All right, readers, what did you find? How is the work you do when you research by observing, experiencing, and interviewing similar to and different from the way you research your topics when you do so simply by reading nonfiction books?"

I called on Matthew, who said, "We thought they were super similar, 'cause in both we had to keep asking, 'Does this make sense?' And then when it didn't make sense, we had to figure out why and come up with ways to tackle the trickiness," Matthew said.

"Turn and talk with your topic group—what strategies did you use when what you were studying didn't make sense?" Students turned and talked, and some got out their text complexity cards to remind themselves of strategies they used. They talked about how they looked for ways their new learning fit with their previous learning, and they discussed strategies for tackling unfamiliar words.

"What other similarities did you notice?" I called on Omnia.

"Just like in our books, we learned a ton," Omnia said.

"Yeah," Iris added, "like when I talked with my brother about video games, he talked about how there are lots of different companies that make video games, and he also talked about the different kinds of video games there are."

"What else?" I asked.

Ways our Primary Research Resembles <u>Reading</u>…	Ways Our Primary Research is <u>Unlike</u> Reading…
• Teaches us new words	• Sometimes takes more time to figure out main ideas
• Often has multiple main ideas	
• Main ides might be hidden	• Can be harder to find
• Have to ask questions when things don't make sense	• Seeing connections across parts is tricky
• Might be confusing at first	

FIG. 10–1   One example of the "Ways Our Primary Research Resembles Reading" chart, built on the responses of students' in that classroom.

"Um, we had an idea, but we . . . we weren't sure. We thought that, maybe, we used what we knew about text structure?" Peter said.

"Hmm, . . . what do you think, readers? We know thinking about text structure helped us as we read. Did you do similar work as you were researching? Turn and talk with your topic group." I gave students a minute to talk and then called them back.

"I heard you say that you actually *did* think about text structure. You noticed problems and that led you to look for. . . ." My voice trailed off.

"Solutions!" students called out.

"The same was true for other text structures too. Were there any differences?"

"Just one big one," Spencer volunteered. "We were reading other kinds of things, not books! Things like photos and videos and our conversations."

"Wow, readers! It's seeming like the research we're doing now is really not that different than when we're learning from an article or a book."

LINK

Remind students to get a sense of their topic, noticing the main ideas, and to notice ways in which their primary research requires similar reading skills as when they read print texts.

"Readers, as you head off to start researching today, you've got a few different jobs. One is to get to know your topic widely, learning about as many main ideas as you can that go with your topic, so that when you return to studying texts in a few days, you've got some ideas about what's important to know. And second, you'll want to continue researching in different ways—maybe interviews, observations, surveys, or videos—and, as you do so, make sure you're *reading*, although what you're reading won't look like books! As you do this, will you watch yourself as a researcher? If you find other ways that researching these real-life sources is like and unlike reading, add them to our chart. Off you go!"

Developing Actionable Plans for Primary Research

AS STUDENTS set about researching through observations, interviews, and surveys, it's likely you'll see them dream big, suggesting ways to conduct primary research that are outside of what's possible during this short study. As I listened in, I noticed Lila had suggested "visiting the Amazon rain forest" as a way to study venomous animals. "I'm not allergic to the medicines they give you if you get bit, so I won't have to worry about getting killed," she said confidently to her partner. Omala had suggested visiting NASA headquarters in Washington, D.C., and traveling to Mars to learn more about aliens, and Matthew was certain a weeklong trip to Antarctica to measure changing ice levels was the best way to learn about global warming.

I gathered these readers together. "Readers, I brought you together today because you're imagining incredibly powerful ways to study your topics, and I think that if these topics turn into lifelong interests for you, maybe even careers, it's likely you'll be able to pursue your ideas. I thought it would be so cool to go on some underwater dives with those scientists who study life at the very bottom of the ocean, or travel with the scientists who work on the International Space Station in outer space and learn about their work. The more I thought about it, I realized that while I might be able to do those things *someday*, I certainly won't be able to do them in the next few weeks. So I thought today, we could think about ways we could research right here, right in our town, really thinking about ways we could research without spending any money or traveling far away."

I decided to use the example of my own research project. "I'm doing a research project on scientists. If I wanted to interview someone, who could I interview? Hmm, . . . I guess I could watch videos of scientists working online. But I'd really love to interview someone in person. Will you all talk together about who I could interview?" I gave students a minute to brainstorm and then called them back.

"What about our science teacher, Ms. Richards?" Matthew said. "I bet she knows a ton about how scientists work."

"I think that would totally work, Matthew. I'll come up with some research questions, and then I'll have to figure out a time to interview her. Let me jot that down. Then, what about observations? Who or what do you think I could observe?"

MID-WORKSHOP TEACHING
Developing Plans for Primary Research

(continues)

—Develop plan: observations/ interviews/surveys

"Readers, I want to share with you the work Matthew, Omala, Lila, and I just did, because I think we could all learn from it. At first, they had some really cool ideas about how to research their topic: traveling to Mars, researching in Antarctica, even visiting the Amazon rain forest. Then they realized something powerful. They weren't going to be able to put their plans into action tonight, or even make them happen this year. So here's what they did. They thought about the research they could do right here, in our town, without spending any money." I asked Lila to share her plan with the class.

"I decided that I could research animal venom by calling my friend's mom and talking to her because she works with snakes. And I have a snake, so I think tonight I'll watch my snake and make a ton of observations of her. And I might even survey people and see how many animals they can list that have venom to see if they know a lot of them," she said, and she posted her research plan for her classmates to see.

"So readers, I thought right now it would help if you all spent a few minutes working on your research plans. Will you jot down ideas you have for observations and interviews and surveys, things you could do right in our town for free?" I gave students a few silent minutes to work.

"Once you have a bunch of ideas jotted down, continue your research."

"Oooh! I bet you could observe a science class, maybe the third or fourth graders when they're in science doing an experiment, or you could come watch us tomorrow when we experiment with our bean sprouts and take a ton of notes," Lila contributed.

"Do you see how we're getting a ton of different ideas for research I could do for my project on scientists, research we can do right here in our town, without spending money or traveling far away? Right now, can you try the same thing with your topic? Brainstorm together research you could do in town for free."

Omala started. "I'm researching aliens, and I was thinking I could go to Mars 'cause it would be awesome to see if there were aliens for myself, but I definitely can't make that happen for free, and I don't think that can happen this week. So I'm stumped."

"Maybe you could go somewhere where you could see the stars, and you could make observations, and maybe you'll see something there that gives you an idea," Matthew suggested. Omala quickly wrote the idea down.

"Yeah, or maybe you could visit the Museum of Natural History. They have a ton of stuff about the planets. . . . I don't know if they have stuff on aliens but they might. It could help. And you can go there online if you can't go for real," Lila chimed in, and soon Omala had a list of ideas.

Quickly Matthew and Lila had lists of their own. Lila decided that to study animal venom, she could interview her best friend's mom who was a herpetologist and find out all about really powerful snakes. And she thought she could watch her garter snake at home and make observations, because she was pretty sure he had venom. Matthew decided to survey the adults he knew to see what they believed about global warming, and he thought he would interview all the people who felt particularly strongly about global warming to learn about why. I had students choose one idea from their research plan to start with, and then I sent them off to begin researching.

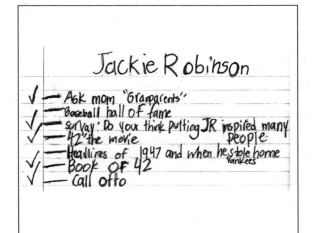

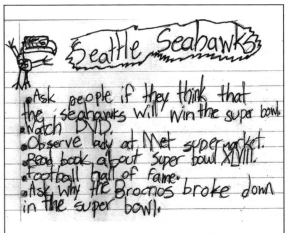

FIG. 10–2   Students generated powerful and realistic research plans.

Breaking Action Plans into Achievable Steps

Share your research plan with students, detailing ways you can accomplish different parts of your research plan.

"Readers, your research plans are really growing. You've got long lists of different plans for your research. Here's mine." I put my research plan, jotted down in my reading notebook, under the document camera for students to see (see Figure 10–3).

"Do you notice how I am considering lots of different research options? Once I have many different options, I'll need to think through how I'll accomplish the different tasks. For example, I think I will need to ask the science teacher when a good time might be for an interview in the next few days, and then I'll have to figure out exactly what I want to ask her. And, for the survey I think I'll need to come up with a ton of questions to ask, read through them and narrow them down to find the questions I most want to ask, and then create a form I can use to collect all the answers I get." I added these ideas to my research plan.

Set students up to read through their research plan and consider how they'll accomplish each part of their plan, jotting notes for themselves in their notebooks as they go.

"Right now, can you do this same work? Read through your research plan, thinking about the steps you'll need to take to accomplish each part of your research plan. Jot down the steps as you think of them in a way that works for you." I coached in as students worked, encouraging them to break complex ideas for research down into multiple steps.

After a few minutes, I stopped students. "Tonight, you'll have a chance to put your plan into action!"

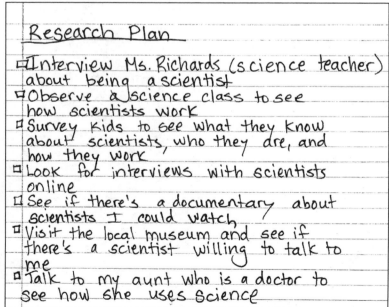

> Research Plan
>
> ☑ Interview Ms. Richards (science teacher) about being a scientist
> ☑ Observe a science class to see how scientists work
> ☑ Survey kids to see what they know about scientists, who they are, and how they work
> ☐ Look for interviews with scientists online
> ☐ See if there's a documentary about scientists I could watch
> ☐ Visit the local museum and see if there's a scientist willing to talk to me
> ☐ Talk to my aunt who is a doctor to see how she uses science

FIG. 10–3   The teacher's research plan models different options for primary research.

PUTTING YOUR RESEARCH PLAN INTO ACTION

Readers, during our share today, you created a powerful action plan, considering ways you could bring each part of your research plan to life. Tonight, will you start putting your plan into action? Perhaps you'll generate interview questions and call a source you'd like to interview. You might find videos online you can watch to learn more about your topic. You could even make observations of something related to your topic. The possibilities are endless! As you study your source today, use all your reading work to help you. Spy on yourself and jot down notes to add to our chart about ways research is similar to and different from the work we've done as readers.

At the same time, start gathering print sources you can bring into the classroom and study. Look for books, articles, and more! Begin bringing these resources into the classroom tomorrow. You need to have your resources in class by _____.

Learning from Primary Research

(?) What is the purpose of Primary Research?

Text: Stu notebook Research Notes

ear Teachers,

We are choosing to write this session as a letter to you, because it will describe the teaching in the classroom that could follow the day previous to this, but it also will offer general suggestions to help students to launch successfully into inquiry projects on topics of their own choosing.

For homework in the last session, you asked students to begin finding sources to read on their topic. You can expect that while probably most students have found at least one article, some may not have access to a home computer or printer, and in any case the number of books that students will be able to gather quickly will likely be very different, depending on the student and the topic. For all of these reasons, it is important to schedule a trip to your school or local library (at a time outside of reading workshop) within the next few days.

Talk to your library media specialist, if you are lucky enough to have one in your school. One amazing library media specialist we know heard about students engaging in personal inquiry projects and began bookmarking helpful sites on the library computers. She also pulled some relevant books off the shelves, making displays of topics that students were studying. She asked for the student topics in advance and was prepared to help particular children search.

Your local library is another good resource. You may wish to take your whole class to the local library, or you might choose to visit on your own, checking out books that will especially help those students who you know will have a hard time gathering sources. The time you spend on this will pay off in leaps and bounds. Not only will you have gotten your children engaged in a project that will feel important and sustaining, but you will have also secured resources to keep them deeply engaged in reading.

If you have access to a school or district computer technology specialist, perhaps you can schedule a visit to the school computer room where students can research online. This specialist, as well, may also want to do a lesson about using the Internet to research, showing students how to craft effective keywords to search, and/or may bookmark sites for students and be able to help particular students who might have trouble. The specialist may also be able to direct students to beneficial websites. Major museums like the Smithsonian (www.si.edu/visit/kids), the British Museum (www.britishmuseum.org/explore/young_explorers/discover/museum_explorer.aspx), or the American Museum of Natural History (www.amnh.org/explore/kids-guide-to-the-museum) have many resources for students to explore. Of course, you can supplement students' resources by finding and printing additional articles on their topics. This can be particularly supportive for students who have difficulty finding their own resources.

These visits must happen quickly, however. You want your students to be able to get right to the work of being immersed in reading and research. And none of these visits should replace reading workshop.

Your students have been engaged in a wide variety of research up to this point, conducting interviews, making observations, and creating and administering surveys. As you saw in Session 11, if a student researching the Loch Ness monster is stuck, you might coach her to think if there is anyone who has visited Scotland and seen Loch Ness. The student might even post that query and your name and class number in the school, asking if there are any parents or teachers in the school who have visited Loch Ness and would be willing to talk with her for a few minutes. If not, then there are undoubtedly travel channel video clips about Loch Ness, websites about traveling there, perhaps even newspaper articles about possible sightings, in addition to *Beastly Tales* or other books on the Loch Ness monster. And students might decide that these options are not quite right. But the point is to push them to consider wider research options. They can end up rejecting these. But pushing oneself to consider multiple possibilities can often offer up more lines of new inquiry than one would have thought of previously.

It is important that students see this primary research *not* as research for research's sake, but instead understand the role this research plays in helping them understand the breadth of their topic. Fifth-graders are called to organize information they are learning across texts into new categories or main ideas. Then, as they read on, they are expected to revise their main ideas to reflect the new information. When contradictory information surfaces, readers have to track these differences and consider why these contradictions exist. To support students in moving toward these fifth-grade expectations for "Cross Text(s) Synthesis" on the learning progression, you might decide to teach a lesson today where you show students that researching widely can help them understand the breadth of their topic and the main ideas contained within it.

FIG. 11–1 Students might store their research in file folders or book bins.

MINILESSON

During your Connection, you could gather students on the rug with their reading notebooks. Ask them to meet with a partner within their topic group and to share the progress they made on the research action plan they began during yesterday's lesson.

You might then craft a teaching point that is large and offers worthy work, perhaps one that sounds something like, "Today I want to teach you one reason researchers do primary research is to learn as much as they can about their topic. By studying your primary research, you can discover patterns and determine main ideas that are significant to your topic."

In your teaching, you could do a brief demonstration, showing students how you reread the notes you've taken on your primary research to discover patterns and determine main ideas. You might show students the notes you took from interviewing the science teacher about being a scientist, the survey you took about people's perceptions of scientists, and the observations you made during a science class about how scientists work. Think aloud about patterns you notice, and then recruit students to study alongside you, turning and talking about patterns they notice and the important main ideas they lead to. Chart a few main ideas you've already noted. The list you generate might look similar to this:

Main Ideas about Scientists

- Scientists work in incredibly different ways.
- Scientists often have a research focus, a topic they know really well.
- Many scientists work for universities.
- Scientists ask a lot of questions, and they do research to answer them.
- Scientists find answers to their questions.

For your Active Engagement, you might involve students in rereading the primary research they've done so far, including their interviews, observations, and survey data, to discover patterns and identify main ideas that are already significant to their topics. As students flip open their notebooks, reread their notes, and get to work, coach in. Encourage students to find a way to record those main ideas after they find them. After giving students a few minutes to work, you might voice over to highlight powerful ways students recorded their main ideas. Highlight how one student recorded main ideas in bubbles in the margins of her page, another added headings to annotate his notes, and a third set up a new page in his notebook to record the main ideas he'd already learned. Remind students to choose a system that works for them.

Finally, for your Link, you will want to emphasize that as students research widely and learn more, they should alternate between conducting additional primary research and studying their primary research notes to identify patterns and determine main ideas.

CONFERRING AND SMALL-GROUP WORK

When you send students off to work today, you'll want to support them in securing print sources on their topics. You'll likely want to work first with the students who do not yet have sources. Students might have trouble due to research access or because their topic does not lend itself to enough age-appropriate sources. If you have students who do not

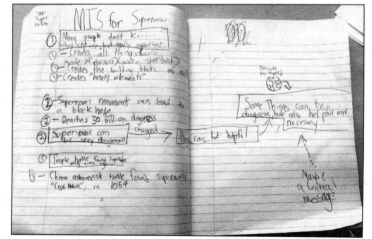

FIG. 11–2 Nathaniel rereads his notes, records main ideas significant to his topic, and annotates his notes to show which details fit with each main idea.

have access to home computers, they will need time to research in school. You might give a bit of that time during reading workshop, but it's likely students will need time outside of reading workshop to research. You might meet with the student and plan times for research. Propose different possible times. They might research during snack time, come in early before school starts, come in a little early from recess, or stay fifteen minutes after school, for example. Let the student decide.

The second trouble tends to be that the topics students choose do not always lend themselves to enough age-appropriate materials. Since you have asked your students to tell you their topics, you know who is likely to find books fairly quickly and easily (mummies, sharks, gorillas, and so on) and whose topic may be more difficult. You will want to meet as quickly as you can with students whose topics do not lend directly to books. Do all you can to support the first-choice topic. Sometimes, the problem is that the topic

Jackie Robinson
"42"
1. Jackie Robinson played during seagragation
2. J.R didn't think he would ever play with white players.
3. Branch Ricky wanted a player who "had the guts not to fight back."
4. Many people mistreated J.R and his wife just because black.
5. Reporters tried to get under J.R's skin.
6. People who supported J.R tried to help him keep his cool.
7. Many people on the Dodger were forced to like J.R.
8. Even Dodgers fans booed J.R because black.
9. Dodgers players don't like J.R.
10. J.R had a good sense of humor.
11. Some white people thought that J.R was a good player and respected him.
12. J.R's dad left him, J.R don't remember.
13. Dodger's minor league manager liked J.R.
14. J.R was forced to play 1st base.
15. Players signed a petition not to play with J.R.
16. J.R doesn't like having a lot of help, he

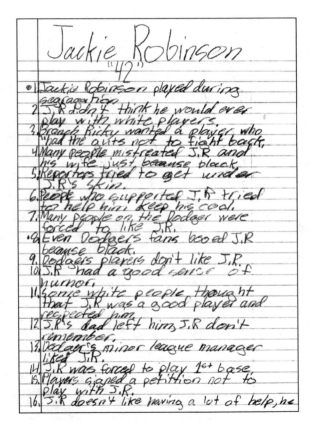

FIG. 11–3 Ben watches the movie *42* and takes notes on his topic, Jackie Robinson.

Interview
Shina
How did you like fashion in the 1980s— comforble because not tite and showy
What was your statement Piece in the 80s—"sweatshirt that I loved—grey with pink hearts and princess sholders!"
How did you wear hair in the 1980s—I wore my hair in the rich girl AKA half up.—sun in dep hair gel
Late 80s— tight ponytail curl in front.
How did you wear your makup—baby soft perfume—Lip Lickers, Max factor rollon lip shine. clearol lighted makup mearor.—kissing posion—bonny bel knock zezmah.

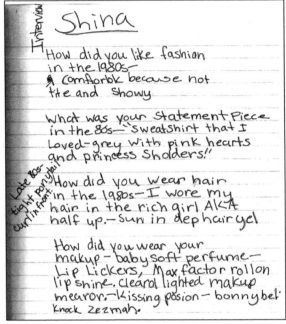

FIG. 11–4 Eva conducts a survey to learn about fashion in the 1980s.

Do you know How J.K Rowling Came up with the Story of Harry Potter?

no	yes	How?
卌 卌 卌 II	IIII	Dad: She came up with it all at once basiclly.
		mom: on the subway
		me: She saw his face on a subway a kings cross and came up with the story.
		Ava: On her way back to the U.K with her daughter she went to kings cross and started from there.

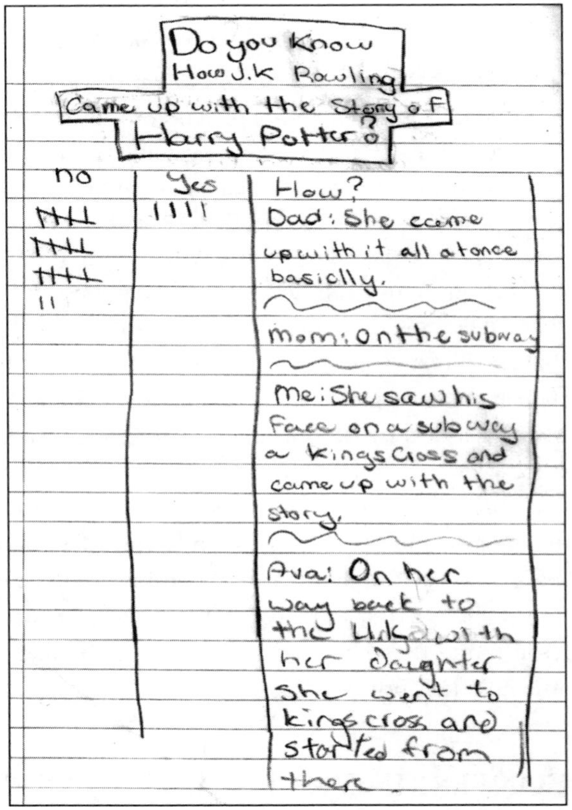

FIG. 11–5 Clementine surveys family and friends to gauge public knowledge about her topic, J. K. Rowling.

is too focused, making it hard for them to gather a wide array of texts. If that is the case, you can suggest a slightly broader topic, which then includes the chosen topic as a part. So, if a student really wants to study the life of a particular rap artist, you might suggest studying "what a career in music is like," or "early lives of famous musicians." You might then channel these students to read biographies of musicians in addition to watching interview clips or other digital texts about the rap artist or reading magazine articles reviewing the artist's latest tour. Students might watch performance clips and observe the artist's performance style or interview other fans. The student usually tends to be happy if his first-choice topic is still part of the project and part of the learning.

Mid-Workshop Teaching

For the mid-workshop teaching, you might choose to remind students of the work they did in Bend I building vocabulary and word solving. Ask students to recall strategies they've already used, revisiting the learning progression as needed. You might ask students to study their earlier word banks or post a few particularly powerful examples for students to study. Remind readers that they should revisit their initial definitions for words as they learn more.

SHARE

For the share you might ask students to gather together in topic groups and share the main ideas they've already generated. As students share, encourage them to look for trends in main ideas across the group. You may want to end with a symphony share, where you serve as the director, signaling to students that they should share a main idea they've developed. Marvel at the sound of so many main ideas filling the room!

Homework

For homework tonight, you will likely want students to continue their primary research, building off of the research plan they began yesterday. Remind them that as they do this work, they need to pay attention to main ideas they are learning about their topic and revise their notes to incorporate their new learning. You might also remind students to continue gathering sources for their topic and to bring those sources in for tomorrow's lesson.

Sincerely,
Katie and the TCRWP team

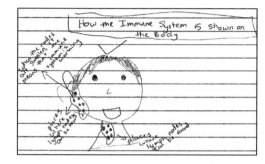

FIG. 11–6   Isabella creates a quick diagram using expert words on her topic.

Session 12

Coming to Texts as Experts

IN THIS SESSION, you'll teach students that readers approach texts differently after having done some primary research on a topic. They know what's important to know about their topic, which leads them to see patterns not noticed by novice readers.

GETTING READY

✔ Prepare an excerpt from *How People Learn: Brain, Mind, Experience and School* to study with students (see Connection).

✔ Display the chart of main ideas from your primary research on your project, titled "Main Ideas about Scientists," from Session 12 (see Teaching and Mid-Workshop Teaching).

✔ Be ready to read aloud a section from pages 17–18 of *Alien Deep: Revealing the Mysterious Living World at the Bottom of the Ocean* by Bradley Hague or a similarly complex nonfiction text on your inquiry topic (see Teaching and Active Engagement).

✔ Ensure students have their text complexity cards handy and are referencing them as they encounter complexities in their texts (see Conferring and Small-Group Work).

✔ Be sure students have access to the "Lenses to Carry When Reading History" chart from Session 7 (see Share).

✔ Prepare a "Lenses to Carry When Reading Scientific and Technical Texts" chart (see Share).

✔ Be sure students have copies of the fourth- and fifth-grade "Cross Text(s) Synthesis" strand of the learning progression (see Homework).

OPEN THE DOOR, and step out for a walk. What do you see? What do you hear? What stands out to you as particularly important? In her book, *On Looking: Eleven Walks with Expert Eyes* (Scribner, 2013), Alexandra Horowitz, a professor in the Barnard Department of Psychology, writes about her experiences doing just that. She describes walking around a city block, first on her own and then several times later, accompanied by eleven different experts. During her first walk, on her own, she set out to note as many different things as she could, and she arrived back home feeling proud of how much she had noticed. Later, as she followed the same path, accompanied by different experts, she realized she had missed pretty much everything on her first journey through.

The book captures her experience seeing the same block differently, with fresh eyes, based on the expertise of the person walking with her. When walking with geologist Sidney Horenstein of the American Museum of Natural History, she felt as if the city almost came to life, and she noted signs of life in every corner. Then, when walking with Dr. Bennett Lorber, president-elect of the College of Physicians of Philadelphia, she found herself thinking about the extraordinary act of walking, paying close attention to the gait of those walking around her.

We've found the same is true of our readers.

For the past several days, your readers have been turning to experts, learning from others what is important to know about their topic. However, "an expert can only indicate what she sees; it is up to your own head to tune your senses and your brain to see it. Once you catch that melody, and keep humming, you are however changed" (Horowitz, *On Looking*, 264). Today's lesson sets readers up to catch the melody of their inquiry topic for themselves. Although they're only a few days into their inquiry projects, their expertise on their topics is already growing, and they've already begun identifying ideas important to their topic. Students are ready to dive into texts on their inquiry topic, seeing more in the texts they're reading because they're tuned in to what is important to attend to.

Coming to Texts as Experts

CONNECTION

Explain the difference between approaching a topic as a novice and approaching a topic with knowledge of what's important. Share research from *How People Learn* to illustrate your point.

"When reading about a topic on which you are a novice, everything is new. This means that often the author seems to be throwing so much new content at you so quickly that it can be difficult to figure out what exactly to hold onto. A few days ago, when you picked up texts on your topic and started reading, you probably felt as if the texts contained an intense density of new information. That's been on my mind because last night I read a book titled *How People Learn: Brain, Mind, Experience and School*. One of the chapters focuses on how learning is different for experts and for novices. The author said there are a couple of key ways in which experts are different from novices, and I wanted to share two of them with you." I projected these:

1. Experts notice features and meaningful patterns of information that are not noticed by novices.

2. Experts have acquired a great deal of content knowledge that is organized in ways that reflect a deep understanding of their subject matter.

Ask students to consider how they'll come to texts differently now they're becoming experts on a topic. Have them turn and talk, and then highlight a few key ideas that were shared.

"This got me thinking that now that we're more expert on our topics, now that we've done all this primary research through interviews and surveys and observations, we're ready to come to our topics differently. And, it seems to me that these principles give us a few ideas about how we'll come to texts differently now. Can you look carefully at these principles with your partner, and talk about how we'll come to texts differently now that we're experts?" After a minute, I called students back together.

"I heard you say that experts really see more than novices, and part of it was that they group information together in bigger ways, based on the patterns they notice. And, you said that once they take what they already know and group it into some categories that make sense, they see more than they could have before."

You are an educator, and it's likely you live your life differently because of that role. It might be that when you enter the bookstore, you search for books you know your most reluctant reader will just love. Or perhaps when you're listening to the radio, you hear a story that one of your book clubs just has to hear. You will forever be changed by your experiences as an educator. This is what you seek to communicate to students here. You let them know that now that they have conducted primary research on their topics, they need to come to texts differently, more expertly, in a changed way.

By suggesting that researching turns children into experts, you invite children to role-play their way into positions of academic importance. Giving kids access to power and influence is no small thing.

❖ **Name the teaching point.**

"Today I want to teach you that readers come to texts differently once they have some expertise on their topic. You'll come to texts with a knowledge of what's important to know about your topic, the main ideas, and you read differently, and see more, because you have this knowledge in mind."

TEACHING

Let readers know their research up to this point will lead them to see more in texts than they would have before.

"Now that we've done several days (and nights) of research on our topics, we're ready to come to our books as experts, with knowledge of what's important to know about our topic, the main ideas, in mind as we read. With this knowledge in mind, we'll see so much more in texts than we would have otherwise, because we'll constantly be thinking about how what we're reading fits with the main ideas we already know."

Model how your knowledge of main ideas from your initial research leads you to approach a text differently, seeing more in the text because you know what's important to pay attention to.

"Readers, yesterday you helped me study the notes I took from my interviews and observations and identify patterns and main ideas." I revealed the list we had generated during the last session.

Main Ideas about Scientists

- Scientists work in incredibly different ways.
- Scientists often have a research focus, a topic they know really well.
- Many scientists work for universities.
- Scientists ask a lot of questions, and they do research to answer them.
- Scientists find answers to their questions.

"Take a minute to read over this list with your partner, and remind yourself of some of the main ideas that are important to our topic. For this first part, I'll need you to think alongside me. Let's read a chunk of our read-aloud, *Alien Deep*, where the scientists are journeying underwater. Instead of just noticing details the author Bradley Hague teaches, let's work to see more by keeping the main ideas we already know in mind. If you see ways the information we're reading about fits with one of our main ideas, will you pop a finger up?"

I started reading from page 17 in *Alien Deep*.

> For mission director Tim Shank, a biologist from Woods Hole Oceanographic Institution, and the ROV team from NOAA, the heart of the operation is the command center deep inside the ship. In the darkened room, faces of the pilots, navigators, and scientists glow in the reflected light of more than two

Your demonstration extends the "Cross Text(s) Synthesis" work you launched in the previous session. Here, you show students how you come to a text with ideas in mind and reorganize your new learning under those headings. This is fifth-grade level work on the learning progression.

Across the lesson, you return to the language of your teaching point repeatedly to increase the likelihood that what you teach will stick with your students, becoming part of their thinking and their language. You will also want to weave the language of your teaching points into your read-alouds across the unit and the year.

dozen computer and video monitors. Live images from the ROV and camera sled cover an entire wall and are beamed out live to scientists worldwide.

I noticed only a few students had their fingers up, so I paused my reading to think aloud, modeling for students how I read actively. "Hmm, . . . well, if I were a novice, I'd probably just rattle off facts I'm learning here—that there's an institute called the Woods Hole Oceanographic Institution, that there's a command center that's deep inside the ship, and so on. But now that I'm becoming an expert on my topic, I need to approach this part differently." I tapped my chart of main ideas.

Reread the passage. Demonstrate how you think about how the information you just read fits with the main ideas for the class research topic.

"Let's reread this chunk, and this time, let's really work to see more. Let the main ideas we already have in mind help you to see more than you did before." I reread the passage to students, and fingers flew up.

"Now that I read with our main ideas in mind, I'm thinking that this part definitely teaches more about how scientists work in different ways. Here they're working inside a ship with lots of technology and, it sounds like, a big crew. There are pilots, navigators *and* scientists. And I think it is important to notice that these scientists seemed to work collaboratively—that there were a bunch of scientists on the ship, and they were sharing what they learned with scientists from around the world. That's a new way scientists collaborate that I didn't know about before! I bet a novice reader would have just skipped right over that detail.

"Readers, do you see how our knowledge of what was important to know about the topic helped us to see more in this text than we originally did, and definitely more than a novice would have?"

ACTIVE ENGAGEMENT

Charge students with studying another section of the read-aloud text with the class's main ideas in mind, noticing how their knowledge of the topic leads them to see the text differently.

"Will you give this a try with the next section in *Alien Deep*? I'm going to read on, and will you listen as an expert, pushing yourself to see more in the text because you'll be reading with the main ideas we already have in mind?"

> *As the distance to the ocean floor tracks toward zero, the first images seem promising. The water is so thick with smoke and silt that it's hard to see anything else. A powerful hydrothermal vent should be in the area. For the vehicles and crew, the search is on.*
>
> *Unfortunately, finding a vent isn't as easy as following its smoke. Down in the depths, a layer of pressure known as a barocline forms an invisible barrier. When vent smoke hits this layer, it scatters over a wide area, obscuring the source. To find the vent, Tim and his team will have to read the signs in the landscape."*

Study your students carefully. If their fingers pop up and they quickly notice ways the information in the text fits with the main ideas you identified yesterday, you will want to skip over this additional scaffold.

This lesson incorporates a new read-aloud text, Alien Deep, which weaves across this bend. Although you can use stand-alone sections of the text in your minilessons, the text has a chronological structure, and students will benefit from hearing sections read in order. Look for ways to incorporate this text into your read-aloud period. For instance, you might read aloud a section with students, modeling ways you take notes on the information important to your scientists inquiry project. Or, if students need more support with word solving, you might read aloud sections of the text and think aloud when you encounter tricky vocabulary.

"All right, experts, get to it! See more in this section of the text by keeping our main ideas in mind." Students jumped into action.

I listened in as Dexter and Lily talked. "Well, it's hardly teaching anything about scientists," Dexter started. "It's telling all about how dirty the water was, how you could hardly see anything."

"Look closer. Choose a main idea and then reread with that main idea in mind," I coached.

"Let's try the first one, that scientists work in incredibly different ways," Lily said, and she and Dexter began rereading.

Debrief, highlighting the transferable work students did.

"Readers, can I stop you for a minute? You're really coming to texts as experts, with main ideas important to our topic in mind, which is helping you to read differently and see more in texts. In *Align Deep*, this helped a lot of you see that some scientists work in incredibly difficult situations. A novice would have read right past that information!"

LINK

Set readers up to reread their research notes, looking for additional main ideas that pop up across their notes, then move to their reading spots and get started reading.

"Readers, yesterday you studied your primary research, noticing patterns and determining main ideas. Today, since you've conducted additional research, it's likely you'll need to spend some time rereading your notes and adding to your main ideas. Use the system you developed yesterday, or a system one of your classmates developed, to help you record main ideas you're learning about your topic.

"As soon as you're ready, you can head off to your reading spots to read. As you pick up your books, make sure you're keeping the knowledge you already have about your topic in mind. You should be reading differently, seeing so much more than a novice would, because of this knowledge!"

As you listen into partnerships, think about the coaching tips you can voice over to support the work of the entire class, in addition to the work you do supporting partnerships. If you overhear two students talking about how the text was not really teaching anything, for example, you can assume that other students in the class are having that same conversation and voice over a tip.

Look for any opportunities you can create to give students choice. Here, rather than telling students how to take notes on their research topic, you put the choice in their hands, suggesting they develop their own system or use a system developed by one of their classmates.

Using Your Knowledge of Text Complexity to Your Advantage

THE FIRST BEND OF THIS UNIT set students up to read with a keen awareness of text complexity, noticing ways that texts were complex and selecting strategies that made sense to help them comprehend the text. We encourage you to draw on this bank of knowledge within the second part of this unit, helping students to see how all their research into text complexity can benefit them as they engage in their personal inquiry projects.

Use text complexity cards to study your own writing about reading.

As you observed students at the end of the minilesson, it's likely you saw several students who needed additional support to determine main ideas from the notes they had

already. Likely there are a few students who boxed out interesting details and others who identified main topics related to their topic but didn't name out main ideas.

You might want to gather these students together with their text complexity cards and reading notebooks, and encourage them to use the cards (and any strategies they've added) to study their own notes. Remind them as they do this that they can consider their own notes as informational writing. Did students simply list everything they observed, with no headings or obvious chunks? Teach them to reread their notes and add in headings with colored pencils or Post-it notes. Remind them that their notes might not be arranged in order, so pull out the text complexity card that reminds them to "Be alert for when things remind you of something you read earlier—go back and reread." Coach students as they reread their notes, noticing when what they're reading now in their notes fits with something that came earlier. Encourage them to jot or otherwise mark their notes to make these connections clear to themselves.

Did students take notes without making their central ideas explicit? Pull out the strategy card that reminds them to "Read a lot before trying to explain the big ideas. Use your own words to try to summarize." Remind them of the phrase "So the big idea here seems to be . . ." and encourage them to use that phrase to see more in their notes. You might show them how they can try out writing big ideas a few different ways, trying to find the right way to word each idea.

Sequence texts based on text complexity.

If you notice the volume of reading has significantly decreased for a group of students, it might be that the texts they are holding are a notch too difficult. These students would likely benefit from a small-group lesson on how to sequence texts for research, starting with the least complex text on the topic and working their way up to the most complex. Gather these students together with their collection of texts.

You might say, "Researchers, I gathered you together today because I want to remind you that as you begin researching a topic, it helps to start with texts that are less

(continues)

"Readers, eyes up here. Remember how at the beginning of the year, you created theories about your fiction books pretty early on, and then you read on with those theories in mind? As you read, you noticed information that fit with your theory, sure, but you also pushed yourself to notice information that led you to refine your theory or revise it totally?

"Well, the same is true when you're reading nonfiction. When you're reading a text with main ideas in mind, you need to collect information that fits with your main ideas. At the same time, you need to be open to learning new main ideas and revising the main ideas you have based on the new information you're learning.

"I was reading on in *Alien Deep*, and I came across this line. 'For two days *Little Herc* and *Seirios* explore the rest of 2-A in search of the vent that created so much smoke, but with no luck.' I almost pushed past it, because pretty much everything that we read in *When Lunch Fights Back* showed that scientists find answers to their questions quickly, with one try. But when information doesn't seem to fit, I know I need to pause and think about it. Will you help me see if this information should lead me to revise one of my main ideas or add a new one?" Students turned and talked, and I revised our main idea chart based on their comments.

"As you read on, make sure you're collecting information that fits with your main ideas and also looking for information that leads you to revise your main ideas or add new ones."

Main Ideas About Scientists

- *Scientists work in incredibly different ways*

- *Scientists often have a research focus – a topic they know really well*   ★ HELLO ★ I'm an **Expert**

- *Many scientists work for universities*

- *Scientists ask a lot of questions, and they do research to answer them*   How...? What if...? Could...?

- *Scientists work hard, often encountering failure, on their way to discoveries*

- ^*Scientists find answers to their questions*

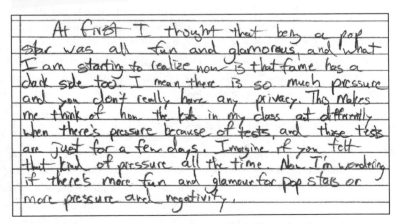

FIG. 12–1   Dexter writes to capture the ways his ideas about pop stars have changed.

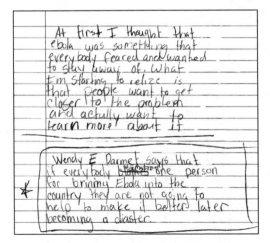

FIG. 12–2   Paloma writes long to explore her new learning about Ebola.

difficult. This helps us build up our background knowledge on our topic and learn lots of new vocabulary words. Then, we can move next to more difficult texts. To sequence these texts, it helps to figure out what makes the texts complex. I thought today we could study the texts in our bins next to our text complexity cards, looking at what makes each text complex. With that in mind, we could order the texts from less complex to more complex. Pull out a text you *think* might be easiest to begin studying first."

Immediately launch students into studying their text, coaching as students look across the text. It will likely be easy for students to notice headings and subheadings that don't help or are misleading, dense texts loaded with lots of details, and captions with a ton of information. Coach them to look into the text more closely, reading a chunk and noticing the vocabulary the author uses and whether the ideas taught seem explicit. While they may not end up with a perfect sequence of texts or a sequence that exactly matches how *you* would have ordered the texts, engaging students in the process of sequencing their own texts will help them recover their reading volume. And, more importantly, it will give students ideas for how to begin research projects they embark on moving forward, long after they leave your classroom.

Orient to texts with the lens of text complexity.

Remember the lesson you taught in Session 2 of this unit? You channeled students to orient themselves to more complex texts, using their knowledge of text features and the topic to help them. You urged students to live in that gray area, tolerating confusion, understanding that ideas might be revealed slowly. As you now look out across your classroom, you'll likely see students who have completely disregarded this teaching. They're easy to spot: they pick up their text, open right to page 1, and start reading without a second thought. Today, you might choose to gather these students together to show them a way to give orienting to a text a new level of engagement—orienting to what the text will teach *and* to its complexities. Look to the "Orienting" strand of the Informational Reading Learning Progression to see ways in which this work becomes increasingly complex and to anticipate possible coaching moves.

You might gather these readers and say, "Readers, remember at the beginning of this unit that I taught you how valuable it was to orient yourself to these more complex texts you're reading? Remind your partner how we did this." Have students turn and talk while you listen in, and then set a purpose for the small group. "Well, I'm a bit shocked to see you not doing this work. Understanding what a text might teach before you jump into it is crucial. Today, I want us to revisit this work with a new twist. That is, we can strengthen our preview by noticing ways that our texts are complex. By that I mean, we can go into our preview with what we know about text complexity in mind, and notice things that make our text tricky. That way, when we read, we can have ideas for what a text might teach *and* already have strategies in mind to help us with those tricky parts. Can you choose a book to preview first? Right now, get started previewing the book. You'll need to do all the work we did before, that work you've let go of, and you'll also need to add in this new work. Ask yourself, 'What's tricky about this nonfiction text?' Lay out the cards that show how your text is tricky to help you if you need." Coach students individually and as a group as they preview, drawing their attention to cards about structure and knowledge demands that they might otherwise ignore.

As students wrap up their previews, gather the group back together and leave them with a powerful link. You might say, "Researchers, when you preview a text in this way, it sets you up for a whole different kind of reading and note-taking. You've got ideas about what the text might teach and how you'll set up your notes based on that, and, as you read, you'll live in that gray area and be willing to revise them. And you've got ideas about what makes this text complex. This will help you as you read because if you get to a part where, for example, the headings are misleading, you can say, 'I see *the headings and subheadings don't help/are misleading*, so I need to be the kind of reader who . . . .'" I let my voice trail off and gestured to students to find the card and suggest a strategy. "Get started reading, and remember to do this work orienting yourself the next time you encounter a new text."

Plan to meet with these small groups again in a few days to follow up on the work you started and offer additional support.

Reading Scientific and Technical Texts

Suggest that readers read many kinds of nonfiction texts: historical, scientific, and technical. Channel students to identify the kind of text they are reading.

"Readers, will you gather on the rug with a familiar text on your topic? Earlier in the unit, we discovered that some of the lenses we carry when reading historical texts can also help us understand scientific texts. Since then, many of you have been carrying these lenses as you read, and they've helped you think about the relationships between people, places, and events important to your topic.

"Some of you are reading historical texts, texts about famous people and places and events. Others of you are reading scientific texts, texts about supernovas and poison dart frogs, and global warming. And a few of you are reading technical texts: diagrams, directions, forms, information displayed in maps and charts. Talk with your partner about whether your text falls into one of these categories: historical, scientific, or technical." I gave students a minute to decide which category their familiar text fell into.

Introduce new lenses readers carry when reading scientific and technical texts. Ask students to read carrying the applicable lenses to notice and analyze relationships.

"I want to introduce you to some new lenses that will be particularly useful to carry when reading scientific and technical texts.

Lenses to Carry When Reading Scientific and Technical Texts

What: Parts

- What are the parts of the topic?

- Are any of the parts especially important?

- How do the parts impact one another?

Why: Consequences

- What changes in this text (people, ideas, numbers, animals, and so on)?

- What do those changes reveal?

- What are the successes? Challenges?

- What are the results of these events?

"So right now, pick up your text and read a bit, carrying the lenses that make sense for your text. If you are reading a scientific or technical text, you might read thinking about the parts of your topic, how they impact one another, and the consequences and results of your topic. If you're reading a historical text, continue carrying the lenses you know to your texts." Students launched into reading, and I knelt down to coach a few students I knew needed extra support.

D'Andre was bent over a diagram of a shark's eye. I asked him what he was noticing. "I'm thinking about parts right now, 'cause this book has a chapter about each part of the shark's body," he said, and then glanced up at the chart. "And one way they impact each other is they all make up the shark's body."

"See if you can push further," I coached. "Is one part particularly important? Or, do the parts impact each other in any way?"

"Maybe the eye is particularly important?" he said tentatively. "It's surprising 'cause the eye is so small, but it says that sharks are 'visual predators,' and visual reminds me of vision, so vision must be important to sharks. It even says here that 'a one-eyed shark would not survive long.' So I'm thinking that the eyes are really important to shark survival, maybe even most important."

After a few minutes, I voiced over, "Talk long with your partner. What relationships are you noticing in your texts? Describe the relationship and then discuss the ideas it gives you."

Lenses to Carry When Reading Scientific and Technical Texts

What: parts
- What are the parts of the topic?
- Are any of the parts especially important?
- How do the parts impact one another?

Why: consequences
- What changes in this text (people, ideas, numbers, animals, etc.)?
- What do those changes reveal?   *I notice...*
- What are the successes? Challenges?
- What are the results of these events?

ACCOUNTING FOR NEW LEARNING

Readers, before you begin reading about your topic tonight, spend a few minutes assessing your work against the "Cross Text(s) Synthesis" strand of the learning progression. First, read across the levels, looking at what's expected of fourth- and fifth-graders. Then, look at your notebook work on your inquiry topic. Figure out where your note-taking falls. Be critical of your work. You'll want to look for ways you can strengthen your "Cross Text(s) Synthesis" work. Maybe you'll revise your headings so they show your new learning. Or, perhaps you'll include contradictory parts in your note-taking. Once you've assessed your work and made revisions, get back to reading with your goals in mind.

Also, spend a little time tonight collecting sources for your research. These sources could be books, articles, pamphlets, interviews, surveys, photos, and more! Bring in whatever resources you find so you can use them for your ongoing research.

Here are some websites that kids in past years have found useful:

- National Geographic: kids.nationalgeographic.com (search terms: National Geographic kids)
- Great Websites for Kids: gws.ala.org (search terms: great websites kids)
- Scholastic News: magazines.scholastic.com (search terms: scholastic news)
- Time for Kids: www.timeforkids.com (search terms: time kids)
- Tween Tribune: tweentribune.com/junior (search terms: tween tribune)

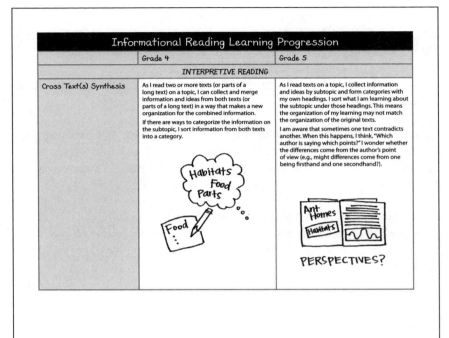

Informational Reading Learning Progression		
	Grade 4	Grade 5
	INTERPRETIVE READING	
Cross Text(s) Synthesis	As I read two or more texts (or parts of a long text) on a topic, I can collect and merge information and ideas from both texts (or parts of a long text) in a way that makes a new organization for the combined information. If there are ways to categorize the information on the subtopic, I sort information from both texts into a category.	As I read texts on a topic, I collect information and ideas by subtopic and form categories with my own headings. I sort what I am learning about the subtopic under those headings. This means the organization of my learning may not match the organization of the original texts. I am aware that sometimes one text contradicts another. When this happens, I think, "Which author is saying which points?" I wonder whether the differences come from the author's point of view (e.g., might differences come from one being firsthand and one secondhand?).

How can I write to understand what I'm reading?

Writing about Reading in Nonfiction

OPEN YOUR STUDENTS' READER'S NOTEBOOKS and spend some time studying their entries from Unit 1 *Interpretation Book Clubs*. Most likely the color and sketches that spring from the page are what you'll notice first. Looking closer, you'll probably see writing that reflects a deep engagement with the text, with your students exploring ideas that stretch far beyond the printed page.

In Unit 1, you and your students worked to create a new vision of writing about reading, one that stretched far beyond Post-it note retellings and repetitive notebook entries. You helped students consider what it meant to write *really, really* well about a text, and they studied their writing about reading, and the writing about reading of others, to determine these characteristics. Later, students learned to approach reading differently because they'd be writing later and to read upcoming sections of text with the ideas they're growing in mind.

Now, continue reading through your students' reader's notebooks, paying special attention to the pages from *this* unit. Up to this point, we've asked students to rely primarily on strategies taught in years past for writing about their informational reading. It's likely that you see pages filled with boxes and bullets, capturing main ideas and details that support them. You might see pages that mirror the text structure the author used: compare and contrast, problem and solution, cause and effect. You'll see the summaries you've asked students to write, and the ones they've created themselves. Are students authoring their own responses to reading? Are students using their writing about reading to help them think deeply about the texts they're reading? Or, is the majority of their writing about reading simply a tool to help them record what the text said?

Today, you'll begin a mini-exploration with your students to move their writing about informational reading beyond simply recording what the text said. We suggest you first tackle this work by letting students in on the situation at hand. Talk to them honestly and straightforwardly and let them know that the writing about reading they're doing now in no way parallels the passionate, exciting writing about reading work they did in the previous unit. Make this new work feel big and important by sharing a snippet of a research article

IN THIS SESSION, you'll teach students that informational readers *write* to understand what they are learning as they read. Specifically, they can angle their writing so that it better explains the information.

GETTING READY

- ✔ Students should bring a nonfiction text on their inquiry topic and their reading notebooks to the meeting area.

- ✔ Prepare a section from "Six Reading Habits to Develop in Your First Year at Harvard" to share with students (http://guides.library.harvard.edu/sixreading habits; search terms: Harvard reading critically). A link is provided to this article on the online resources (see Connection).

- ✔ Choose a section of a familiar read-aloud text on your inquiry topic. We suggest pages 38 and 39 from *When Lunch Fights Back* (see Teaching).

- ✔ Be sure your "Main Ideas about Scientists" chart is easily accessible (see Teaching).

- ✔ Have your reading notebook or a white board and dry-erase markers ready to demonstrate your writing about reading (see Teaching).

- ✔ Be sure students have copies of the four strands of the learning progression they studied in Session 3: "Main Idea(s) and Supporting Details/Summary, "Analyzing Author's Craft," "Comparing and Contrasting," and "Inferring Within Text/Cohesion" (see Homework).

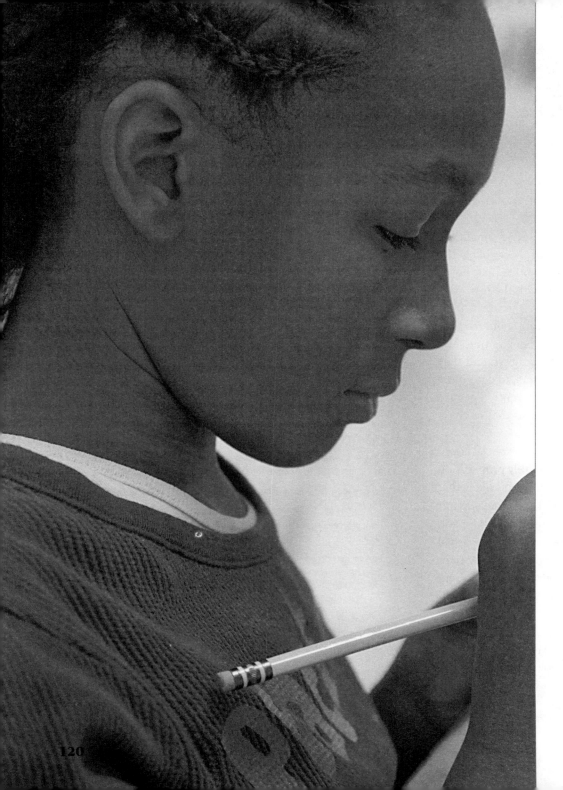

from Harvard University's Library website on "Six Reading Habits to Develop in Your First Year at Harvard." We pull in just one reading habit to today's lesson, but the document is a worthy read, and you'll likely see ideas for how to bring the other five reading habits into future lessons (and you'll see this article come up again in Unit 3 *Argument and Advocacy*).

Once you've rallied students to the big work they'll take on today, you'll show students how you reread a text and design your own response to the text, based on the main ideas you've already identified as significant to your topic. You'll model creating a chart that takes the information you're learning and rearranges it into a new form, yielding information that helps you learn more about your inquiry topic. Then, you pass the reins onto students.

As in the first unit of study, your tone when studying students' writing about reading will be critical. Resist the urge to funnel students back into predetermined forms that may match the author's structure but would likely not match their purpose for reading. And, above all, celebrate students' early attempts at designing their own responses in their reader's notebooks. Linger near a reader, touch a particularly beautiful part in their writing about reading, and compliment the reader in a loud whisper, loud enough for others around to hear. "That sketch you made really brings the content you're writing about to life. I bet this sketching really helped you understand that dense chunk of text you were reading," you might whisper to one reader. Then, pull up to another reader and share a new compliment. "Wow! You're really thinking about how the information you're reading fits with the main ideas you've already noted on your topic. Those arrows you're drawing are letting you show how information really fits together. Keep it up!" These little compliments will have a remarkable impact on the writing about reading work your students do today.

Writing about Reading in Nonfiction

CONNECTION

Talk to students about how their reader's notebooks show how much they've grown as readers since the first unit, but tell them they could be making better use of their notebooks now.

"Readers, I was looking through your notebooks while you were at art yesterday to see the work you have done on your inquiry projects and how it's going so far. I also wanted to just leaf through them, looking at how you have grown at using your notebook since the start of the year. When I was looking through your notebooks, I was sort of struck. I definitely do see notes on your research focus, but I am not sure that I see you *really* using your notebooks as tools. Let me explain what I mean by that. Earlier this year, you studied how to make your writing about reading about *literature* as beautiful and meaningful as your other writing, and these pages overflow with work that helps you crawl deeper into the story, to see different layers to the novel. I can feel your passion, your energy for your reading when I read through these pages.

"But then I turn to the sections where you are writing about informational texts, and the notebook suddenly has a very different feel. There are mostly pages of notes with sometimes a sketch or a timeline or a web, but it doesn't feel like you are using the reading notebook pages to help you *think*, *really think* in the same way you are when you write about your literature reading."

Let students know that this has made you think hard about writing about reading in nonfiction.

"So, this has made me think more about writing about reading in nonfiction. Because, of course, it shouldn't be exactly the same as writing about reading in literature. But if writing about reading in literature should help you to see different layers to the story and make deeper interpretations, then what should writing about reading in informational texts help you to do?"

Read a snippet of an article that relates to writing about reading about informational texts, and let students know that you think this research could be helpful for the class to consider.

"I wasn't totally sure, to be honest. So I started to do some research and I came across this really interesting article. It is posted on Harvard University (you know the famous university) Library's website and the article is called 'Six Reading Habits to Develop in Your First Year at Harvard.' Basically, it is about things that Harvard thinks you should do to be a

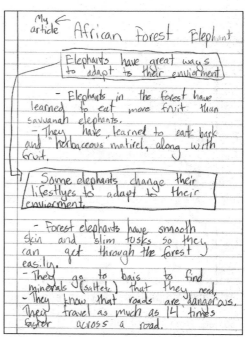

FIG. 13–1   It's likely many students' note books look like this, filled with boxes and bullets (or even lists of facts!).

Your tone here (as always) is critical. You've got to convey that this is truly something you are wondering about, a hard thing to figure out and that it is worth considering.

better reader. I know you're all ten or eleven and not on your way to Harvard this minute, but when I read this I thought that it would be really interesting for us to consider. I think it could help us think more about how to use notebooks as tools to write about reading of informational texts. Let me read you just a part of it.

"This is the third habit Harvard wants students to develop. I'll read, and will you think: 'How might that relate to my writing about reading of informational texts?'"

> Outline, summarize, analyze: Take the information apart, look at its parts, and then try to put it back together again in language that is meaningful to you.

> The best way to determine that you've really gotten the point is to be able to state it in your own words.

I paused to look at the students, some of whom looked puzzled. "Let me read it once more." After I had again read the snippet of the article, I looked at the students. "Talk with your partner about how this might relate to your writing about reading of informational texts." I gave students a minute to talk, and then called them back together.

"I agree! It feels like maybe what Harvard might be saying here is that the real goal is to deeply understand the text and truly be able to explain what it is saying to yourself. And to truly explain the whole, you need to look deeply at the parts. And so I think that's what we might try in our writing about reading about informational texts. We might try taking information apart and looking at the parts to try to explain things to ourselves better."

❖ **Name the teaching point.**

"Today I want to teach you that informational readers *write* to understand what they are learning as they read. Specifically, you can angle your writing so that it better explains the information."

TEACHING

Involve the class in thinking along with you as you demonstrate how you might use writing about reading to better explain parts of the class read-aloud to yourself.

"So, let's try a little of this work together. It feels like the first step when you break something down into parts is to figure out which of the parts you want to look at closely. So, if we consider our class read-aloud *When Lunch Fights Back* (you all know I'm using this as a source for my personal inquiry project), I think the first part I want to really focus on closely is the 'Science behind the Story' sections." I flipped through some pages, stopping at page 38. "Oh, you all remember this one. This is about the science behind the two-spot astyanax, remember those fish that injure each other?" The class nodded.

"Okay, so if I wanted to explain this part better to myself—think with me—I could ask, 'What is this part really trying to get me to understand?' Hmm, . . . well maybe it's trying to get me to understand exactly why the two-spots injure each other. So if I wanted to use writing about reading to think about this part, I could use my writing about reading

The article "Six Reading Habits to Develop in Your First Year at Harvard" can be found on the Harvard University Library's website at http://guides.library.harvard.edu/sixreadinghabits (search terms: Harvard reading critically). It is a worthy read, and it may give you more ideas for bringing the other five reading habits into future lessons. We'll return to this article again in Unit 3 Argument and Advocacy.

To accentuate what you hope students do not do, it can help to do that thing, and then show students how you self-correct. It also helps demonstrate the positive learning mindset of approximation, that it is okay to make mistakes and brush the dust off one's pants and to try again—a learning attitude that research has shown to produce achievement in student learning.

to understand exactly why the two-spots injure one another. I guess I could make a cause-and-effect diagram to help myself understand it," I mused.

Deliberately model revising your thinking about how to use writing about reading. Recruit students to help you revise your writing about reading with your main ideas in mind.

I paused. "But that's not really what *our class's* inquiry project is about. We are *not* researching the two-spot. Instead, we've got to keep our main ideas in mind about scientists in mind." I tapped our "Main Ideas about Scientists" chart.

"So, I want to use writing about reading to help me better understand our main ideas. Hmm, . . . How could I use my notebook to better understand scientists?" I tapped my pencil on my notebook. At this point some students were on their knees, some waving their hands a little. "Tell your partner what you're thinking." Students turned and talked.

"Okay, you guys are giving me an idea. How about this? What if I made a chart in my notebook like this . . ." On the white board, I quickly jotted a big rectangle, made three columns and recorded the title of the book.

<u>When Lunch Fights Back</u> by Rebecca L. Johnson

"And then, what if in one row, I put the scientists' names, since there are different scientists in each section? And then, since a couple of my main ideas are about how scientists have a research focus and ask a lot of questions, those could be my next sections. So I could have rows for their research focus and for the questions they ask, and maybe what their research process is like, since another one of my main ideas is that the scientists I've read about have all researched in really different ways." I started making hasty rows by drawing lines quickly across the columns, nothing fancy.

<u>When Lunch Fights Back</u> by Rebecca L. Johnson

Scientist(s)		
Research focus		
Questions asked		
Research process		

This *demonstration moves students toward fifth-grade work in "Growing Ideas," which calls students to sometimes come to texts with their own ideas, their own agendas, and to see their text through the lens of that idea. Skim the "Critical Reading" strand of the learning progression to see how expectations for students are increasing.*

Main Ideas About Scientists

- Scientists work in incredibly different ways

- Scientists often have a research focus — a topic they know really well
  HELLO I'm an Expert!

- Many scientists work for universities

- Scientists ask a lot of questions, and they do research to answer them
  How...? What if...? Could...?

- Scientists work hard, often encountering failure, on their way to discoveries

- ^Scientists find answers to their questions

Project MI About Scientist

"And then maybe one more row for . . . 'other'? Because I know the scientist who studied the hagfish got slimed, and that is interesting information. Maybe there are other things like that for the other scientists."

<u>When Lunch Fights Back</u> by Rebecca L. Johnson

Scientist(s)		
Research focus		
Questions asked		
Research process		
Other		

"So, I'll reread all of the 'Science behind the Story' sections and use this chart to help me capture and think about the parts about the scientists' careers. If I filled this chart in for each of the different scientists in the book (I'll have to add more columns, of course), it could really help me understand the relationships between the scientists. And I could better refine the main ideas I already have about scientists. I could see patterns and points of disconnect. That would help me better explain to myself how scientists work and their exciting careers."

Pause to debrief the replicable steps you have taken that you want students to follow.

"Readers, do you see how I really thought about what part of the text I wanted to take apart and better understand, and especially what would help me learn more about my inquiry topic and my main ideas? And did you see how sometimes it isn't the first thing you think of? Sometimes you have to be willing to revise how you are going to take the text apart. You need to really push yourself to think about what kind of writing about reading you could do to better understand and explain things to yourself."

ACTIVE ENGAGEMENT

Set students up to try out thinking about what kind of writing about reading they could do about their text that would help them better explain information to themselves.

"Okay, so as you've seen, this isn't easy work. I want to give you a chance to try out some of how this work might go for your text. You're going to really need to squeeze your brain. You probably want to start by thinking the same way I did, 'How do I want to break this down? What part (or parts) seem important for me to help me to learn more about my topic?' Flip through some pages and think about that for a minute." I gave them some time as I watched them turning pages. "Put a finger on a page that you're considering studying more closely." Most students did so.

Resist the urge to pull out the ruler and fuss over whether your lines are straight. By demonstrating how quickly you sketch out a tool to help better understand a text, you model for students how they can do the same. What matters most here is that your writing about reading is tied to the main ideas you've already identified, and that your writing about reading helps you think more deeply about the text you're reading.

Your demonstration here supports students in meeting fifth-grade expectations for "Inferring Within Text/Cohesion" on the learning progression. Students are expected to discuss major relationships that occur across discipline-based texts, and come up with their own ideas about those relationships, even when the author has not specifically outlined them.

If, when studying your students' reader's notebooks, you notice many students are already drawing charts to help them learn from texts, you will want to modify your demonstration. In that case, you might decide to bring in sketching, showing students how you quickly sketch out the steps in a scientist's research process. Or you might create a flowchart, showing how a scientist moves from generating a research question to formulating an answer from that question.

It often helps to break the steps of a process down for students during an active engagement. I knew that if I gave all the directions at once, some students would primarily concentrate on choosing a section of the text and not make it to the real meat of the active engagement. Because of that, you will want to break down the active engagement into different steps and move students quickly through each step in the process.

"Okay, now for the really hard part. Think about the main ideas you've already found for your topic. What do you need to understand about this? What do you need to explain to yourself? And how could you maybe use your notebook to help you to do that?" I trailed off, again giving students space to think.

I lowered my voice. "Try out using your notebook in some way to help you to understand something you need to explain to yourself. Just give it a try." I was quiet, watching some students slowly putting pen to paper, others still studying pages. I stayed quiet as more students started tentatively jotting.

Push students to share and talk about what they are trying with a partner. Listen in and coach.

After about two minutes I said quietly, "Turn and share what you are writing and thinking with a partner."

Nina and Iris had their heads over Nina's notebook. "So a main idea that keeps popping up for me is that people aren't sure if the Loch Ness monster is real," Nina said.

"Is there a lot of evidence?" Iris asked.

"Well, different people think different things and have different evidence," Nina answered. "So I made a big T-chart and on one side I wrote *Yes* and the other side *No*, and I think I can write all of the evidence for each side."

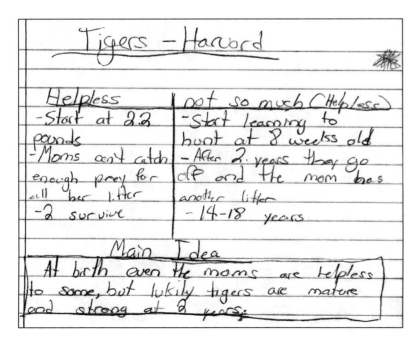

FIG. 13–2   Sabrina designs her own way to write about her reading.

In third and fourth grades, your students learned that one way they could hold on to the information they were reading in the text was to take notes in a way that mirrored the text's structure. When reading a text that was arranged sequentially, they could jot notes using a timeline or numbers to capture steps in order. Or, when reading a text that was organized using a compare-and-contrast structure, they could write first about the similarities between two topics and then about the differences. If you notice students having trouble getting started, you might remind them of this earlier work.

Meanwhile, Peter was telling Jonathan that he knew different parts of the medieval castle served different purposes, so he thought he could draw labeled diagrams of castles on the outside and castles on the inside, and add on to these as he read more. "And maybe that will help me understand why the different parts of the castle were important," he said.

Debrief what you heard, emphasizing that these ways of writing about reading allow students to better understand what they wanted to explain to themselves.

"I saw many of you doing this powerful kind of thinking, really asking, 'What kind of writing will help me to understand my main ideas and learn new ones? That is not easy work and I really see you pushing yourselves. And already, I see more energy shining out of your notebook pages."

LINK

Send students off to continue to read and research, reminding them to make use of their notebooks as a helpful tool.

"Readers, in a minute, I'm going to send you off to continue to read and research. I want to remind you that your notebook should be a helpful tool for you. It should help you to hold on to information you have read and *think* more about it. It should help you to take information apart, study those parts, and then explain what you have learned in ways that are meaningful for you. So, as you go off today, consider carefully how to use your notebook as the most helpful tool possible to you. Okay, head off!"

Addressing Predictable Problems with Writing about Reading

TEACHING IS A CONSTANT BALANCING ACT. The teaching point of today's minilesson is designed to support students in using writing as a tool for thinking. Here we outline several predictable problems that can tend to surface in reading workshop classrooms when we prioritize writing about reading, with suggestions for conferring and small-group work to address these concerns.

Whenever we spotlight writing about reading in our teaching, we need to anticipate this could divert students' attention from reading large swaths of text, causing reading volume to fall dramatically. Look at students' reading logs next to their writing about reading. If you see students taking copious notes, but when you look at their reading log you see only six pages of reading completed in forty minutes, you'll want to pull these readers together to discuss the importance of balancing reading with writing about reading. You might gather students with their logs and notebooks, and remind them how in Session 1, they studied their reading log to determine if they were reading three quarters of a page in a minute. Ask students to study their logs with a partner now to see how close they are to that goal, and help them set goals to boost their reading volume moving forward. They might suggest placing a Post-it at the end of a section as a speed bump to remind them not to stop and jot until they come to the end of a chunk of text. Or, they might jot inspiring goal Post-its for themselves with phrases like "Keep reading! Just a few more pages!"

Then, too, a study of students' reader's notebooks is likely to reveal students who are recording everything, almost transcribing the text, instead of writing in response to their reading. You might gather a group of readers to address this need. Pull out the models of note-taking you've been creating during your read-alouds, the reader's notebook you're keeping on your research project, or student exemplars from this year or previous years. Invite the group to do an inquiry into what strong writing about reading looks like. Ask students to study examples of writing about reading in partnerships and name out qualities of strong writing about reading. Students might notice that readers use short phrases or symbols/codes to capture their thoughts quickly or that readers organize their notes based on the main ideas they're studying, rather than based on

the headings from the text. Then, students could revise their notes based on what they learned, while you coach in and support their work.

MID-WORKSHOP TEACHING   **Keeping Track of Sources**

"Readers, as I see you all using your notebooks as tools to help you think and explain things to yourselves and as I see you getting more excited about your writing about reading of informational texts, I want to compliment you and also give you a word of caution. No matter how you are using your notebook to think about your reading, it's absolutely critical to keep track of your sources. You're going to want to put the title and author on the top of your notebook pages, I'd imagine, and also jot page numbers when you take notes, whether you're using boxes and bullets or a diagram or creating your own way of writing about your reading.

"And, also, remember that anytime you include the exact words from the text—a direct quote—you have to put it in quotation marks in addition to putting the page number, okay? Remember that. The rules of note-taking from sources do not go out the window just because we're playing with different ways to use our notebooks. Keeping track of sources and giving them credit is nonnegotiable work. It's likely some of your texts will contradict each other or say something in slightly different ways, and we'll want to be able to revisit those texts and those pages.

"So pause right now, wherever you are, and be sure you've listed the title and author from the source you're writing about in your notebook. Also be sure that you've used quotation marks and included page numbers when you used direct quotes. Then get back to reading and research!"

Alternatively, you could address this by teaching students to paraphrase, asking students to read a section of the text, then close the text and turn and teach someone else what they just read. Students could practice this work several times, alternating between turning and teaching, and turning and recording what they just read. Of course, students can learn to check back in the text to be sure their facts and details are correct, but learning to write and teach with the book closed will dramatically decrease the number of students recopying the text directly.

Of course, you're also likely to see students quoting from the text in dramatically different ways, some using no quotes at all and others quoting long paragraphs from the text. You'll want to teach students to seek balance when quoting. You might pull out a long quote from *Alien Deep*, showing students how you reread the quote to determine what precise words you want to quote, whittling a paragraph down to the most essential sentence. Next, you could ask students to reread their notebook and try whittling down their quotes to their most essential parts. Coach in with prompts like "See if you can shorten it" and "Look for the most important part, the part that would be lost if you paraphrased it."

BEFORE

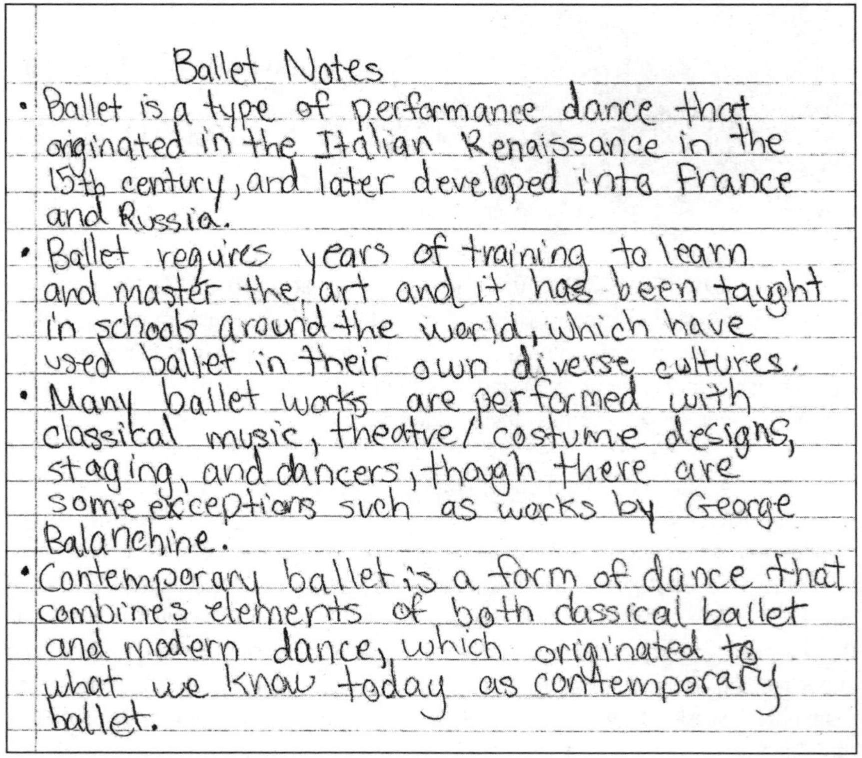

> Ballet Notes
> - Ballet is a type of performance dance that originated in the Italian Renaissance in the 15th century, and later developed into France and Russia.
> - Ballet requires years of training to learn and master the art and it has been taught in schools around the world, which have used ballet in their own diverse cultures.
> - Many ballet works are performed with classical music, theatre/costume designs, staging, and dancers, though there are some exceptions such as works by George Balanchine.
> - Contemporary ballet is a form of dance that combines elements of both classical ballet and modern dance, which originated to what we know today as contemporary ballet.

AFTER

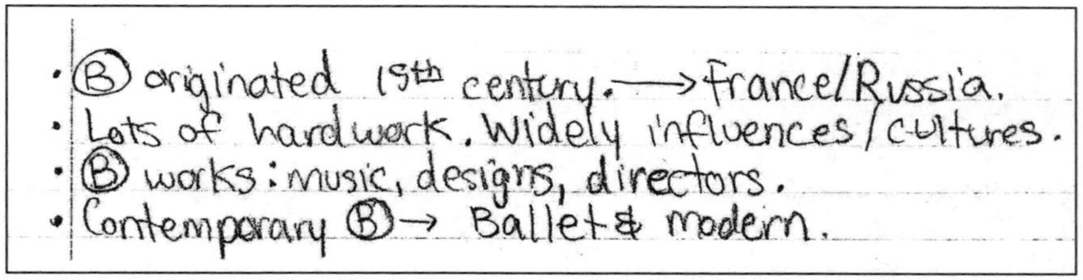

> - B originated 19th century. → France/Russia.
> - Lots of hardwork. Widely influences/cultures.
> - B works: music, designs, directors.
> - Contemporary B → Ballet & modern.

FIG. 13–3   This student revised her writing about ballet. Her new notes capture the same information in a streamlined way.

Learning from Each Other's Writing about Reading

Ask students to skim through the pages in their reader's notebooks to select a powerful example of writing about reading that their group could benefit from studying.

"Readers, in just a minute, you'll have time to meet in your topic groups. Instead of teaching each other about what you learned, will you teach each other about the writing about reading work you've been doing? You've developed so many powerful ways to write about your topics, and I think you'll really benefit from studying the work your group mates did. Take a minute right now to look through your writing about reading and choose the page you think your group could learn the most from." Students silently flipped through their notebooks. I waited until most students had settled on a page, and then continued.

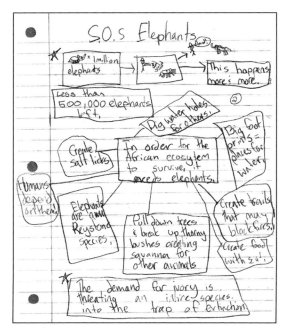
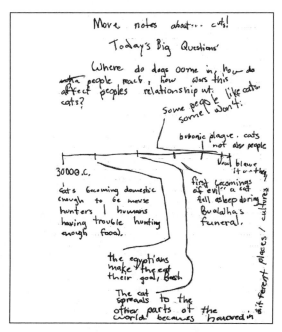

FIG. 13–4   Members of the animal topic group huddle together to learn from these samples of writing about reading.

Channel groups to make plans for studying each other's writing about reading, and then direct students to start studying together. Coach in as groups work to lift the level of their work.

"Make a plan for how you want to study each other's writing about reading. Maybe you'll put one notebook in the center for a minute and all study it, and then ask the writer questions about what she did. Or maybe you'll pass the notebooks around your group, studying each one before you share out the big things you learned about writing about informational reading. However you decide to study, make sure you're studying what your group members did while they were writing about their reading and learn some new moves you can try tonight!"

Groups sprang into action, and I moved around the room, coaching into groups to support their work. I noticed the first group was passing their notebooks quickly, so I said, "Make sure you're really studying each sample of writing about reading carefully. Linger on the page, pushing yourself to see more." To another group, I said, "Find a way to capture what you're learning, maybe jotting down what you're learning on Post-it notes or in your notebook. You want to hold onto all this brilliance!"

SESSION 13 HOMEWORK

 ## REFLECTING ON YOUR GOALS

Readers, on Day Three of this unit, you studied your initial writing about scientists at work next to four strands of the learning progression:

- Main Idea(s) and Supporting Details/Summary
- Analyzing Author's Craft
- Inferring Within Text/Cohesion
- Comparing and Contrasting

Based on what you noticed, you set goals. You've been working toward those goals for a few weeks now, and I bet you've made tremendous progress!

Tonight, will you take a close and careful look at your goals? Where do you already see evidence of working toward your goals? Celebrate the ways you've already grown! Mark up your evidence in a way that makes your growth clear. You might put small Post-its in your notebook or add symbols in the margins.

Will you also look at what you still need to do, in this final bend of the unit, to really meet your goals? Make a plan for how you still need to improve, and start putting that plan into action as you read tonight.

Be sure to spend a majority of your time tonight reading through your sources.

Session 14

Lifting the Level of Questions (Using DOK) to Drive Research Forward

ONE WAY TO BUILD our students' agency is to let students in on the secrets we know and rely on in our daily instruction. In today's lesson, you'll do just that. You'll let students in on some of your teacher knowledge around questioning, introducing them to Webb's Depth of Knowledge (DOK) levels and teaching them how they can use these new insights to lift the level of the questions they pose around their inquiry topic.

Webb's DOK levels correspond to how deeply students understand and engage with content. Webb lays out four different levels of questioning. Level 1 questions are right there in the text, with correct answers that can be memorized. Questions build to level 4, where students answer open-ended questions, working across multiple texts, in more in-depth inquiries. You'll notice this lesson delves deeper into these levels.

Although Webb's DOK levels are numbered, they are not presented in a taxonomy, and they're not leveled hierarchically. The goal is not to provide kids with a steady diet of level 4 questions, as often some level 1 and 2 questions are necessary for foundation building. But it *is* important that kids are given opportunities to ask and to wrestle with high-level questions. You'll notice references to movement across DOK levels all throughout the lesson. You'll notice the acknowledgment that at the start of an inquiry, students may ask more DOK level 1 and 2 questions to help them make sure they are comprehending the text. Eventually, they generate higher-level questions that launch extended investigations.

Of course, you do not need a complex text to do complex thinking, so you'll notice that in this session, you also emphasize to students that they are all capable of doing this work. You'll show them how they can ask level 1 or level 4 questions of any text, regardless of how simple or complex the text appears. Then, too, you'll show students how not only can they ask questions, but they can reflect on the questions they ask, becoming more metacognitive about their questioning process.

IN THIS SESSION, you'll teach students that researchers ask questions at different levels—from basic comprehension questions to those requiring in-depth exploration. They question the text they're reading, the topic they're studying, and their own agenda.

GETTING READY

✔ Prepare a "Webb's Depth of Knowledge Questions" chart, and cover each level so you can reveal the information separately (see Connection).

✔ Students should bring their reading notebooks and a pen to the meeting area (see Connection).

✔ Choose a section of a text on your inquiry project to demonstrate how you question as you read. We recommend page 25 from *When Lunch Fights Back* (see Teaching).

✔ Have your reader's notebook handy to jot in (see Teaching).

✔ Prepare to share pages 9–10 of *Align Deep* with students (see Active Engagements).

✔ Prepare a chart titled "To Pursue Deep Research Questions . . ." (see Share).

✔ Jot down your research plan to share with students (see Share).

Lifting the Level of Questions (Using DOK) to Drive Research Forward

CONNECTION

Introduce students to a new tool teachers use to analyze their questioning, and invite them to think about ways they can use this tool to strengthen their research.

"Researchers, when you were unpacking this morning, Lily and I had a fascinating conversation about the research she did last night. Can I tell you about it, and will you think about if what's true for her was also true for you? She said that as she was reading her sources and writing to help herself understand what she was reading, she kept coming up with new questions about her topic, things she just *had* to know. And then as she read on, her questions just kept getting answered. You should see her notebook page. It's just filled with questions and answers, questions and answers. Was that true for any of you?" Several students nodded.

"It got me thinking about a tool I've been using as a teacher. It's been helping me plan strong questions for our read-alouds and for the minilessons we do together. I want to share it with you, because I think it will help you research, too.

"It was created by a researcher named Norman Webb in the 1990s. Webb created this thing he calls *Webb's Depth of Knowledge*. He thought about how deeply you could know things. Are you up for studying this tool with me?" The kids nodded. "Great! As we study together, will you start brainstorming ways this tool could help us with our research? Jot down what you find."

Explain the characteristics of each level of Webb's Depth of Knowledge, revealing a premade section of a chart. Give students an example of what a question at each level might look like.

"Webb decided that at the first level—level 1—a reader's questions would be very basic. They would sound like, 'Where do hagfish live?'" I added a Post-it note with that question to the chart. "These kinds of questions would have answers that were right or wrong, and the answers would be right there in the text."

"To get up to Webb's level 2, you have to take the information you're learning and do something with it. You might organize it in a new way, maybe according to your own agenda, or you might figure out what the multiple main ideas are. Here, a question would sound like, 'What are the main ideas of this section?'"

Note the way students' homework is occasionally referenced in minilessons. You needn't do this each day, but giving students opportunities to share their homework reminds them (and you!) that it is not busy work. Instead, it is an important component of the reading workshop.

Notice that students are regularly active during the Connection. It would be easy for students to sit back passively here, watching as you reveal parts of the chart. Instead, you recruit students to be active participants, saying, "As we study together, will you start brainstorming ways this tool could help us with our research?" Look for students to be watching actively, jotting along the way, and be prepared to voice-over if they need reminders to jot.

I paused to remind students to continuing thinking as I taught. "We've got two levels to go. Keep thinking about how we could use this chart to strengthen our research. Jot what you're thinking!" I gave students a moment to jot, then continued.

"Well, Webb kept thinking about questions that would require more thinking, and those were the next two levels he developed, levels 3 and 4. I'm putting these up at the same time because, in a lot of ways, they're really similar." I uncovered the two levels. "See how at both levels there's not just *one* right answer or *one* right way to go about answering the question. Instead, there can be *multiple* right answers. Next, questions at both level 3 and level 4 are based on the evidence and details in the text, but at these levels, you have to go beyond that.

"Here's the big difference between the two levels. At level 3, you're thinking really deeply about *one* text, probably the text you're reading at that moment. At level 4, though, you're going deeply into *multiple* texts, maybe two or maybe a ton of texts, and thinking across all of them."

I posted sample questions for levels 3 and 4. Our chart looked like this:

Resist the urge to elaborate on your descriptions of each level of Webb's Depth of Knowledge. Later in the lesson, as students generate questions, you will coach them as they differentiate between the levels of questions and clarify their understanding of each level. Now is the time to give a brief introduction to each level. Move through this part of the lesson quickly, aiming to keep your introduction of each level and students' note-taking under three minutes.

Webb's Depth of Knowledge Questions

Level 1 (or RECALL)
- Has a right or wrong answer
- Answer can be memorized
- Answer can be found *right there* in the text

| Where do hagfish live? |

Level 2 (or SKILLS/CONCEPTS)
- Still has a right or wrong answer
- Have to take information and use it
- Have to think and search for the answer

| What are the main ideas of this section? |

Level 3 (or STRATEGIC THINKING)
- Has multiple right answers or approaches
- Uses evidence, but goes beyond it
- Goes deep into one text

| What does Rebecca Johnson want me to think about animals that fight back? |

Level 4 (or EXTENDED THINKING)
- Has multiple right answers or approaches
- Uses evidence, but goes beyond it
- Goes deep into multiple texts
- Takes time to investigate

| What benefit can studying how animals fight back have to humans? |

Level 1 - Recall
- What school do you attend?

Level 2 - Skills/Concepts
- What is 236, in Expanded form?

Level 3 - Strategic Concepts
- According to our math notebook, what are some strategies to solve multiplication?

Level 4 - Extended Thinking
- How can I use mult to solve real-world scenarios?

"Take a minute to brainstorm with your partner, and think, 'How could this information be useful to us as we research?' I listened in as partnerships shared.

"Maybe it would help us know where to find answers, like we could know if we needed to look for an answer in the book or to really think about it," Nina suggested.

"Right now I think most of my questions are right there, level 1," Peter added, "so it could help me ask different kinds of questions."

❖ **Name the teaching point.**

"Today, I want to teach you that when readers dig deep into a topic, it pays to ask questions at different levels. Some questions will help you understand the text you're reading, and other questions will get you to think beyond the text, to question *across* texts, *across* your topic and even to question your own agenda."

TEACHING

Demonstrate how you read a section of a text, pushing yourself to ask questions on different levels. Recruit students to think alongside you, generating their own questions as you read.

"Will you try this work with me? Let's first look at a section of *When Lunch Fights Back*, and then later, since we'll be pushing ourselves to ask questions at all levels, let's hold it next to *Alien Deep*. As we read a chunk of each text, let's spy on ourselves, and notice the kinds of questions we ask. When we find ourselves asking questions, let's hold up fingers to show which level question we *think* we have—three fingers for a level 3 question, two for a level 2 question, and so on. Ready?"

I projected page 25 in *When Lunch Fights Back* so students could follow along, and said, "This is the section on the science behind the fulmar chicks, the ones that vomit on predators attacking them." Then I started reading:

> The word fulmar *means "foul gull." The name refers to the fulmar chicks' horrid, fishy-smelling vomit, which they spew onto anything that threatens them.*

Immediately I paused, looked up, and held up one finger. "I've already got questions, don't you?" Several students nodded. "I'm so curious about this vomit, like how far can the vomit reach? How close do predators have to be?" I gestured to students to suggest other questions, and students called out, "Yeah, what's the vomit made of? Who do they vomit on?"

Your teaching across this lesson supports students in moving toward fifth-grade expectations for the "Critical Reading" strand of the learning progression. The questions students ask of one text and across several texts will spark ideas that they can later investigate.

Fifth-graders are expected to monitor for sense as they read. Particularly as texts become more complex, they will often need to generate initial questions at DOK levels 1 and 2, and then read on with those questions in mind. Look to the learning progression for additional information.

Demonstrate asking questions at different levels, and weave in tips along the way to help students strengthen their questioning.

"We're asking a ton of level 1 questions right now, which makes sense. We're just getting into the text. Let me give you a tip: As researchers read more and more on a topic, their questions often get deeper. So right now, let's push ourselves as we go on to ask questions on another level." I continued reading.

> *A fulmar chick can hit a moving target up to 6 feet (2 m) away.*

"Well, that definitely shows my first question was a level 1! It was right there in the text, one answer. I didn't have to do a lot of work to find it." I continued reading.

> *It can also hurl out half a dozen blasts of vomit in quick succession. Scientists have discovered that fulmar chicks can even defend themselves with vomit while hatching, before they are completely free of their shells.*

I glanced up. Hands around the rug held up a range of fingers.

> *Fulmar vomit is mostly a mixture of oily substances secreted by the bird's stomach wall. It has a vile odor and is as sticky as glue. Once the vomit gets on another bird's feathers, no amount of cleaning and preening will remove it.*

"Now that I've read a bit more, I want to push myself to ask other kinds of questions, questions that will be interesting for me to study. One question I have is 'Why do scientists do all this research?' I mean, it seems pretty awesome to be researching bird vomit as your job, and science research being cool is the agenda I've had so far as I've been reading, but I figure there must be something deeper. I'm not sure we'll find a straightforward answer to that in this text (or in any text, really), so this is probably a level 4 question. I think it will require a ton of research to investigate.

"And another question I'm growing is 'Do all scientists work in the same way?' I'm thinking I could read across all 'The Science Behind the Story' sections to get some ideas, so this could be a level 3 question. I'll jot these down in my notebook.

"Do you see how we're asking these deep questions now, but we had to ask some level 1 and 2 questions first to make sure we understood the text?"

As you read on in the text, it becomes clearer what level many questions fall at. My initial question was a level 1 question because the answer was right there in the text, presented to us as we read on. Rather than dwelling on the precise level at which questions fall when students ask them, you might choose to clarify the levels later, when questions are answered, as I did here. Alternatively, you could ask students to justify why they believe a question falls at a different level.

Demonstrating how you briefly jot in your reader's notebook is incredibly powerful. It shifts the notebook from being a school tool—something kids use just because they're told to—to a tool that readers use to record their thoughts and grow their ideas.

ACTIVE ENGAGEMENT

Set students up to develop their own plans for studying a second text.

"Readers, it's your turn. Let me give you a second tip before you get started: To dig deep into a topic, it helps to think across texts and across subtopics. Push yourself to ask questions that will cover more than one text or more than one part of a text.

"Can you try this right now with pages 9 and 10 from *Alien Deep*? We've read these pages before, but will you reread them now, really questioning them? Make a quick plan for how you'll read the text—together, silently, taking turns— and how you'll talk about your questions along the way.

"Get started reading and questioning!"

Coach partners to ask questions at a variety of levels as they work collaboratively through the text.

I listened in as Iris and Nina questioned the first paragraph on page 9. "How far down are they?" Iris asked. "And, what does their research vessel look like?"

"Remember to think about where your question falls," I coached as both girls held up one finger. "Those seem like 'right there' questions—you can probably answer them by reading on in this text. What questions could you ask to push yourself deeper into both texts?"

"Hmm, . . . well, like before, I'm still wondering if all scientists work the same way," Nina began. "I'm thinking they might all have surprises, 'cause here in *Alien Deep* the author says there's an 'unexpected discovery' as part of their work, and in *When Lunch Fights Back* it says they were 'surprised to discover.' So maybe we could think more about ways scientists' work is the same and different."

Debrief, naming the work of questioning across texts in a generalizable way.

I reconvened the class. "Readers, you're doing some powerful work here. Many of you started by asking level 1 questions, questions with answers you could find right there in the text. Instead of stopping there, you next did something that was key. You held *Alien Deep* right next to *When Lunch Fights Back*, and you thought, 'What other questions could we ask here, questions about more than one text?' Thinking about multiple texts helped you push for deeper questions, ones like 'How are the ways different scientists work similar and different?' This will really help us push our research."

Fifth-graders are expected to consider who wrote a given text and what the author might stand to gain from a text, as well as to consider what a text is saying about an issue and whether they agree with what the text is teaching. Be on the lookout for partnerships you could coach to do this work. Look to the "Critical Reading" strand of the learning progression for more information.

LINK

Invite students to spy on themselves as they ask questions of the text, noticing which are ones they can answer quickly, and which are ones that require more research, to look across texts.

"Today as you read, will you spy on yourself? When you ask a question, notice, and jot it down. As you do this, be honest with yourself. Jot down all your questions on Post-it notes or in your notebook—the ones that take all of ten seconds to answer, as well as the ones that could take ten years. Remember, it's important to have a balance of questions, and recording your questions, and then studying them will help you maintain this balance.

"As you do this, you'll likely need to question inside the text you're reading. It will also help you to question across texts, holding two or more texts next to each other and letting that pairing spark questions. And—this is big—you might even need to question your own agenda like you helped me do, when you said, 'This isn't just about how cool the work scientists do is. We have to ask, "Why does this work matter?"' Off you go!"

After you say, "Off you go!," be on the lookout for readers who disregard all earlier teaching and focus solely on amassing a growing pile of questions on Post-it notes. You might pause at one table and say, "Remember that researchers draw on all they've learned as they read," and then encourage students to scan the room, noting charts that signify earlier teaching and using those to guide their thinking.

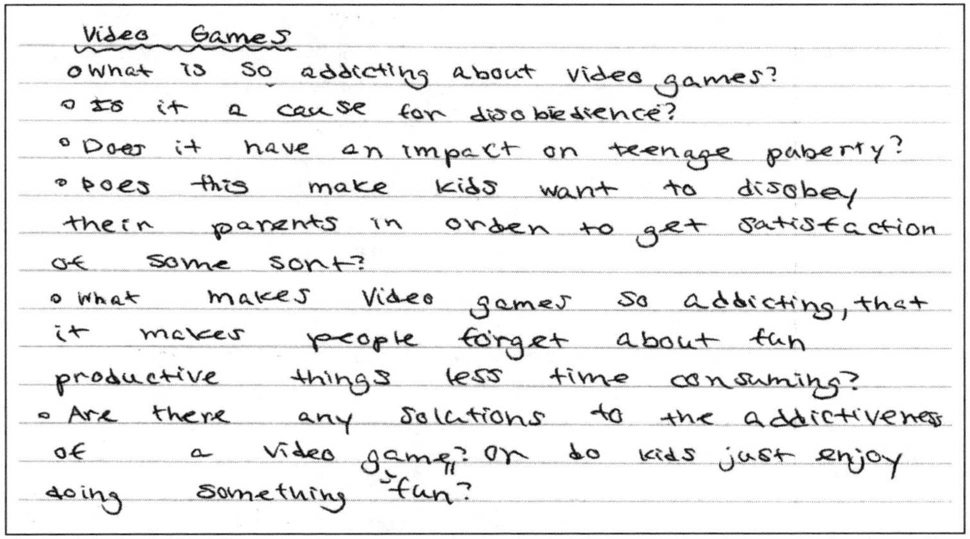

> Video Games
> ○ What is so addicting about video games?
> ○ Is it a cause for disobedience?
> ○ Does it have an impact on teenage puberty?
> ○ Does this make kids want to disobey their parents in order to get satisfaction of some sort?
> ○ What makes video games so addicting, that it makes people forget about fun productive things less time consuming?
> ○ Are there any solutions to the addictiveness of a video game? Or do kids just enjoy doing something fun?

FIG. 14–1   Iris asks questions that push her to think across texts and even question her own agenda about video games.

Supporting Readers to Ask and Answer Questions

NONFICTION FEEDS INTO A CURIOUS STANCE that most children take toward the world, and you'll likely see students asking a range of powerful questions. However, asking questions as an activity in and of itself can lead to a kind of complacency if students don't return and try to figure out answers to their questions. As teachers, we need to support readers in taking an active stance when reading, teaching them that one reason we read is to answer the questions we generate.

I was reminded of this in a recent conference when I pulled alongside Lila. Last time I'd met with Lila, she'd set a goal to strengthen her writing about reading, so I started the conference by asking her to tell me about the progress she'd made toward her goal. "Last time we met, you set a goal to strengthen your writing about reading. How's that going?"

"Pretty good," she said, notebook closed. "I've been doing a ton more writing, and I've been organizing it in really cool ways, like based on what I want to think about, even if it doesn't match the way the text's teaching it."

"Can you take me on a tour of your recent writing about reading, the pages you're particularly proud of?" I asked. Lila immediately opened her page to the writing work she'd done based on today's minilesson. This was no surprise. Lila was the kind of reader who always tries out the day's minilesson. My goal was to celebrate the work Lila has done, while figuring out how to extend it.

"Lila, can I give you a compliment?" She nodded enthusiastically. "Well, you're really doing some tremendous work here today pushing yourself to ask all different kinds of questions about animal venom. And I see here, that when you realized all your questions were those level 1 questions, the kinds you could answer *right there* in the text, with right and wrong answers, you pushed yourself to go beyond the text and to ask those level 3 and 4 questions that stretched beyond the page, and maybe even beyond the text. This is powerful work, and I bet those questions are already helping you think

more deeply about your topic." By this point, Lila's grin stretched from ear to ear, so I decided to link my compliment for Lila to my teaching point.

"And, can I give you one tip that will help you make this work even stronger? When readers ask the kinds of questions you're asking now, the kinds that go beyond the text, it helps to stop sometimes and try to answer those questions. Sometimes, you can turn to another text for an answer, and other times you'll have to try out multiple possibilities for what an answer could be. Are you up for trying this?" Lila nodded. "Okay, will you reread all those questions you've been asking and find one you think is worth studying deeply to try to answer, one you don't know the answer to right away?"

Lila bent over her notebook. "Maybe this one, where I ask, 'Do venomous animals live everywhere?' That's important to find out, 'cause then I'd know if everyone needs to learn about venom, or if only some people do. That I think I could google."

"Hmm, . . . if that's an easy one to find an answer to, keeping looking through your list to find one that's a bit harder to answer." Lila studied her notebook again.

"Umm, this one, I think," she said. "Should people try to save endangered animals that are venomous or not?"

I thought Lila's question would definitely pay off to research further, but I wanted to make sure she felt the same way and had reasons to back up her choice. "Why do you think this would make a strong question to try and answer?" I asked.

"For one thing, people feel a *ton* of different ways about it. I bet there are a bunch of reasons for each side, money reasons and life reasons and animal rights reasons. It seems super complicated," she said. "I've been trying to figure out how i feel about it, so studying it could help me."

"Researchers, I see your piles of questions growing! Take one minute to jot down any last questions you have right now."

After a moment, I continued. "Will you and your partner spend a few minutes looking across your piles of questions? Sort them into different levels—with a pile for level 1 questions that were easy to find answers to and another pile for level 4 questions you'll have to look across texts to answer and, well, you get the picture."

Students immediately got to work sorting their questions into piles, and I coached in, encouraging them to use our questioning chart to accurately evaluate their questions.

"As you look across your piles, you can get a sense of yourself as a reader, of the kinds of questions you're currently asking. Can you look at your piles of questions and set a goal for yourself? What can you do to deepen the questions you're asking? Record your goal so you can work on it going forward."

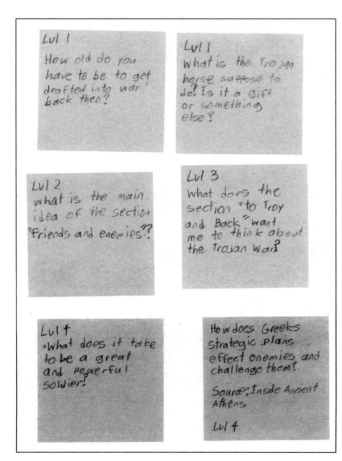
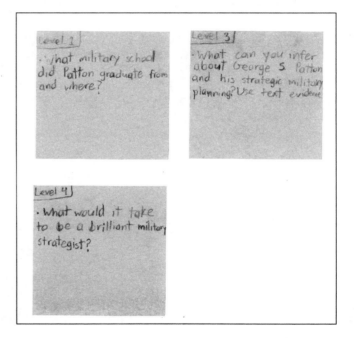

FIG. 14–2   Students' notebook pages showing how they sorted some of their questions into piles.

"When you find a question like this, it helps to generate some possible answers. You might say, 'Maybe . . .' and try out one possible answer, and then say, 'Or perhaps . . .'" and try out a second answer, and push yourself to say, 'Or could it be . . .' and try out a third answer. Then, you can read on with your question and possible answers in mind, looking for evidence that proves or leads you to revise your thinking. Ready to try this?" I asked. "Let's start with 'Maybe . . .'"

"Maybe . . . maybe people should try to save them because all living things deserve to be saved. Like, venomous animals are really no different from the cuddly panda bears we love to save. And, they're endangered because of us, because of the things we've done, so it should be our job to save them."

"Try out 'Or perhaps . . .'" I prompted.

"Or perhaps we shouldn't save them? 'Cause saving them costs a lot of money, and mostly they're just causing problems for people, and people are getting poisoned by accident and having to go to the hospital and that costs a lot of money too."

"Lila, this is powerful work you're taking on. You're pushing beyond asking questions and starting to answer them, generating a few possibilities for what an answer could be. Now you're ready to read on with your possible answers in mind, seeing if your answers are confirmed, or if they need to be revised. Will you try this with a couple more questions over the next few days, being sure you're asking *and* answering those questions?"

I ended by asking Lila to make a plan for how she'd try out this work in the future, and she jotted down her plan while I recorded my observations and ideas for Lila's next steps in my conferring notes. Glancing at the "Critical Reading" strand of the learning progression, I noted that Lila was coming to texts with her own agenda, and reading and note-taking with that agenda in mind. Looking at the "Questioning the Text" thread, I recorded that it seemed Lila was taking her texts at face value, not considering the author's intentions and background. This could be a possible next step for Lila.

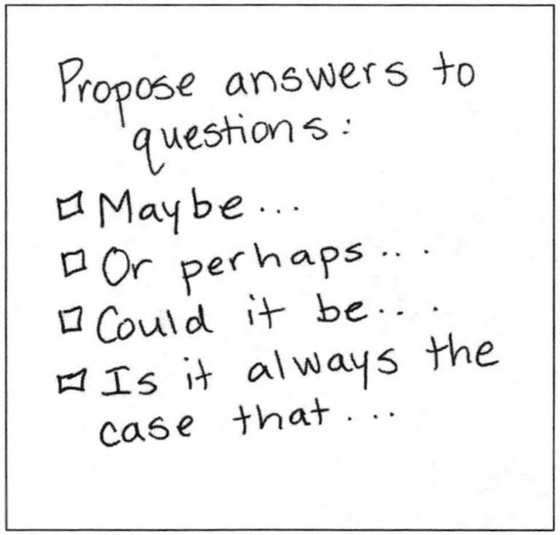

FIG. 14–3   A quick Post-it note, created by the teacher or student at the end of the conference, serves as a powerful reminder of what was taught.

Collaborating on Questioning and Research

Explain to students that researchers, like scientists, strengthen their inquiries in the company of others.

"Readers, can I share with you something I uncovered in my research that I think will help us all? At first, when I started reading about scientists, I thought they worked in isolation. That means by themselves. I pictured them in a lab, white coats on, working all alone. Then, as I read more, I realized that scientists definitely don't work in isolation. Even when they're working on their own experiments, scientists are constantly talking, sharing questions, making suggestions to each other. I thought we could try some of this same work with our questions today."

Engage students in a study of your major research question, asking them to suggest possibilities for research. Model jotting those suggestions down as a way to plan for future research.

"Let me show you what I mean. I'm noticing that all the research that scientists do is cool, but I want to think more deeply about it, so I came up with these questions: 'What's the purpose of scientific research? Why would scientists research creatures like the hoopoe chicks and giant clams? Who does it help?'

"Right now, will you all be my topic group? Imagine I came to you with this question: What's the purpose of scientific research? Here are some ways you could help me." I posted a chart titled "To Pursue Deep Research Questions . . ." "With your partner, come up with at least two pieces of advice for me." I listened in and jotted while students turned and talked.

"Well," Nina said to her partner. "I think that reading about research people do on made-up creatures might be helpful. Like maybe you could borrow one of my articles about the Loch Ness monster and read that."

"Yeah, it might help to read about other kinds of research that scientists do, too. I'm studying football and there are a ton of people studying injuries that football players get. That could be interesting," Marcus agreed.

Set students up to work with their research groups.

"So right now, get back into the research groups. This time, instead of sharing your research plans or your writing about reading, share your questions. You'll want to share one question at a time, laying it out and getting lots of feedback on

---

To Pursue Deep Research Questions...

- Think about other texts, topics, or concepts that might be related to your study

- Brainstorm keywords that could help you in your research

- Consider other sides or perspectives to the question   Maybe...   It could also...

- Use our "Webb's Depth of Knowledge Questions" chart to make your question stronger   LEVEL **1** → LEVEL **2** → LEVEL **3** → LEVEL **4**

---

how you might pursue it or make it stronger. Take lots of notes when your question is being discussed because you'll probably get ideas for research you need to do. You can use my notes as a sample."

I posted my notes for students to see (see Figure 14–4).

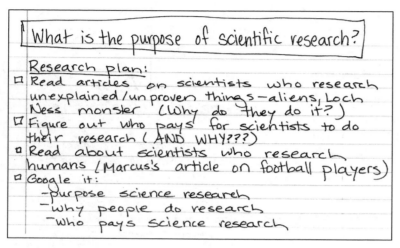

FIG. 14–4   Teacher-modeled research question notes

Students launched into group conversations and worked for several minutes, taking turns sharing their questions and giving feedback to group members to strengthen their questions.

SESSION 14 HOMEWORK

 ## ASKING MORE QUESTIONS, RESEARCH MORE DEEPLY

Readers, as you continue researching your topic tonight, keep your updated research plan in mind. It's likely you'll need to find additional sources to help you answer your questions. These additional resources might be directly related to your topic. They might be about a related topic that you believe will pay off to study. Either way, collect a few more sources today. Then spend time studying them.

Also, pay attention to the questions you're asking as you read. Jot down all the questions you're asking. Include the questions with answers right there in the text. Also include the questions that require you to go deep into multiple texts to find the right answer. Remember you need to ask questions at lots of different levels. If you notice that all of your questions are at the same level, push yourself to ask other types of questions. I'm including a mini-version of the chart we studied today for you to use at home.

Webb's Depth of Knowledge Questions

Level 1 (or RECALL)	Level 2 (or SKILLS/CONCEPTS)
• Has a right or wrong answer	• Still has a right or wrong answer
• Answer can be memorized	• Have to take information and use it
• Answer can be found *right there* in the text	• Have to think and search for the answer
Where do hagfish live?	**What are the main ideas of this section?**

Level 3 (or STRATEGIC THINKING)	Level 4 (or EXTENDED THINKING)
• Has multiple right answers or approaches	• Has multiple right answers or approaches
• Uses evidence, but goes beyond it	• Uses evidence, but goes beyond it
• Goes deep into one text	• Goes deep into multiple texts
	• Takes time to investigate
What does Rebecca Johnson want me to think about animals that fight back?	**What benefit can studying how animals fight back have to humans?**

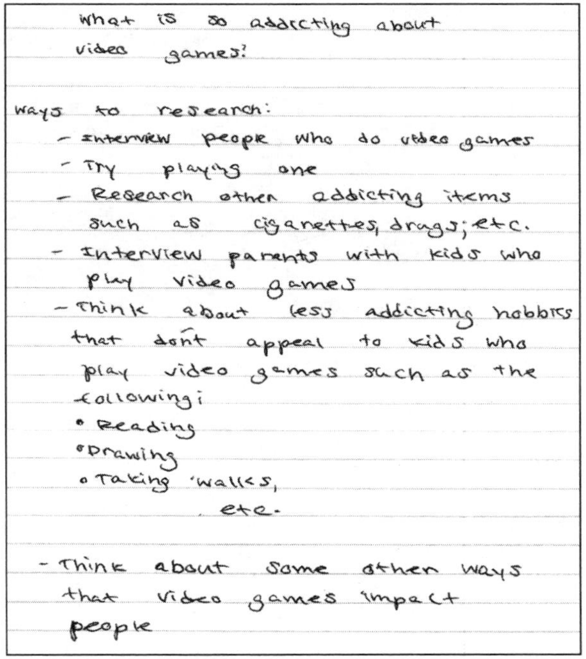

What is so addicting about video games?

ways to research:
- interview people who do video games
- try playing one
- Research other addicting items such as cigarettes, drugs, etc.
- Interview parents with kids who play video games
- Think about less addicting hobbies that don't appeal to kids who play video games such as the following:
  • Reading
  • Drawing
  • Taking walks,
     etc.

- Think about some other ways that video games impact people

FIG. 14–5 Iris generates a research plan to investigate a big question: What is so addicting about video games?

Synthesizing across Subtopics

IN THIS SESSION, you'll teach students that readers synthesize information across subtopics, both within a single text and across texts. They explain how parts of the text work together and determine why one part of the text is important to the rest of the text or the rest of the topic.

GETTING READY

✔ Students should bring their reading notebooks and multiple texts on their inquiry topic to the meeting area (see Connection and Active Engagement).

✔ Create a "To Synthesize across Subtopics, Researchers . . ." chart (see Teaching).

✔ Show the article "Hagfish Slime Could Be Eco-Friendly Fabric," or another article on your class inquiry topic, to your class. A link to the "Hagfish Slime Could Be Eco-Friendly Fabric" article is available on the online resources. (see Teaching).

✔ Take notes on "Hagfish Slime Could Be Eco-Friendly Fabric" to highlight note-taking on a subtopic, or display the sample notes from the online resources (see Teaching).

✔ Prepare a section of your class read-aloud on the same subtopic to demonstrate how you study a subtopic across texts. We suggest pages 7–8 from *Alien Deep* (see Teaching).

✔ Display "Webb's Depth of Knowledge Questions" chart from Session 14 for reference (see Connection).

✔ Create a "Readers Synthesize within a Text By . . ." chart to help students synthesize within a text (see Conferring and Small-Group Work).

✔ Use the text complexity cards from Session 8 to help students integrate text features into their synthesis (see Conferring and Small-Group Work).

✔ Be sure students have their copies of the "Comparing and Contrasting" strand from the Informational Reading Learning Progression for grades 4 and 5 (see Share and Homework).

B Y THIS POINT, students have amassed and read several texts on a topic, and they've used primary research to learn even more. Their brains are likely overflowing with all the information they've learned. While some students will naturally group information on similar subtopics together as they read across texts, other students will benefit from direct instruction and opportunities to practice that skill. This session sets out to do just that, supporting students in synthesizing the information they're encountering across subtopics into a coherent and usable form. Students are first asked to consider how a part of the text they're encountering on a subtopic fits with a part of another text on the same subtopic. During the mid-workshop teaching, you'll teach students that it's not enough to consider how texts agree, or fit together; they also have to consider places where texts disagree, contrasting what those two texts teach. As you wrap up the lesson, you'll ask students to self-assess their work synthesizing against one strand of the Informational Reading Learning Progression, setting goals for their comparing and contrasting work moving forward.

Today's lesson builds off of work your students did last year during fourth grade in Unit 2 *Reading the Weather, Reading the World*. Your students learned that as they read across many texts about a similar subtopic, they needed to read subsequent texts differently than they read the initial text, because they had the notes and information from the first text in mind. They learned to read a second and third text on a subtopic, asking, "Does this add to what I've already learned? Change what I learned?" As they encountered new information, your students learned to revise their notes to reflect their new learning. Last year, your students did this work with the support of a club, and this year, you'll ask your students to lift the level of their synthesis work, while working with increasing independence.

This is work you'll want to support within your read-aloud. Up to this point, you may have been reading through sections of texts and talking about what authors taught in isolation. Start looking at ways to bring cross-text work into your read-aloud, so students have regular opportunities to synthesize information across subtopics in a text. You might read aloud a part in *Alien Deep*, ask students to turn and talk to recall parts where the same subtopic was addressed in *When Lunch Fights Back*, and then reread a part from *When Lunch Fights Back* that students identify, considering how the information in the parts of the two text fits together.

There are many ways to extend this work. One teacher we work with asked students to bring their copies of "Lessons from the Deep" with them to the meeting area. She distributed a few copies of *When Lunch Fights Back* around the rug. Then, she read aloud parts from *Alien Deep*, asking students to consider how the information she was reading fit with the parts they were holding. Another teacher we work with gave each topic group copies of a different article from the *Science* section of *Tween Tribune*, the Smithsonian's online news site for kids. He asked the groups to first study their individual article, and then he read aloud sections from *Alien Deep*. At regular points, he asked topic groups to discuss how the text they were holding fit with and contradicted the class read-aloud.

This session also prepares students for the critical literacies work they'll take on in Sessions 19 and 20, where you'll teach students that following only one author's perspective on a topic gives you an insufficient understanding of that topic. You'll notice we begin laying the groundwork for this work in the Mid-Workshop Teaching, asking students to compare and contrast texts on the same subtopic. Students will only dabble in this work today, but heightening their awareness of these disagreements will help students become more critical consumers of text for the rest of their lives.

Synthesizing across Subtopics

CONNECTION

Remind students of their initial research focuses, and ask them to revisit their notes and notice how much more sophisticated their knowledge of their topic is now.

"Researchers, I've got to say, I'm floored by how far our research has come already. In just the last few days, we've gone from these topics that were kind of broad and vague to understanding that our topics are actually far more complicated. Take our class topic, for example. Remember how we started with scientists? And now, we've noticed all these subtopics that were tucked inside our topic." I ticked the subtopics off on my fingers when I named them. "How scientists work, what makes scientific research exciting, why people choose to become scientists, who scientists work for, even that big question you helped me come up with yesterday about what the purpose of science research is.

"Right now, will you look over your inquiry project in this same way? Start with your topic from Day One, remind yourself what it was, and then study your notes on the lookout for all the subtopics you've already noticed. Collect them on your fingers, and get ready to list them all out for your partner."

For students to transfer what you teach and model about synthesizing across subtopics to their own topics, they will need to know the subtopics that make up their topic. Giving students a minute now to think about their subtopics and name them with a partner will set them up to be successful as they access the more challenging work still to come in the lesson.

After a moment, I continued, "Share all those subtopics with your partners." Students turned and shared, while I listened in.

"Give yourself a pat on the back. You've certainly come far as researchers. Let me introduce you to a new step you can take in your research, something that will help you once you've started to uncover all these subtopics."

❖ **Name the teaching point.**

"Today I want to teach you that as researchers investigate a topic, they often encounter multiple subtopics hidden inside their topic. You read on with those subtopics in mind, notice when multiple texts teach about the same subtopic, and ask, 'How do these parts fit together? Why is this part important?'"

TEACHING

Tell students that synthesizing across subtopics is a step-by-step process, and let them know you'll be going through those steps together. Show a chart with the steps.

"Researchers, let me show you how this synthesizing across subtopics work can go. There are usually some predictable steps that researchers take to do this work. I've put them on a chart for us to see." I revealed a chart titled "To Synthesize Across Subtopics, Researchers..." "We'll go through these steps first for our class topic, then you'll get a chance to try going through them for your own research topic."

Demonstrate for students how you look back over your research and identify a subtopic you want to study further. Read a section of an article, learning all you can about that subtopic.

"So first, researchers, we need to identify a subtopic we want to study further and what we already know about it. Let's take the one we were asking questions about yesterday: What's the purpose of scientific research?' Now, we don't really know much at all about that subtopic yet, right? So, to find a text to help us learn more, last night, I googled 'purpose for scientific research' and I came across this incredible article from National Geographic. It's all about the hagfish's slime. And, check out this section! I wanted to call all of you when I read it last night, it was that cool. It quoted that same scientist, Douglas Fudge, who we know from *When Lunch Fights Back*." I shared a snippet of the article. "Here's what it said."

> But Douglas Fudge, an interactive biologist at Canada's University of Guelph, in Ontario, has given us a reason to embrace the goo: It may one day be used to produce a strong, eco-friendly fabric.

Jaws dropped in awe. "Isn't that crazy? Can you imagine that gross slime dripping down from Douglas's hands being used for *fabric*? And as I read on, the article even said that 'hagfish slime threads are almost as strong and light as spider silk,' which people have been trying to use as fabric. Let me show you what I jotted down in my notebook when I finished reading." I projected a page (see Figure 15–1).

Read a new text, and rally students to consider how the information they are learning in the new text could fit with what they read about the subtopic in the first text.

"That's all I've found so far on this subtopic, so let's keep this as our lens as we read a chunk of a second text, *Alien Deep*. There isn't a section titled 'The Purposes of Science Research'—we know that's not how texts work anymore as they get more challenging—but let's read this first section in the text thinking, 'How does this part connect to what we already know? How do these parts fit together? Why is this part important?'" I began reading aloud halfway through page 7.

To Synthesize Across Subtopics, Researchers...

- Identify a subtopic to study further, reminding themselves what they already know about it

- Read a section of a text to learn about the subtopic and ask how it connects to what they already know

- Read another section of text and ask,
  - "How does this connect to what I already know?"
  - "Why is this part important?"

You'll notice that I explain to students how I research to find the article, rather than just posting the article for them to study. Look for opportunities to support the development of twenty-first century research skills.

A whole new world has been discovered right here on Earth, and it is being explored by a whole gallery of amazing scientists. It is a world of exotic creatures and extreme environments as bizarre as anything in my favorite science-fiction novels. It is a world of lethal landscapes where some of the most basic assumptions about life are being questioned. Even better, it is a world that, until its discovery, scientists never thought possible: the world of deep-sea hydrothermal vents.

In the 35 years since the first one was discovered in 1977, hydrothermal vents have revolutionized our understanding of life: where it came from, how it evolved, and what its limits are. But our knowledge is still fragmentary.

Model doing what students will predictably do when they read with subtopics in mind. Demonstrate how you reread the text, digging deeper to notice connections.

"Well, this part doesn't fit at all. Nowhere does it say, 'Scientists research because it helps . . . .' I guess we should just keep reading." I picked up the book to keep reading, and then said, "No, wait. I know the text won't come out and say the words I'm looking for like *research*, *purpose*, and *benefits*. Let me see if I can push myself deeper. How could this possibly fit with our subtopic, the purpose of science research? "Let me reread and see if that will help. As I do, let's all be thinking 'How does this part connect to what I already know? Why is this part important?'" I reread the section.

"Hmm . . . well, maybe this part about hydrothermal vent research could fit with what we read earlier about hagfish slime being made into thread because they both show that scientific research can have benefits. I'm thinking, though, that *Alien Deep* introduces a new reason why scientific research matters—that it teaches us more, and, that as we learn, it helps us question everything we thought we knew about the world. So maybe this part is important because it's raising a different perspective on our subtopic I hadn't thought of before. Reading with our subtopic in mind really helped us to see more, and now we can add these new ideas to our notes." I projected my notebook, showing what my page of notes looked like now (see Figure 15–2).

ACTIVE ENGAGEMENT

Set students up to transfer the work of synthesizing across subtopics from the class topic to their individual inquiry topic. Remind students to follow the steps on the chart.

"Readers, will you give this work of synthesizing across subtopics a try with your topic? Just like we did with our class topic, you'll follow the steps on the chart to help you. So, remember first you need to identify a subtopic. Earlier in this lesson, you thought about all the subtopics you've already encountered on your topic, and you listed them with your partner. Right now, choose one you already know a bit about. Then, read through your notes with that subtopic in mind, thinking, 'What do I already know about my subtopic?'" I gave students some time to reread their notes and then pointed to the second bullet on our chart.

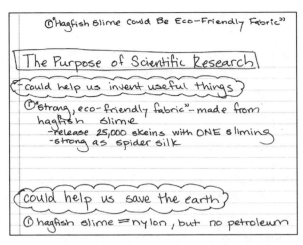

FIG. 15–1   These sample notes provide a model for note-taking on a subtopic.

FIG. 15–2   These revised notes show connections between two texts on the same subtopic.

"As soon as you're ready, will you pick up one text that teaches about your subtopic and reread it with your subtopic as a lens, seeing what that text teaches you about your subtopic?" Most students quickly found a spot in their first text to study, and I reminded a few students to use the table of contents to help them.

"Now, read on in the same text with your subtopic in mind, or pick up a new text that also teaches about your subtopic. As you read this new part, will you think, 'How do these parts fit together? Why is this part important?' Jot down what you learn."

As students worked, I coached in. When I saw Peter scanning down a page and then flipping to the next one, I said, "Remember to read looking for any possible connections to your topic. You know your page will probably not say exactly what you're researching." Working together, we quickly generated a list of words related to his subtopic of *life for servants in a medieval castle*: workers, orders, difficult, strenuous, and labor. He continued reading, looking for ways what he was reading could possibly fit with *life for servants*, and I moved around the rug coaching other students.

"Share your initial findings with your partner." I listened in as Omala and Nina shared.

"My subtopic is how people fake seeing UFOs. It was super easy for me to find my subtopic in a ton of books, 'cause all the books I'm reading have sections about how people fake seeing UFOs. The article I read just told a story about how people thought they saw something and it ended up not being real. But check this out." Omala opened her copy of "Investigating UFOs and Aliens" and started pointing out sections to Nina. "It teaches different things."

"Like what?" Nina asked.

"It goes into all the awesome ways that people fake UFO sightings, like how they don't give any real evidence, they just say it *had to be*," Omala said.

Nina's face lit up. "That's totally what I found on the Loch Ness monster, too, like, people have pictures but I don't know if that's real evidence."

LINK

Remind students to read new texts with their subtopics in mind, considering how the information they learn fits with what they've already read and with the questions they have.

"Readers, as you go off to continue to read and research, remember that it pays off to read with your subtopics in mind. As you do this, keep asking, 'How do these parts fit together? And, why is this part important?' Reading in this way will help you understand your subtopics more deeply."

As you listen in, be on the lookout for partnerships that are having trouble synthesizing across texts. You might choose to provide these students with a short list of familiar sentence starters they used in Grade 4 Unit 2 Reading the Weather, Reading the World *when they were synthesizing information across texts on a subtopic. These familiar sentence starters include: Author's name tells more. She writes . . . ; Author's name tells something that sort of builds on this . . . ; Author's name provides more detailed information. This text says . . . ; and Author's name gives an example. She writes . . . Have these ready on small sheets of paper to distribute to partnerships as needed.*

The research groups you have organized can have unexpected benefits. Groups might notice that they have the same subtopic—faking evidence or adaptations or unexpected discoveries—and then synthesize not only across texts on their topic, but also across the topics represented in the group. If your students do not naturally gravitate toward this work, use some of your conferring and small-group work time to support this.

I touched the "Webb's Depth of Knowledge Questions" chart we started in the previous session, listing the characteristics of four levels of questions. "And be sure you're keeping your questions in mind as you read across subtopics. Remember that those level 4 questions will require you to go into multiple texts, to really dig deep, to answer them.

"So, as you go off today, work to see how parts within a text and across the text fit together to help you learn more and generate answers to your questions. Go get started!"

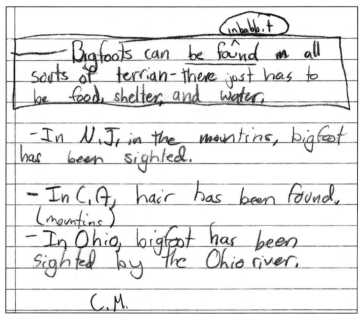

FIG. 15–3   A student synthesizes information about where Bigfoot can live by reading across several texts on the subtopic.

Supporting Foundational Work in Synthesizing Texts

YOUR WHOLE-CLASS INSTRUCTION supported students in synthesizing across texts. At the same time, it's likely you'll have students who need support synthesizing information within a text, particularly as the texts they read become increasingly complex. Below are suggestions for small groups or conferences to support students with this foundational work.

Support students in synthesizing parts within a text.

I gathered a group of readers together and asked them to select a text from their research set. "Readers, today I want to teach you another way readers synthesize within texts that I think will especially pay off for you. Specifically, I want to teach you that readers pause after reading each part of their text, and think, 'What does this part teach?' Then, as readers read on, they think, 'How does this part fit with the part I read before? How are they similar and different?' This helps us explain how each part of the text builds on the parts that came before."

I posted the questions for the group:

I asked students to pull copies of the level 5 version of "Lessons from the Deep" from their folders. "Will you help me practice with this text?" I read aloud the first paragraph and asked students to turn and talk, thinking, "What does this part teach?" Students agreed that the first paragraph said the octopus was amazing and gave tiny bits of evidence, such as how there were so many types and how they could be found all over.

"With that in mind, let's read the second part, and think, 'How does this part fit with the part I read before? How are they similar or different?'" I read aloud paragraphs two and three (several sessions before, we had decided these two paragraphs should be chunked together), and asked students to turn and talk again. I tapped the chart to remind students about the kinds of questions they should be asking.

FIG. 15–4   This mini-chart supports students with synthesizing within a text.

I reconvened students and set them up to transfer what they had just learned to their inquiry project texts. "Readers, this is work you can, and should, do whenever you're reading. At first, you'll likely have to stop after each chunk of text, thinking, 'How does

(continues)

"Readers, as you've been researching today, you've come across the same subtopic in multiple texts. Right now, can you get out two texts you've already studied that teach about the same subtopic and turn to the places where those texts teach about that subtopic?" I gave students a minute to find those places.

"So far, today, you've been reading across texts on the same subtopic, thinking, 'How do these parts fit together? Why is this part important?' Well, what I want to teach you is that researchers notice agreement (how parts fit together), but they also notice disagreement—places where parts don't fit together, places where parts say completely different things or choose really different words to teach something.

"So, right now, can you reread the two parts you have open? This time instead of giving them the agreement test, give them the disagreement test. Think, 'In what ways are these parts different? How do they contrast?'" I gave students a couple of minutes to work independently, and then asked them to share with their partner.

I listened in as Dexter talked with Lily about the discrepancies he had noticed. He had two articles laid out: "Rocking with R5" (www.timeforkids.com/news/rocking-r5/166331, search terms: rocking R5 Time) and "Taylor Swift Wants You to Read" (tweentribune.com/junior/taylor-swift-wants-you-read, search terms: Swift wants read). "At first, I thought these articles both were about the same thing—pop stars getting you to do things—because the articles talked about how the pop stars were using videos to get their fans to think a certain way. But when I think about differences, maybe it's that they're both trying to sell different things. Like, Taylor Swift is trying to sell reading and convince kids that they can get a lot out of books. But R5, they're selling Ring Pops, a candy. That feels really different."

I gave students another minute to share and then paused their conversations. "Back to reading, and as you continue today, be sure you're thinking about how the texts you're encountering on the same subtopic can be compared and contrasted."

this part fit with the part I read before?' and you'll push yourself to notice similarities and differences. As this work becomes easier, you'll probably start doing it without thinking. Right now, can you open up the book you brought with you and give this work a try?" I coached in for a few minutes as students worked, and then sent them off to continue researching with this new learning in mind.

Support students in integrating complex text features into their synthesis.

I noticed another group of students were synthesizing sections of text but were ignoring the complex text features on each page. I pulled them together, hoping to build off of the powerful work they were already doing. "Readers, I gathered you together today because I'm noticing you have a particular strength at reading sections of a text and thinking about how they fit together. This synthesizing work comes pretty naturally to you. So today, I want to give you a tip to help you make your synthesizing even stronger. It's this: when readers synthesize, they combine the text *and* the text features on the page. This becomes increasingly important as the texts you're reading become more complex."

I laid out a few text complexity cards. "Remember that now *there are complicated numbers and statistics*, *the visuals present new information*, and *the captions give MORE information*. As readers, we have to put all these together with the text when we synthesize."

"To practice this work, can you find a place in the text you brought with you where you can try this work?" I opened to page pages 30 and 31 in *When Lunch Fights Back*. "I chose these pages because they have lots of visuals and longer captions that I'll have to synthesize across." Students flipped through their books, settling on pages and opening them on their laps. "Tell your partner why you chose that particular page. What's complex about it that will make it interesting to synthesize?" Students turned and talked, touching and naming the text complexity cards as they described what made their page an appropriate choice.

"Right now, read the text on the page and think, 'What does this part teach?'" After about a minute, I voiced over, "Now, study one of the text features. Think, 'What does this part teach?' Once you know what both parts teach, put them together!" I coached students through a few rounds of reading parts of their texts and thinking about how those parts fit together. As they worked, I offered lean prompts to some students, saying, "Now add in another text feature!" or "Think about how that part fits!" To other students, I provided more scaffolding, using *When Lunch Fights Back* to demonstrate how I did the work.

At the end of the small group, I restated the teaching point and then asked students to jot down on a Post-it note what I had taught them that they needed to work on. Their jots gave me a quick sense of what they learned from the small group and set them up to practice the strategy more independently moving forward.

Analyzing Comparing and Contrasting Work

Ask students to study the "Comparing and Contrasting" strand of the learning progression with their research groups and set goals for their work moving forward.

I asked students to pull out their copies of the "Comparing and Contrasting" strand of the learning progression they studied during our assessment day and for homework the night before. "Readers, earlier in the unit we had a chance to study the "Comparing and Contrasting" strand. Right now, will you reread the strand with your research group? Mark it up, making sure you really understand what it means." After a few minutes, I paused the groups.

"Now, working independently, look back across your recent work and think, 'In what areas is my comparing and contrasting work already strong? In what areas can my comparing and contrasting work be strengthened?' If you already have a goal around comparing and contrasting, see if you need to revise it. If you do not yet have a goal around this work, get one!"

After about two minutes, I asked students to share out their "Comparing and Contrasting" goals with their research groups. "It will be important for you to work on this goal tonight, and for the next few days until this work becomes automatic for you."

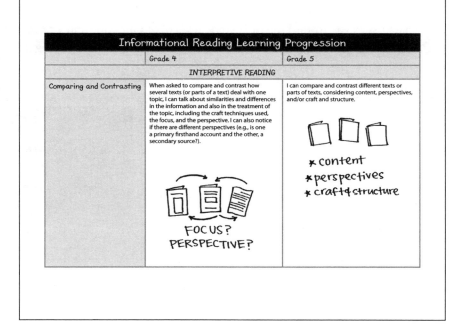

Informational Reading Learning Progression		
	Grade 4	Grade 5
INTERPRETIVE READING		
Comparing and Contrasting	When asked to compare and contrast how several texts (or parts of a text) deal with one topic, I can talk about similarities and differences in the information and also in the treatment of the topic, including the craft techniques used, the focus, and the perspective. I can also notice if there are different perspectives (e.g., is one a primary firsthand account and the other, a secondary source?).	I can compare and contrast different texts or parts of texts, considering content, perspectives, and/or craft and structure.

★ content
★ perspectives
★ craft & structure

FOCUS?
PERSPECTIVE?

STOPPING TO COMPARE AND CONTRAST WHILE YOU READ

Readers, tonight, make sure you're not reading texts in isolation. By that, I mean, make sure you're reading with your subtopics in mind. Notice when multiple texts teach about the same subtopic. When you notice this, stop and ask, "How do these parts fit together? Why is this part important? Notice similarities between the two texts as well as differences." Make sure your notes reflect what you learn.

As you do this, work on the "Comparing and Contrasting" goal you set today. Make sure your work toward your goal pushes you toward the fifth-grade level of "Comparing and Contrasting." Be sure you're comparing and contrasting texts in different ways. Use the section of the learning progression we studied for your reference.

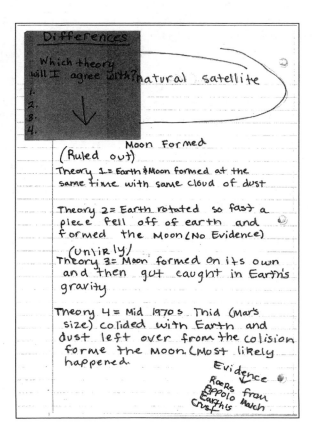

FIG. 15–5   Students create ways to write about their reading that capture contradictory content.

Session 16

Writing about Reading

From Big Ideas to Specifics

YOUR STUDENTS are tackling their own individual inquiry topics and writing about reading in ways that are incredibly unique to them. It would be easy to stop students today and to teach a minilesson where you demonstrate one specific way to write about your reading and then ask all students to write about their reading in that same way. The challenge for today, however, is to determine how to support students' personalization of their writing about reading about their own topics, while still teaching in ways that help them lift the level of that writing about reading across the board.

To do this, we suggest you teach into characteristics that make up all powerful writing about reading. This session teaches students that to write *really*, *really* well about your reading, it helps to move back and forth from specific details to big ideas. In his 2006 book *Writing Tools: 50 Essential Strategies for Every Writer*, Roy Peter Clark, vice president and senior scholar at Poynter Institute, describes this as movement up and down the ladder of abstraction. The "ladder of abstraction" was a term first popularized by linguist and semanticist S. I. Hayakawa. Clark writes, "Good writers move up and down the ladder of abstraction. At the bottom are bloody knives and rosary beads, wedding rings and baseball cards. At the top are words that reach for a higher meaning, words like 'freedom' and 'literacy'" (106).

While it's likely your students are not writing about bloody knives and freedom, they are ready to begin writing up and down the ladder of abstraction, moving between specific, concrete details and big ideas. They might move between noting that there are 70,000 UFO sightings, reported worldwide each year—a specific detail—to growing a big idea about how people everywhere seem to hope we're not alone on Earth, and they look for evidence to support that wherever they can. This movement between specific details and big ideas is something we'd be delighted to see in every student's writing about reading.

If you are following the writing units of study, then this is likely not the first time students have heard about the ladder of abstraction. During their personal and persuasive essay writing in fourth grade, for example, students learned to move back and forth between concrete specifics and more abstract generalizations. But it is more than likely that students, even if they remember hearing about this ladder of abstraction before, will need help in seeing

IN THIS SESSION, you'll teach students that the best writing about reading moves back and forth from specific details to big ideas. You'll help readers see that they need both ideas and details to develop strong thinking and identify what they really want to say about their topic.

GETTING READY

✔ Students should bring their reader's notebooks to the meeting area so they can study and revise their writing about reading (see Connection and Teaching and Active Engagement).

✔ Select two student samples of writing about reading to highlight: one written with specific details and another focusing on big ideas or use the samples in the online resources (see Teaching and Active Engagement). 👆

✔ Have blank chart paper and markers ready to create a ladder of abstraction chart (see Teaching and Active Engagement). 👆

✔ Prepare a "Ways to Push Our Thinking" chart to support students in writing about big ideas and specific details (see Mid-Workshop Teaching). 👆

✔ Have quiet music ready to play during a gallery walk (see Share).

how that previous learning applies to this new work. During this minilesson, you'll then reintroduce students to the ladder of abstraction, highlighting examples of students in the class who have produced powerful writing at the two ends of the ladder. You'll show the work of a writer who wrote with specific details, and you'll invite students to study their writing for examples of this work, and then you'll highlight a writer who wrote about big ideas. As you do this, you'll build a ladder of abstraction with your students, introducing them to the fact that the best writing includes both specific details and big ideas. Then, you'll invite students to study several entries in their reader's notebooks, noting if they're the kinds of writers who write with specific details or with big ideas, and then to set a goal to write up and down the ladder.

"To write really, really well about your reading, it helps to move back and forth from specific details to big ideas."

Later in this session, in the mid-workshop teaching, you'll introduce students to a series of thought prompts that they can use to push their thinking whenever they're writing long. They'll see that some prompts help them ground their entries in specific details and other prompts push them to state, restate, and refine their big ideas. You'll ask all students to try out these prompts, moving up and down the ladder as they do so.

Finally, the session ends in a share, where you'll ask students to lay out their very best examples of their writing about reading on their desks, and to study each other's samples through a gallery walk, noticing what their classmates did as readers and thinkers and learning moves they can try in their own writing.

Writing about Reading
From Big Ideas to Specifics

CONNECTION

Channel students to study their writing about reading work, noticing the qualities of their best work. Have students share those qualities with a partner while you listen in.

"Readers, will you gather with your notebooks? Look through your notebook and find your very best example of writing about reading you've done for your inquiry project. When you find it, take a minute to study it closely. See if you can name three things that make your writing about reading strong." After giving students a bit of time to study, I asked them to share what they found with their partners, and I listened in closely.

"Readers, as I listen into your conversations and look over your shoulders, it's clear your writing about reading is getting stronger and stronger. And I think you are ready to hear a huge tip that will, I hope, help you make your writing about reading even stronger. Now, part of the reason I want to share this particular big tip with you today is because of the work I see some of your classmates doing, work I think we could all benefit from seeing. Although each of you has writing about reading that I think we could study and learn lessons from, today we are going to learn from Liam and Lila's work. But first, let me share the big tip to help you raise the level of your writing about reading. Ready?"

❧ **Name the teaching point.**

"Today I want to teach you that as readers craft powerful writing about reading, they constantly move from big to small. You might start with a big idea—your own or one of the author's—and then you support that idea with the specifics from the text. Readers and writers constantly shift between these two places."

TEACHING AND ACTIVE ENGAGEMENT

Begin creating a chart that captures what students have shared and what you think, too. Highlight that good writing about reading contains specific, text-based details.

I jotted down "Include Specific Details" on the bottom of a new piece of chart paper.

"One way you can make your writing about reading particularly powerful is by including specific details. By this, I mean you can include facts, statistics, specific descriptions, and more that help capture your topic really specifically.

I knew I wanted to share with students two specific ways they could make their writing about reading strong: writing with specific details and writing with big ideas. Because of this, I looked and listened in for students whose work could serve as examples of these strengths, and I noted the students I could use in the day's minilesson. I also jotted down other ideas students shared for future lessons. If you prefer to prepare all of this ahead of time, you could ask all students to mark their best example of writing about reading with a Post-it note before today's minilesson and leave those examples for you to look through.

While we often recommend building a chart in advance and unveiling key sections during your minilesson, we find this chart is particularly powerful to create in front of students. You will want to first add the two extremes onto the chart, specific details and big ideas, and then show students how you bridge the gap between the two. Of course, the minilesson is not the time to make a perfect version of this chart. If you are worried about how the chart looks, you can always remake it later.

"Let me show you how Liam did this. You know he's been researching all about elephants—he wants to learn a ton before he goes to see one in the zoo in a few weeks—and here's what he already found." I projected his notes page for the class to see (see Figure 16–1).

"Liam's work jumped out to me because it feels like he's using a ton of specific details. He's got the height of the elephant, how much it weighs . . ." I let my voice trail off, and gestured to the students to call out ideas.

"How often calves are born!"

"How old they are when tusks grow!"

"I agree! Those specific details help u̲ ̲ ̲ ̲ ̲ ̲ ̲ ̲ ̲ ̲ ̲ ̲ ̲ d.

Set students up to reread their en̲ ̲ ̲ ̲ ̲ ̲ ̲ ̲ ̲ ̲ ̲ ̲ ̲ ̲ ̲ ̲ tails, and to do some quick revision of places where thei̲ ̲ ̲ ̲ ̲ ̲ ̲ ̲ ̲ ̲

"Right now, read through your recent ̲ ̲ ̲ ̲ ̲ ̲ ̲ ̲ ̲ ̲ d very specific details. Also look for places where your details ̲ ̲ ̲ ̲ ̲ ̲ ̲ ̲ ̲ 'The team won a lot of games.' When you find them, do so̲ ̲ ̲ ̲ ̲ ̲ ̲ ̲ ̲ ̲ umber of games the team won—say, seventy-five.

"Grounding your writing about reading i̲ ̲ ̲ ̲ ̲ ̲ ̲ ̲ ̲ ̲ ̲ cifics of your topic."

Highlight that good writing about rea̲ ̲ ̲ ̲ ̲ ̲ ̲ ̲ ̲ ̲ ̲ ̲ ̲ ow the big ideas are connected to those details.

"There's another big way you can strengthe̲ ̲ ̲ ̲ ̲ ̲ ̲ ̲ ̲ ̲ ̲ ̲ ̲' on the top of our chart paper. "To write particularly well abo̲ ̲ ̲ ̲ ̲ ̲ ̲ ̲ ̲ ̲ ̲ ̲de big ideas. These might be central ideas the author described across a text or ̲ ̲ ̲ ̲ ̲ ̲ you grew while studying several texts."

I projected a page from Lila's notebook and invited students to study it with me. "Let's check out how Lila really explored big ideas with her topic, animal venom." I read the page aloud (see Figure 16–2).

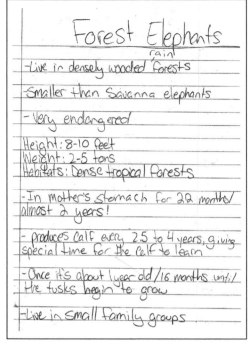

FIG. 16–1 Liam's notebook entry captures specific facts about forest elephants.

Stage One:
Include Specific Details
• *examples from the text*
• *specific numbers, dates, people and places*

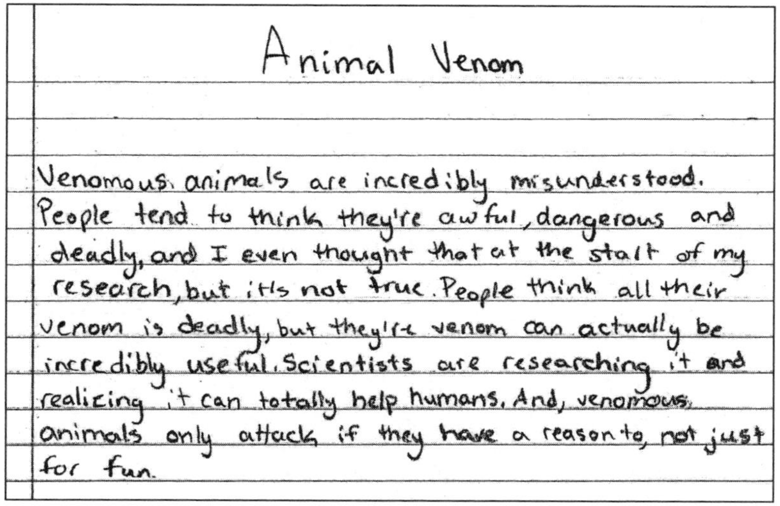

Animal Venom
Venomous animals are incredibly misunderstood. People tend to think they're awful, dangerous and deadly, and I even thought that at the start of my research, but it's not true. People think all their venom is deadly, but they're venom can actually be incredibly useful. Scientists are researching it and realizing it can totally help humans. And, venomous, animals only attack if they have a reason to, not just for fun.

FIG. 16–2   Lila explores big ideas about animal venom by writing long.

"Do you see how Lila tells a few big ideas she has about her topic? She says what she used to think and what she thinks now, and what other people think compared to what she thinks.

"Right now, can you reread the writing about reading you studied earlier? What are some big ideas you or the author had that you could add to your entry?"

I gestured to students, and they called out the big ideas they were growing.

"Soccer players wouldn't be half as good without their coaches!" Sophia said.

"Being a pop star isn't all sunshine and roses," Dexter added.

"Being an archeologist is incredibly tough, and it requires a ton of patience," chimed Jonathan.

"I love how you came up with big ideas that you could support by naming out the specific details in the text. The ideas you came up with could be true for lots of soccer players, researchers, and artists, not just the ones you found in your books."

> **Stage Two:**
> _Include Big Ideas_
> • the author's ideas
> • your big ideas
> • huge questions

> **Stage One:**
> _Include Specific Details_
> • examples from the text
> • specific numbers, dates, people and places

While many classes piloting this unit chose to showcase work from students in their classroom, some teachers chose instead to show the samples of writing about reading included in this session. You could introduce these samples as work from other fifth-graders around the country, or you could pretend that Liam and Lila were former students whose work you just had to save.

Your teaching today particularly supports students in strengthening their critical reading skills. Look to the "Growing Ideas" and "Questioning the Text" threads of the learning progression for ideas of how to support students with this work.

Highlight the importance of writing with specific details and big ideas by sharing Roy Peter Clark's advice about writing up and down the ladder of abstraction.

"Okay, so you have learned some lessons from Liam and Lila's work. Now, I want to remind you of my big tip. Remember, you need small details *and* big ideas, and the best writing about reading moves back and forth between the two. The other day, I was reading a book titled *Writing Tools* by Roy Peter Clark, and in it, he gave advice about fifty things all writers could do to strengthen their writing. One of his pieces of advice was that writers need to 'climb up and down the ladder of abstraction.' I know you have probably heard about this before, like when you were in your essay writing units in writing workshop, but considering the ladder of abstraction can help you in *reading* workshop with your writing about reading as well as in writing workshop. So let's remind ourselves of how it works."

I added a ladder to the chart, so it connected "include specific details" at the bottom of the chart to "include big ideas" at the top.

"What Roy Peter Clark meant is that it's important for writers to climb up the ladder—to write about ideas, theirs or the author's—and to climb down the ladder—and support those ideas with the specific details. He said the very best writing has both—big ideas and specific details. This is true of the writing we do during writing workshop, and it's also especially true of the writing we do about our reading. Writing about your reading in this way, where you climb up and down the ladder, will help you grow strong ideas about your inquiry topics."

LINK

Invite students to notice whether their writing about reading relies more on specific details or big ideas. Have them set a goal for how to strengthen their writing about reading.

"Before you head off to research today, take a few minutes to study your notebook entries. Read through your last three entries, thinking, 'Am I the kind of writer who writes big? Or am I the kind of writer who writes with specific details?' Either way, set a goal for what you'll work on today in your writing about reading."

I gave students a few minutes to study their writing about reading. "If your big goal for your writing about reading is to write with big ideas, head off to your reading spot and start reading. And, if you're going to work on writing with specific details today, off you go!"

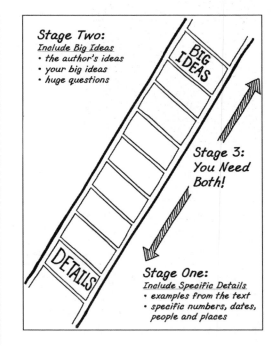

FIG. 16–3 Sophia rereads a recent notebook entry, coding where she wrote with specific details (D) and where she wrote with big ideas (BI).

Lifting the Level of Writing about Reading

OFTEN OUR INCLINATION is to gather students who are in need of support and to nudge, coach, and scaffold them to move them forward. However, it is important that we also set aside time to meet the needs of our strongest readers. Here, our role is often to enrich and extend the work these readers are doing. As I studied students' reader's notebooks, I noticed Leela, Omala, Marcus, and Jonathan were primed for some more advanced writing about reading work to support growing ideas around nonfiction. All four were moving between big ideas and specific details as they wrote, and they were growing powerful thinking as a result. I decided to pull them together for a strategy group.

"Readers, I am so proud of the work that you are doing growing ideas about your topics. You're moving between big ideas and specific details that illustrate those big ideas. Listen to how Omala did this here. She wrote, 'There is so much unexplained evidence out there that points to life existing on other planets. Think about the burps of methane that are being found on Mars. People blow them off. It's like we're too narrow-minded and can't be open to the possibilities that we are not alone in the universe.' See how she went from a big idea to details and back to big ideas?

"In fact, you are doing such excellent work growing ideas that it seems like you are ready to take your ideas to the next level. How does that sound?" The grouped nodded enthusiastically and leaned in closer.

"I want to teach you when we're growing deep and powerful ideas, it sometimes helps to turn to metaphor, turning to a concrete image to make an abstract idea that much clearer. You tried some of this last year when you were trying to lift the level of your thesis statements when you were writing personal essays. Metaphors can also be applied to our ideas when writing about nonfiction reading.

"Will you help me do this with my inquiry topic, scientists? Let me share with you some of the writing I did earlier, and can you rack your brain for a metaphor that will help make up my ideas clearer?" I read aloud my notes.

"One big idea I'm growing is that scientific research can be done for different reasons. Take someone like Douglas Fudge, for example. He's researching hagfish slime to create fabrics, and he hopes those fabrics will be more environmentally friendly than fabrics like nylon, things made of oil that pollute our planet. That's totally different from Tim Shank. His research on trenches deep below the surface of the ocean had really different goals, like understanding life underwater and even life in outer space. That's cool, but I'm wondering if that kind of research actually benefits anyone."

"Talk with a partner about what metaphors I could use." I gave students a minute to brainstorm, and then I asked Marcus to share.

"You could totally compare scientific research to an octopus," he said chuckling. "There are so many kinds of science research, just like there are a ton of kinds of octopus, and they're all really unique, just like scientists themselves."

"Or, you could compare it to a snowflake, how each snowflake is different. You could use that to show that every scientist researches for different reasons," Leela added.

"Readers, this is powerful stuff you're doing, generating a few different metaphors that could help me capture my ideas on my topic. When we do this, it lifts the level of our ideas, giving our readers a clearer picture and firmer grasp of the ideas we are trying to convey. For now, can you try this out with your topic? Find an entry in your reader's notebook, reread to remember your big ideas, and then think about a metaphor you could use to capture your ideas."

While the students sprang into action, I knelt beside Jonathan and scanned his reader's notebook entry. The big idea on the page was "An archaeologist's work can be incredibly boring and tedious at times, but it has big payoffs at the end." "Ooh, that's a huge idea. What metaphors are you considering?" I said.

"Readers, your notebook entries are growing, and you're really pushing yourselves to include both specific details and big ideas in your entries. Here's the thing, though. It pays to explore your ideas and details further. Writing is one tool that can really help you explore your ideas and the big questions you have. I'm putting up a chart of 'Ways to Push Our Thinking' that you used last year when you were writing personal and persuasive essays. Some of these prompts will help you write about big ideas and questions, and other prompts will help you write about specific details."

I posted the chart for students.

"Right now, will you spend a few minutes writing long about your reading? If you already know what to say, just pick up your pen and start writing. If, however, you're not sure what to say, look up at our 'Ways to Push Our Thinking' chart, choose a prompt, and write long off of it until you need another one.

"When you've pushed your thinking as far as you can, pick up your source and keep reading! Remember you should still be reading big chunks of text before you stop to write."

Ways to Push Our Thinking

- In other words . . .
- That is . . .
- The important thing about this is . . .
- As I say this, I'm realizing . . .
- This is giving me the idea that . . .
- An example of this is . . .
- This shows . . .
- Another example of this is . . .
- This connects to . . .
- I see . . .
- The thought I have about this is . . .
- To add on . . .
- I used to think that . . . but now I think that . . .
- What surprises me about this is . . .
- Many people think . . . but I think . . .

"Maybe I'll compare it to being a detective, how most of the time you're following these tiny clues or in your office doing paper work but then, sometimes, there's a huge exciting breakthrough," Jonathan said. I prompted him to try out another option. "Or, I could compare it to a snail, like, the archaeologist is moving along, so, so slowly, brushing sand off here and there, and it takes what feels like forever before they reach their goal, so they're slow like a snail, but also steady, and they get there in the end."

"Readers, take a few minutes to share what you're thinking with your partner, and then, will you write long about your ideas right here before you leave the group?"

Learning from Others

Have students reread their notebook entries and identify a page where they wrote up and down the ladder of abstraction, moving between specific details and big ideas.

"Readers, to wrap up our work today, let's admire and learn from the work of our classmates. Right now, will you look through your notebook and find a page where you tried some of this new work, where you wrote with specific details and with big ideas? If you have several entries like this, choose one you're particularly proud of." I gave students a minute to find a page.

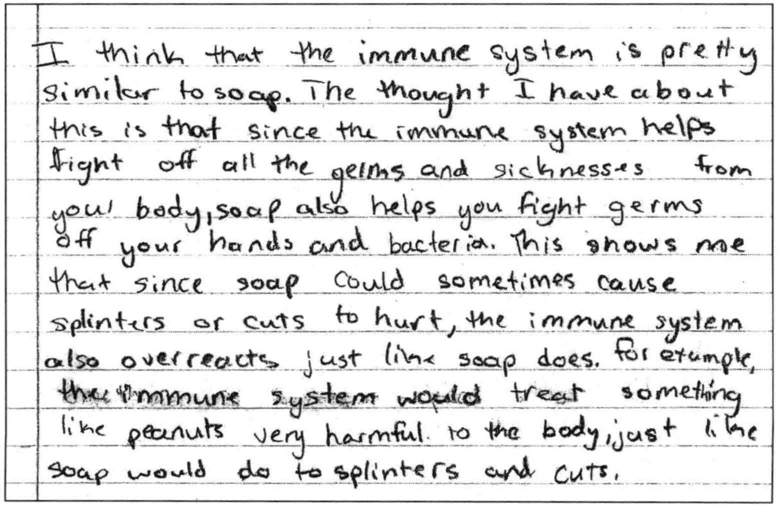

I think that the immune system is pretty similar to soap. The thought I have about this is that since the immune system helps fight off all the germs and sicknesses from your body, soap also helps you fight germs off your hands and bacteria. This shows me that since soap could sometimes cause splinters or cuts to hurt, the immune system also overreacts just like soap does. For example, the immune system would treat something like peanuts very harmful to the body, just like soap would do to splinters and cuts.

FIG. 16–4 Isabella uses a metaphor to capture her ideas about the immune system.

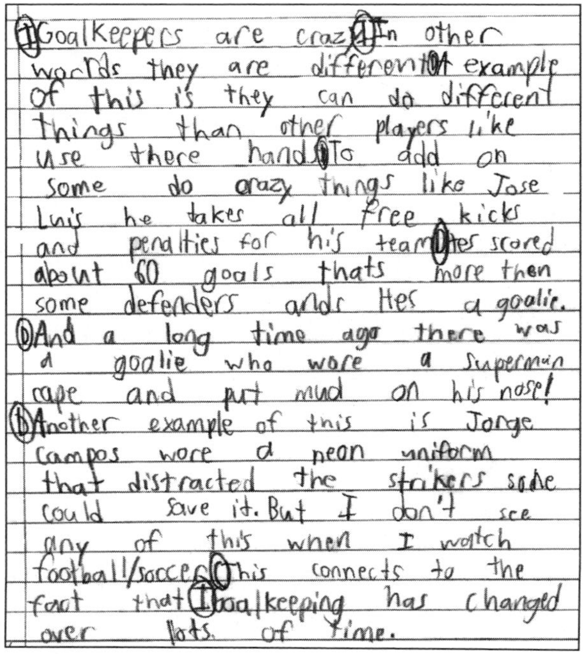

Goalkeepers are crazy. In other worlds they are different. An example of this is they can do different things than other players like use there hand. To add on some do crazy things like Jose Luis he takes all free kicks and penalties for his team. He scored about 60 goals thats more then some defenders and. Hes a goalie. And a long time ago there was a goalie who wore a superman cape and put mud on his nose! Another example of this is Jorge Campos wore a neon uniform that distracted the strikers so he could save it. But I don't see any of this when I watch football/soccer. This connects to the fact that Goalkeeping has changed over lots of time.

FIG. 16–5 Iris uses boxes and bullets to capture her big ideas and specific details.

Set students up to read entries written by their classmates, jotting down notes about methods their classmates used they can add to their repertoire of writing about reading techniques.

"Let's have a gallery walk. I'll put on some quiet music. Will you grab some Post-it notes and a pen or pencil? When I say, 'Go,' travel to a desk, sit down, and study the work your classmate did. See if you can determine what precisely he or she did as a reader and a thinker that helped him or her move from specific details to big ideas. On your Post-it notes, will you jot down notes to yourself about techniques your classmates used that you can also try in your writing about your reading? I'll give you about five minutes to study, so you'll probably get to two or three of your classmates in this time.

"Ready? Go!" I pressed play on the CD player, and classical music quietly filled the room. I joined students as they settled in at a desk, pulled a reader's notebook close, and started studying. I jotted down my own notes.

SESSION 16 HOMEWORK

WRITING WITH SPECIFIC DETAILS AND BIG IDEAS

Readers, continue researching your topic tonight. But also set aside at least ten minutes to write long about what you're learning. Your writing should reflect what you've learned about writing about reading over the past few days. Specifically, you should be writing about reading in ways that help you understand the text you're reading. Make sure your writing moves back and forth between specific details and big ideas.

At the end of reading workshop, you studied your classmates' writing about reading. You also jotted some ideas for how to make your writing about reading even stronger. Tonight, be sure that your new writing reflects what you learned today. After you do some writing, reread and annotate what you've written so it's clear what you tried as a reader.

Enjoy growing ideas and grounding them in details!

> The rain forests of the world is disappearing very fast. People cut down trees to create man-made objects. This shows how people aren't realizing the danger of the world. Animals are becoming extinct. This connects to the world weakening because of the heat in the atomsphere. As I say this, I am wondering how the remaining animals are surviving. What surprises me about this is that only a few people realize that and are trying to help those animals. Animals need space to live in. There can be no food to go around in the crowd of animals. Some scientists believe that 100 & 1,000 species out of every million are disappearing or becoming extinct.

FIG. 16–6 Leela uses familiar prompts to grow ideas about animal extinction and global warming.

Comparing and Contrasting
What Authors Say
(and How They Say It)

ONE OF THE GREATEST TEACHING POINTS of nonfiction reading was delivered by a fictional spider who was a master of literacy in her own right. As E. B. White's Charlotte spun words into her web, she stated, "People are very gullible. They'll believe anything they see in print." Charlotte, like all great writers, knew how to pick words with care and to use her literacy to persuade and convince.

As we help our students roll up their sleeves and do the work that nonfiction readers the world over do, it becomes increasingly urgent to address what Charlotte referred to as the "gullibility" of readers. As ambitious teachers of literacy, we hope that our kids' literacies will enable them to look at a text with an expert eye and see how the text was put together, why trouble was taken to put it together in a certain way, and who benefits from its publication. We want our students to grow up able not only to read words but also to read intentions—and implications—behind words.

In this unit so far, we've helped readers to read intertextually and encouraged them to adopt an insider's lingo on a topic. We've stressed the importance of responding to reading and especially of picking up a pencil to record and to follow the ideas that occur to them about the topic. This minilesson and the few that follow will feel slightly different from the work we've been doing thus far. From deep immersion we now shift to a deconstructive stance, adopting a certain distance from a text to study it critically.

Your teaching today supports students in deepening their compare and contrast work, and you'll teach students that in addition to comparing and contrasting content, they also need to consider differences in perspectives, craft, and structure. The "Analyzing Author's Craft" strand of the learning progression will prove invaluable to you and your students as you take on this work. Analyzing author's craft is a critically important skill within this unit and on the high-stakes assessments many students take. You may find you need to extend this work and add an additional session where you explore author's craft further. Should you choose to do so, you might revisit the Goals and Techniques cards your students used in fourth grade to guide their conversations about goals authors' aimed toward and techniques they used. These are available in the online resources.

IN THIS SESSION, you'll teach students that as researchers read across subtopics, they pay particular attention to how authors portray topics in similar and different ways. They compare and contrast the central ideas authors teach, and they examine how authors teach those central ideas.

GETTING READY

✔ Choose sections in your read-aloud texts on your inquiry topic that you can use to study an author's craft moves. We suggest page 38 from *When Lunch Fights Back* and pages 10 and 12 in *Alien Deep* (see Teaching and Active Engagement).

✔ Prepare a one-day chart titled "Prompts to Compare and Contrast Texts" (see Teaching and Active Engagement and Share).

✔ Be sure students have copies of the "Analyzing Author's Craft" strand of the Informational Reading Learning Progression for grades 4 and 5 (see Mid-Workshop Teaching).

✔ Be sure students have the "Main Idea(s) and Supporting Details/Summary," "Analyzing Author's Craft," "Inferring Within Text/Cohesion," and "Comparing and Contrasting" strands of the Informational Reading Learning Progression for grades 4 and 5 (see Homework).

✔ If you choose to extend today's session, reference the Informational and Goals and Techniques cards.

The upcoming sessions lay the foundation for this work, taking advantage of children's inquiry stance on a single topic to help them read with enough depth that they'll be able to consider how each text reports from its own angle. All texts, even those that report "facts," are deliberate human constructions, and they position the reader. Reading can, in the end, impart the wisdom that there is no absolute truth—there are only reports on this truth—and that a report, no matter how well meaning, cannot claim total freedom from bias.

"All texts, even those that report 'facts,' are deliberate human constructions, and they position the reader."

Perhaps this is what literacy boils down to—a reading of the texts on paper as well as texts that codify human behavior and life in all its richness and diversity. In the sessions that follow, we begin this exciting work of taking texts apart like a researcher and a critic might. This leg of the journey, even as it culminates the work on nonfiction reading, will open up possibilities for lifelong observation and inquiry in our kids' lives.

We hope, in the end, to have children who read in a way that might meet with E. B. White's Charlotte's approval. We hope our children look at the words in a web and glance not just at the pig, but also up at the spider, wondering not merely at the meaning but also at the origins, source, motivation, angle, and implications of the words they've been served.

Comparing and Contrasting What Authors Say (and How They Say It)

CONNECTION

Share a story with readers about a time you encountered two reactions to an event, and ask students to compare and contrast the two reactions.

"Readers, I've got a story I'm dying to share with you that I'm hoping will be useful as we take on some new work. I was about your age, in the car with my family, and we were headed to my grandparents' house. They lived pretty far away, and as soon as we got on the highway, I started asking my parents that question kids just love to ask on road trips. I bet you can guess which one it was. Are we . . . ?"

"There yet!" the kids cried out.

"Exactly! The first time I asked my mom turned around, smiled and said, 'No,' and went back to her conversation. But, by the twentieth time, my mom turned around and snapped, 'No, and stop asking!'" I changed my tone dramatically between the two versions of *no*, making sure the second version sounded short and angry.

"With your partner, will you compare and contrast my mom's two responses? How were they similar and how were they different?" I gave the readers a minute to talk.

"So even though my mom seemed to be saying something similar each time—*no*—the *way* she said it was different. Like the first time, my mom sounded . . ." I gestured to the students to call out suggestions.

"Nice!" "Sweet!" "Patient!"

"I agree. And the second time, my mom was . . ."

"Frustrated!" "Angry!" "Exasperated!"

Connect this story to the work readers do to compare and contrast information taught across texts.

"Readers, I am telling you this story because it relates to some of the work we need to do as readers. Sometimes, it seems like our texts are saying something similar—like how my mom said *no* in both these situations. But, even though

Really play this up. Make sure your voice and your mannerisms clearly illustrate the difference between these two versions. You will support students in comparing and contrasting what a person said and how they said it here, when the work is obvious, so they have some success with this work before you ask them to try it with texts.

Give students just a few moments to do this work. You want to move quickly through the connection to the heart of the minilesson.

texts can *seem* to say the same thing, they'll say it kind of differently. The same way my mom made very different choices in how to deliver her message to me, authors can make different choices in what they want to say and how they want to say it, even when they are writing about the same topic. And it's important for us as readers to pay attention to when that is happening and ask why the authors might have made those different choices."

❖ **Name the teaching point.**

"So, today I want to teach you that after researchers read a few sources on a topic, they compare and contrast those texts, noticing how they portray the topic in similar ways—and how they are different. Then, they speculate about why authors made these craft and structure decisions, thinking, 'Does this relate to the main ideas they're teaching?'"

TEACHING AND ACTIVE ENGAGEMENT

Channel students to study one text on a subtopic. Involve students in thinking along with you as you read a section of text and think aloud about the central ideas.

"This can be a bit tricky, so I thought today we could all practice this work together as a class. So to do this work, we need to start by reading one text on a subtopic. Last night, I came across a section in *When Lunch Fights Back* that we thought was pretty interesting when we first read it during read-aloud, and I thought we could reread it now and study it together. It's about the two-spot fish, do you remember what a bully he was? Let's read, noticing the central ideas Rebecca Johnson is teaching, and let's also notice *how* she taught them, her craft and structure moves. Here goes." I read aloud from a section of the text and projected it for students to see.

> *Biologist Robert Young studies animal behavior. When he started working with two-spot astyanax in Brazil, his goal was to help protect them from a human-made danger. Two-spots are common in rivers throughout South America, including rivers with hydroelectric power plants. Two-spots often swim into power plant turbines. It's a fatal mistake, because the turbine's spinning blades can kill fish. Young wanted to devise a way to keep the two-spots out of the turbines. He wondered if scaring the little fish away with models of predators might be a solution.*

"Hmm, . . . let's first figure out what this part wanted to teach. Well, it seems like one idea Rebecca Johnson wants to teach us is that scientific research could help animals, particularly when they face all these problems, right?"

Set the class up to study the craft and structure decisions the author made. Coach in as students study, then share out what they noticed, marking up the projected copy of the text as you do so.

"This half of the room," I gestured toward the right half, "will you reread this section and notice how Rebecca Johnson structures this section to teach that scientific research could help animals, and the other half of the room, will you reread noticing the craft moves she uses to teach? Get started!" Students turned and studied the text together. As I listened in, I coached partners as they worked together.

After a bit I reconvened the class. "So the half of the room that studied structure," I indicated my right side. "I heard you say that Rebecca Johnson used a problem-solution text structure to teach us how scientific research could help animals. You said that word *solution* was a dead giveaway, plus the fact that she told you about all the problems they face." I jotted the words *problem and solution* next to the section of the text.

"And *this* half of the room," I indicated my left side, "you were looking at the author's craft moves, and you talked about how her word choice made the problem feel big and important. I see the word *fatal*, which sounds really serious. Any others?" Students called out answers, and I quickly circled *human-made danger*, *kill*, and *fatal*.

"And you said maybe she taught by showing contrasts, like showing how the fish were just *little fish*, and that they were kind of helpless against the *spinning blades*."

Channel students to study a second text on the same topic, using the same process of determining what the author teaches and how the author structured and crafted that information, transferring increasing responsibility to the students.

"Now, let's try this again with a second text. First, we'll study a part of *Alien Deep* closely—a part that seems to be about some of the same ideas, noticing what this author teaches and studying how he teaches it, his craft and structure moves. Then, we'll compare and contrast what these two texts teach and how they teach it." I read aloud a chunk of *Alien Deep*.

> *Science doesn't always follow a clear-cut path. Sometimes discoveries happen that completely derail everything we thought we knew. Think of Galileo and the discovery that Earth orbits the sun, not the other way around, or Charles Darwin, whose theory of evolution took biology into completely new and unexpected directions. Scientific revolutions happen when we stop seeing the world we expect and start seeing the world as it is.*

> *The incredible biological world of the vents may never have been discovered had scientists not been trying to solve a geological puzzle.*

"Get started thinking and talking with your partner. Think about what the author Bradley Hague is teaching you here and how, exactly, he's teaching you. Remember to think about his craft and structure moves." I knelt down to coach partnerships as they worked. After a minute, I called students back together.

Support students as they compare and contrast the two texts, speculating about similarities and differences in the way they portray the topic.

"Now, here's the challenge. When we read two texts about the same subtopic, we have to read them next to each other, noticing how they portray the topic in similar and different ways. Are you up for it?"

I projected the two chunks of text next to each other so students could engage in a comparative study. "I'm posting some prompts that might help you and your partner. Get started!"

When analyzing an author's perspective, sixth-graders are called to point to specific places in the text that provide clues to the author's perspective, such as a particular word choice, and then to discuss how that part shows the author's perspective. Your questioning here moves students toward these expectations on the learning progression.

As you read aloud sections of Alien Deep *outside your minilessons, keep in mind the "Inferring Within Text/Cohesion" strand of the learning progression. Sections like this one are ideal for supporting students in thinking about the major relationships that occur across discipline-based texts, an expectation for fifth-graders.*

While most partnerships sprang to work, I noticed Giovanni and Omnia were silent. "We're stuck. They're the same and different, but we can't really say why," Omnia said.

"Let me give you a tip: it helps to talk about one thing at a time. You might talk about what they taught, the words they used, or how they organized their information. Then, you can talk about how the two texts are the same and different related to that one thing. Why don't you start with what they taught?"

"Well, they taught about the same topic," Giovanni said.

"Think about what one text said, and then tell what the other text said," I added.

"The first one said that research helps animals, but the second one . . . It didn't mention that, not at all. It just told about how all the research would help people," Omnia said. I left Omnia and Giovanni to try the same work with craft and structure moves.

About two minutes in, I voiced over to the class. "Now you've got some ideas about how the information the authors are teaching is similar and different. Now it's time to speculate *why* authors might have made these decisions. Ask yourself, 'Does this relate to the main ideas they're teaching?'" I gave students a few more minutes to talk.

While the majority of students talked, I grabbed two quiet partnerships, and said, "Let me remind you of some craft moves you might talk about." Quickly I jotted some craft moves I thought students would be familiar with:

Author Craft

Some craft moves to remember

- word choice
- structure choices
- repetition
- text features

Debrief, naming the work the class just did as transferrable reading work.

"Readers, this work you just did is work you can do whenever you're researching on a topic. It's likely you'll encounter texts like we did today, texts where there are a lot of similarities and some subtle differences. When this happens, it pays off to think about how the information the authors are teaching is similar and different, and then, with that in mind, to speculate about why authors might make those decisions. This helps us understand the scope of our topic."

Prompts to Help You Compare and Contrast:

- *The two sources are similar in the way they each...*

- *Both sources also...*

- *However, the sources differ in that...*

- *On the other hand...*

- *This text says... but this text does not say / also says...*

- *While the first author / source... the second author / source...*

LINK

Set readers up to generate plans for the reading work they'll do today, and then send them off to read, putting their plans into action.

"Readers, there's powerful new work you can take on today. If you've already uncovered contradictions in your research, they might be tiny or really huge, you might start by revisiting those sections, comparing and contrasting what those authors teach and how they teach them. Or, you might read on in your text with this new idea in mind, noticing places when authors teach about the same subtopic and comparing the different texts to one another. There's lots to do!

"Right now, will you talk with your partner and make a plan? What's the reading work you need to do today? Why? Give me a thumbs up once you have a plan." When most partners had their thumb up, I said, "Share your plan with your partner. Tell what you'll do and *why* that's your plan.

"Off you go!"

Using the Learning Progression to Support Students

DURING THE MID-WORKSHOP TEACHING, we are suggesting that you remind students of the "Analyzing Author's Craft" strand of the Informational Reading Learning Progression for grades 4 and 5. This learning progression is a tremendous resource for students, helping them assess where their current practice is and set goals for the future. It's likely the "Analyzing Author's Craft" strand will be particularly important in your small-group work today. As readers, we need to consider not just what the author says, but how they say it—and the *how* can include word choice, structure, perspective, and visual/media elements that are embedded in the text. We need to support readers in understanding that nonfiction isn't truth—rather, it is one person's view of a topic of subject. It is this viewpoint that shapes the choices that an author makes in terms of structure, language, and text features to include in a given text.

You might choose to gather a group of students around a chart-sized version of this strand, or another strand you feel they'd benefit from studying, and ask them to collaboratively assess their work, sharing samples of their writing about reading with one another and giving each other feedback. To see a video of this work in action with literature reading, visit our Vimeo site at http://vimeo.com/55951743 and watch the video titled "Using a Learning Progression to Support Self-Assessment and Writing about Themes in Literature: Small Group Work (3–5)."

It's important to remember that the learning progressions are also tremendous teaching tools, and we suggest you carry several with you as you confer each day. Carrying several strands helps you ensure your conferring supports the repertoire of work your readers are doing. Today, you might carry the "Analyzing Author's Craft" strand of the progression with you as you confer, as well as the "Cross Text(s) Synthesis" and "Comparing and Contrasting" strands you asked students to study a few days ago. Depending on the range of readers in your class, you might carry strands for levels 4, 5, and 6 (or others) with you as you confer.

When you pull up next to a reader, keep these strands close by. During the research phase of your conference, listen to readers, look closely at their work, and consider where, precisely, they fall on the learning progression. Use the progression to create a teaching point. You might notice a reader doing some of the work of a level but not all the work, and your teaching point might address the part of the work the reader is not yet doing. For example, you might pull up next to a reader and notice she's questioning choices an author makes within one text in a variety of ways, considering the

Main Idea(s) and Supporting Details/ Summary (Level 4 to 5)	Main Idea(s) and Supporting Details/ Summary (Level 5 to 6)	Main Idea(s) and Supporting Details/ Summary (Levels 3 to 4)
Peter Giovanni Eva Isabella Luna	Leela Dexter Nina Adjua	Omnia Lily Nathaniel Ben
Inferring within Text (Level 4 to 5)	**Inferring Within Text (Level 5 to 6)**	**Comparing and Contrasting (Level 4 to 5)**
Lila Ben Omala Spencer Giovanni	Iris Matthew Clementine	Marcus Dimitri Sophia Iris Omnia
Analyzing Author's Craft (Level 4 to 5)	**Analyzing Author's Craft (Level 5 to 6)**	
Jonathan Adjua Clementine Paloma Leela	Nina Luna Peter	

FIG. 17–1 This grid helps a teacher see information about her students' nonfiction reading skills at a glance.

MID-WORKSHOP TEACHING   Thinking Deeply about Craft

"Readers, let me stop you for a minute. I wanted to compliment all of you because, as you're comparing and contrasting across texts today, you're paying careful attention to the words different authors use. When you've seen one author using the words *alarming* and *major threat* to talk about climate change, and another using the words *typical* and *unproven*, you've been questioning why authors would use those different words. This is important work, work you'll likely do every day for the rest of your lives.

"What I want to remind you is that when we're comparing how authors are teaching information, there are many craft moves we can consider, beyond word choice. Right now, will you and your partner pull out your copy of the "Analyzing Author's Craft" strand of the learning progression for fourth and fifth grades? With your partner can you read through thinking, 'In what ways am I already analyzing craft and structure? And, how else can I analyze craft and structure?'" I gave students a few minutes to study the strand with a partner, while I moved around the room holding *When Lunch Fights Back*, using the text to illustrate unfamiliar words and phrases for students.

"As you continue researching today and every day, and especially as you compare and contrast across texts, keep in mind all the ways you can analyze an author's craft choices."

author's word and structure choices, and then you can build on that by suggesting the reader do this work across different texts on a topic or event. Alternatively, you might find readers who are regularly demonstrating the work of a level and are ready to be pushed to the next level.

Of course, it will help to have copies of these strands, in addition to your teacher-sized versions of the learning progressions. These small versions of the progressions make great leave-behinds in conferences, and you can give them to readers as records of what you've taught them.

Acknowledging Conflicting Information in Summaries

Ask students to recall what they have already learned about summarizing. Explain that they use the same process to summarize across a subtopic that they used to summarize a single text.

"Readers, earlier in this unit, we worked to summarize information, so we could create a short, concise version of a text. With your partner, list out the work you do as a reader whenever you summarize a text." I listened as students named out the steps they went through: identifying main ideas an author taught, determining how those main ideas fit together, and naming out key supportive details the author gave to support the main ideas.

"To make sense of what they're learning, especially when they're reading information about the same subtopic across texts, researchers often summarize what they're learning about a subtopic across texts. They do this in much the same way as when they summarized a single text: identifying the main ideas they're learning about a subtopic and naming out the key supportive details that fit with those central ideas.

"Right now, can you identify one subtopic you've really been on about, one that you've learned enough about that you think you could summarize what you've learned? As you find that subtopic, reread your notes, and be on the lookout for the main ideas you've learned about that subtopic and the key details that support those ideas."

Explain to students that summarizing becomes more complex when texts contradict. Introduce new prompts students can use to discuss these contradictions in their summaries.

After a few minutes, I stopped the students. "Readers, can I give you a tip? Sometimes you discover that some of the information about your subtopic actually contradicts. When this happens, you can't just ignore that controversy in your summary! You have to acknowledge it and say something about it.

"If I were summarizing a section about how scientists work, I might say, '*The two sources are similar in the way they each* teach that scientists work in a variety of settings. *While the first author* shows scientists only working in isolation, *the second author* presents the work scientists do as far more collaborative.'

"Use the prompts on our chart to help you. Make sure your summary accurately captures the controversy!" I gave students a few more minutes to work on their summaries.

"Meet with your research group and share what you found."

Prompts to Help You Compare and Contrast:

- The two sources are similar in the way they each...

- Both sources also...

- However, the sources differ in that...

- On the other hand...

- This text says... but this text does not say / also says...

- While the first author / source... the second author / source...

REFLECTING ON YOURSELF AS A NONFICTION READER

Readers, today you studied a strand of the Informational Reading Learning Progression, and you used that to strengthen your analysis of craft and structure. This isn't the only strand of the progression you've seen so far this unit. Tonight, bring home your copies of all the major strands you've studied for this unit. Will you spend some time tonight rereading your notes and evaluating your work on these strands and your progress toward your goals? Mark up your notes in some way—perhaps with Post-it notes or by leaving annotations in the margins—to show what you notice. If you see ways to strengthen your work, make some revisions.

Of course, you'll also want to devote a good chunk of time to reading. Be sure that as you read tonight, you're paying close attention to what different texts on the same topic teach and how they teach it. Add your new learning to your notes.

Critically Reading Our Texts, Our Topics, and Our Lives

IN THIS SESSION, you'll teach students that readers pay attention to an author's perspective and how the author might be swaying readers to think, even when the author's perspective is not explicit. Then readers also consider the trustworthiness of sources and develop their own perspective.

GETTING READY

✓ Select a section from a read-aloud to highlight reading for an author's perspective. We suggest pages 30–31 from *When Lunch Fights Back* (see Teaching).

✓ Students should bring to the meeting area a familiar text on their topic that they can reread to determine an author's perspective (see Active Engagement).

✓ Prepare a chart titled "To Check If a Source Is Trustworthy . . ." You could prepare the chart with students during the small group suggested in the Conferring and Small-Group Work section or you could make the chart in advance (see Conferring and Small-Group Work and Mid-Workshop Teaching).

✓ Prepare a chart titled "To Determine Your Perspective, Ask . . ." and list questions readers can ask themselves (see Share).

MOST OF OUR TEACHING, up to this point, has focused on helping students think about what the texts they're reading are teaching. But teaching toward students' understanding a text is only one step along the way. A danger with this kind of teaching is that students will become complacent, thinking about what the text teaches without questioning it. We certainly want students to acknowledge and work to understand the author's perspective, but we also want them to be able to talk back to it.

This is important work, and your students are ready for it. When you've only read one text on a topic, particularly a topic you're a novice on, it's difficult to determine the author's perspective. But by the time you've read several texts on a topic, you've noticed information that repeated, and started to pick up on different authors' perspectives.

Today, you'll first support students as they read to determine an author's perspective on their topic. As the texts students read become more complex, the author's perspective is often hidden, so you'll teach students to pay attention to the words and phrases the author uses, seeing those as clues to the author's perspective. We suggest you use a section of your read-aloud text, *When Lunch Fights Back*, to teach this, questioning the author's perspective on scientists, which is never directly stated in the text.

Later, you'll set students up to question the credibility of the authors they're studying as one way to determine if they should trust the author's perspective. You'll coach students as they study copyright information, research an author's biography, and investigate the websites the information comes from, among other sources of information.

We suggest you wrap up today's lesson by suggesting that it's not enough for students to determine the perspectives of different authors on their topics; now that they're becoming more expert on their topic, they're ready to determine their own perspective about it. This lesson lays the foundation for the critical literacy work students will take on, headfirst, in the Argument and Advocacy unit of study, where they'll deeply explore the persuasive, biased undertones that live within texts.

Critically Reading Our Texts, Our Topics, and Our Lives

CONNECTION

Share an example of an author clearly communicating her perspective on the topic. Explain that although an author's perspective will sometimes be explicit, it will more often be implicit.

"Readers, have you noticed that sometimes authors will make their perspective clear and explicit, coming right out and naming it for us as readers, with words and phrases that really clearly show the author's opinion? Let's say we wanted to make our perspective on ice cream *really* clear. What would you say?" "Ice cream is the very best dessert ever!" Marcus called. "It's the only treat you should ever eat on a hot summer day," Peter added.

"Sometimes authors make their perspective clear, almost coming right out and saying it for the reader. Take *When Lunch Fights Back*, for example. It feels like Rebecca Johnson's perspective on animal defenses is pretty clear. Take the title, for instance: *When Lunch Fights Back: Wickedly Clever Animal Defenses*. She could have just said *Animal Defenses*, and instead she said *Wickedly Clever Animal Defenses*. What ideas does that give you about her perspective about animal defenses?" Students turned and talked, naming out that her perspective might be that these animal defenses are really creative and awesome. "Well, more often, particularly in the texts you're reading right now, authors won't make things that easy. You'll have to read closely to figure out what the author might be thinking about her topic."

❖ **Name the teaching point.**

"Readers, I want to teach you today that readers don't just think about the information in a text. They also figure out the perspective of the author of that text and how he or she might be swaying you to think a certain way about that topic, even when the author's perspective isn't explicit."

In just two minutes (or less) you will have provided students with two clear examples of perspective, showing students first they can generate a perspective on a topic from their own life and then supporting students in identifying a perspective in a text when an author states it explicitly. You will want to save the challenging work of noticing and naming an author's implicit perspective for later in the lesson.

TEACHING

Set students up to read and reread a section of a text alongside you, working to determine the author's perspective on her topic.

"Let's think about *When Lunch Fights Back*. I mean . . . I think Rebecca Johnson's perspective on animal defenses is pretty clear—she told us in the title, and there are lots more clues for that we could find all across the text. But when it comes to her perspective on scientists, well, frankly, I'm a bit stumped by it. Are you up for helping me study the section on the scientists who studied the peacock mantis shrimp to determine what her perspective is on scientists?" Kids nodded in agreement.

"Let's be on the lookout for ways the author is getting us to think a certain way about scientists." I projected *When Lunch Fights Back*, making sure students could see the picture of Sheila Patek on page 31, and then I read the text aloud.

> *A peacock mantis shrimp's punch isn't just fast. It's so powerful it can crack the rock-hard shells of snails and other animals the mantis shrimp eats. Working at Duke University, Patek designed experiments to measure the power of that punch. She tricked a mantis shrimp living in an aquarium into punching an instrument that measures the force of a blow. The technical term is impact force.*
>
> *Patek recorded mantis shrimp punches again and again. She could hardly believe the results. The mantis shrimp typically struck the instrument with well over 200 pounds (890 newtons) of force. "The hammer impact is massive," she says. "These animals are producing thousands of times their body weight in peak impact force. As far as I know this still holds the record as the highest force generation of any organism that has been measured on the planet."*

"Huh? Well . . . Rebecca Johnson's definitely not saying, 'Here's what I think about scientists! Scientists are . . .' so maybe she doesn't have a perspective about scientists? I guess we should read another section to see what we can find.

"No, wait, wait. We know that as texts get more complex, determining an author's perspective can also become more complex. So, let's really push ourselves. How does Rebecca Johnson want us to feel about scientists here?

Demonstrate how you analyze the author's words and images to consider the author's perspective on a topic.

"I'm thinking she feels positively overall about scientists, because she's using a lot of words that make their work seem important: *designed experiments* and *recorded*. And she's taking a whole section in each chapter to talk about their work, which she probably wouldn't do if she thought their work was insignificant." I underlined the words as I mentioned them.

"But I need to be more specific. . . . Well, her perspective on scientists might be that they do fascinating work. That phrase 'She could hardly believe the results' makes her work seem really exciting, since she's discovering things she couldn't have believed before. Oh, and I'm also noticing that it sounds like her experiments turn out the first time. There's no description of how she had to try dozens of times (or more!) to make her experiments work. Instead, it sounds like she designed something, tried it, and it gave her the results she wanted. This is giving me the idea that Rebecca Johnson's perspective on scientists could be that scientists do important and exciting work and that they're often successful."

Fifth-graders are expected to notice when two texts on the same topic are written from different perspectives and consider ways in which the content of those texts or the author's craft varies based on those perspectives. Look to the "Analyzing Perspective" strand of the learning progression to see how expectations for this work build across the grades. This will be a major focus in the upcoming Argument and Advocacy unit.

Knowing that many students would read past sections of text where the author's perspective was not explicitly stated, I decided to model this. I wanted to show students how I could initially read a section thinking it was not teaching much and then revisit that section, noticing so much more when I reread it.

Debrief, naming what you did in transferable language.

"Readers, did you see how I pushed myself to dig into a section of my text, reading and rereading to notice the author's perspective even when the author didn't come right out and tell us? To do this, I noted the author's word choices and image choices, and I thought about what the author included as well as what the author left out."

ACTIVE ENGAGEMENT

Channel readers to study a section of a text on their topic, reading and rereading that section to determine the author's perspective.

"Right now can you choose a text you'd like to work with today, a text where you're not sure what the author's perspective on your topic is? Once you choose that text, find a spot in the text, likely it's a spot you've already read, where you think you could do this work." I gave students a minute to choose a text on their topic and find a spot in the text to study.

"Now read a short section thinking, 'How does my author want me to feel about this topic?' Remember, the author's perspective might not be explicit! Look for words, visuals, or examples that help you understand what the author's perspective might be."

I gave students a few minutes to work. I saw a group of students looking closely at their pages without doing any writing. "You're doing so much smart thinking in your head," I whispered to one topic group. "Find a way to capture it. Look up at the model we did together to get ideas."

To another partnership, I said, "If you're unsure of the author's perspective, try to get the gist of it. Does the author's perspective seem mostly positive? Mostly negative? Share what you're finding with your partner."

LINK

Debrief, naming the work the students just did in a way that's transferrable to other texts.

"Readers, this is powerful work. You're diving into your texts, noticing the information the author's teaching, of course, and then pushing yourself further so you notice the author's perspective on your topic. It will pay off to notice how the author might be swaying you to think and feel about a topic, particularly when the author doesn't come right out and say so. Off you go!"

As you watch students working to determine an author's perspective, be on the lookout for students who draw on only one piece of evidence to come to a decision or students who disregard information that does not fit with their initial idea. Another predictable problem is students who bring in their own perspective on their topic. Jot down what you notice to inform your upcoming instruction. You can do more teaching into these predictable problems during your small-group and conferring work across this unit (and year).

Considering the Trustworthiness of Sources

WHEN YOUR STUDENTS GO OFF TODAY to read and research, pause for a rare moment to note the tremendous growth students have made over the past few weeks. Your students have learned to recognize and tackle challenges in complex nonfiction texts, and they are doing this work independently as they read texts on their inquiry projects. While some students might still be regularly drawing on their text complexity cards, it's likely that others have tucked the cards away, because the strategies are now automatic and they no longer need the temporary scaffold. Celebrate this growth, and name it for students. Then, too, as you glance first at students' reading notebook entries from the early days of the unit and then look to the work they're doing today, marvel at how entries have evolved to include big ideas and a critical analysis of sources. This is tremendous work, and you'll want to help students notice and celebrate the ways they have grown.

But there is more growth ahead. Now, you'll likely want to continue to support their burgeoning critical literacy skills. One way to support students in becoming more critical readers is to push them to consider trustworthiness and credibility of sources. Recently, when I pulled a small group of students to involve them in considering trustworthiness, I carried *When Lunch Fights Back* with me and started the group this way, "Readers, I'm deep into my study of scientists now, and one of the things I've been noticing is that sometimes the texts I'm reading actually contradict each other. One book will say, 'Oh! Being a scientist is super rewarding because you set out to research something and you're successful,' and then the next article will say, 'Actually, being a scientist is really challenging because you go down a lot of dead ends, you try out a lot of experiments that don't go anywhere at all.'

"How many of you have noticed this already in your texts, that one will teach something and another will actually contradict it? What contradictions have you noticed so far? Tell your partner." I gave students a minute to talk.

"When books contradict like this, we, as readers, have to decide which source we want to trust. When my brother and I were little, my dad had to do this a *ton*. We'd coming running to him with some story—I might say that I was just playing quietly and not doing anything wrong when Nathan came up and knocked over my Legos and Nathan would say that he was just walking and tripped on my Legos *on accident*. My dad would have to decide which one of us, which source, was more trustworthy.

"Will you help me check to see if my sources are trustworthy? Let's start with *When Lunch Fights Back*. It can help to read the author's biography." I turned to the blurb on the book jacket and read it aloud.

> *Rebecca L. Johnson has brought science to life in dozens of books for children and young adults.*

"Oh, she's a writer. Well, I guess that makes sense because she wrote this book. I'm wondering if she has a science background, too, aren't you? Maybe she worked as a scientist? Let me continue reading to see whether this source is trustworthy." I continued reading the blurb aloud, gesturing for students to read along with me if they wished.

"What do you think about that? Does that information make her book more trustworthy? Talk with a partner about what you're noticing?" Student sprang into conversation. After a few minutes, I stopped them and asked some of the students to share what they were talking about in terms of trustworthiness. As they shared, I continued to offer lean coaching.

"Readers, we can also think about the book's copyright date. We find that information right in the first few pages of the book. We can look at if the information was published recently or if it was published a long time ago, and that can help us get ideas about the trustworthiness of the source."

I projected the book's copyright page. "Hmm, . . . 2015 . . . talk with your partner. Does that seem trustworthy?" After a minute, I called students back.

MID-WORKSHOP TEACHING
Evaluating the Trustworthiness of Sources

"Readers, I was just talking with some of your classmates, and we realized that some sources, some authors, are more trustworthy than others. In addition to reading sources thinking about what they teach and what the author's perspective is, it also pays to think about how trustworthy an author is. That way, you know if you can trust the information you're learning, or if you need to get a second source to back up what you're finding.

"We came up with some tips we hope will help you check if the source you're studying is trustworthy. Here they are." I pointed to the "To Check If a Source Is Trustworthy . . ." chart we had generated in our small group.

"Take a few minutes right now to study the source you're using. Use our chart to help you, and try out any other ways you can think of to figure out if your source is trustworthy." After a few minutes, I stopped students.

"Share what you're finding with your partner!"

Leela turned and said, "I'm reading 'Al Gore's global warming debunked—by kids!' And I hadn't noticed before, but it turns out there's no one writer. It's just from this site, wnd.com, but I've never heard of it before. So I'm feeling like this source might not be very trustworthy at all. Plus, the information here's been contradicted in a ton of other places—that's another thing we should add to the list—because that makes me think what's here is not true." I gave her a thumbs up and went to listen to another partnership.

"Mine is 'Video games could make kids better, healthier people' and I think it's really trustworthy, 'cause the writer's a doctor *and* she works at Yale, and she talks about data a lot, and she even links to other articles. So, I vote trustworthy," Iris said.

"Make sure you try this work whenever you're studying a source. Spend some time to investigate the source and make sure it's trustworthy."

"Right now, can you try this with your book? Look through your sources and find one text that's contradicted, in some way, with another text you have. Take a few minutes to check and see if that source is trustworthy. Use our two checks, and see if you can develop any others!"

As students worked, they found additional ways to determine whether their sources were trustworthy, and I asked them to add them to our chart.

To Check if a Source is Trustworthy...

• Read the author's biography and think about his/her background

• Check the copyright date

• Look at all the stuff at the back of the book

• Think about the balance of facts and opinions

• Figure out what website the information came from

"Readers, this work of checking whether or not your source is trustworthy is critically important. Think with a partner for a minute about how this work could help you as you continue reading, today and every day!" I decided I would share the chart the group had made with the class and let them in on the work the group had done.

"I heard you say, 'Well, that's really recent, so that could mean the information here is pretty accurate and trustworthy. There probably hasn't been a ton of new research done since this book was published.'"

I put out a small chart for the group to see.

Forming Your Own Perspective on Your Topic

Explain how thinking about an author's perspective can lead readers to consider their own perspective.

"Readers, today as you read different articles, you thought about the perspective of each author. Noticing an author's perspective, and thinking about how that perspective influences the information an author includes or excludes, is important work. And, as we read the ideas of others, it helps us to grow our own ideas. I think now, since you've been studying about your topics for a few weeks, you're ready to determine your unique perspective.

"Right now, in your notebook, will you write long to figure out your perspective on your topic? I'll post some questions that might help you. Use them if you need them, or just write long and let your thoughts grow. Remember it can help to go back and forth between big ideas and details as you write!"

To Determine Your Perspective, Ask:

- What do I think about my topic?

- What parts of my topic feel particularly significant?

- What do I feel about my topic?

- What feelings do I want to instill in others?

- What is it I want to say to the world about my topic?

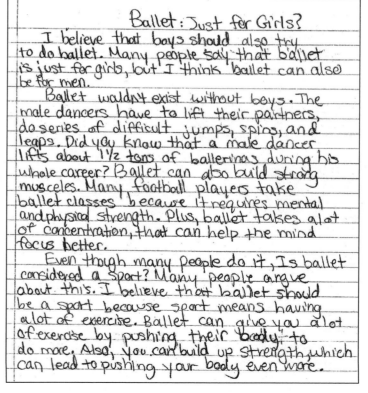

Ballet: Just for Girls?

I believe that boys should also try to do ballet. Many people say that ballet is just for girls, but I think ballet can also be for men.

Ballet wouldn't exist without boys. The male dancers have to lift their partners, do series of difficult jumps, spins, and leaps. Did you know that a male dancer lifts about 1½ tons of ballerinas during his whole career? Ballet can also build strong musceles. Many football players take ballet classes becaue it requires mental and physical strength. Plus, ballet takes alot of concentration, that can help the mind focus better.

Even though many people do it, Is ballet considered a sport? Many people argue about this. I believe that ballet should be a sport because sport means having alot of exercise. Ballet can give you alot of exercise by pushing their body to do more. Also, you can build up strength, which can lead to pushing your body even more.

FIG. 18–1   Omnia writes long to clarify her perspective on ballet.

WRITING TO IDENTIFY AND DEVELOP YOUR PERSPECTIVE

Readers, your research over the past few weeks has made you more expert about your topic. Today, you identified your unique perspective on your inquiry topic. Tonight, will you spend more time thinking about your perspective on your inquiry topic? I'm including the questions we asked ourselves in class today as reminders. Ask yourself some more of these questions and write long in response. Try out a few different ways to word your perspective. Remember that the words we write first are usually anybody's words. It helps to write something a few times to determine what exactly we're trying to say. And, if there are any parts of your perspective that you're not sure about, do a little more research tonight to fill in any gaps.

In our next session, you'll be teaching someone else about your topic. So tonight, you'll want to make sure you know everything you want to know about your topic. For your reading tonight, you might choose to reread the sources that taught you the most. Or you might reread a source that was hard for you a few weeks ago that you think you could understand better now. Or you might read sources that match your perspective (or even sources that contradict with your perspective).

To Determine Your Perspective, Ask:

• What do I think about my topic?

• What parts of my topic feel particularly significant?

• What do I feel about my topic?

• What feelings do I want to instill in others?

• What is it I want to say to the world about my topic?

Living Differently Because of Research

IN THIS SESSION, you'll teach students that when readers study topics deeply, they allow the research they've done to change the way they think and feel about their research topic. They live differently because of this research, planning for and taking action.

GETTING READY

✔ Before this session, work with other teachers to set up audiences for your students' presentations. Ideally, each audience would have 4–6 children, and each presentation should last no more than ten minutes (see Connection, Teaching, Active Engagement, Link, and Mid-Workshop Teaching).

✔ Have your reading notebook handy to model rereading your notes and planning your teaching (see Teaching).

✔ Students should bring their reading notebooks to the meeting area (see Active Engagement, Link, and Share).

✔ Prepare a chart listing who students will present their research to (see Active Engagement).

✔ Prep to show a plan from a recent small group (see Link).

✔ Display the "To Teach Well . . ." chart from Session 4 (see Conferring and Small-Group Work).

ONSIDER THIS FOR A MOMENT. Presumably neither you nor I have scoured the Scottish highlands looking for the Loch Ness monster, or attended a feast at a medieval castle, or observed guinea pig behavior in different settings, or visited research stations in Antarctica to observe changing levels of sea ice, or scored a winning goal in the Manchester United stadium. By the end of this unit, however, you and your readers will have experienced and learned from all this and more. Scotland will no longer be an obscure location on a map; guinea pigs will be more than the charming creatures that live in a cage in the living room.

Nonfiction reading does this. Nonfiction reading pushes readers into deeper connections with the very real world around us. From the true story in a magazine that inspires its reader to pledge the donation of a heart or an eye to the book on teaching reading that helps a teacher reimagine the tone and texture of life within her classroom, nonfiction reading has the power to spill out of its covers to affect what readers think about their world.

Writer Annie Dillard describes experiencing this at a very personal level. She writes about how, at age ten, she got hold of a nonfiction book called *The Natural Way to Draw* (Nicolaides, 1969) that changed her life. "This book would ignite my fervor for conscious drawing . . . For the rest of August, and all fall, this urgent, hortatory book ran my life. I tried to follow its schedule: every day, sixty-five gesture drawings, fifteen memory drawings, an hour-long contour drawing . . . I outfitted an attic bedroom as a studio and moved in. Every summer or weekend morning at eight o'clock, I taped that day's drawing schedule to a wall" (1987, 78). She lived differently because of her experiences reading.

What opportunity this unit provides! How important it is for nonfiction reading to help your children connect to that big wide world out there. If we conceive of a unit of study as being a vehicle that drives children's consciousness down a path of learning, we might regard the skills and strategies involved in reading nonfiction texts as the starting point of this journey. Certainly strategies are precious, especially those that have the transferability to propel kids onto a higher plane of thinking. But more than this, we'll want to honor the joy of learning, the thrill of being one who can launch learning expeditions of our own.

We will want to memorialize ways that nonfiction reading can spur a legacy of thought and action in the reader.

On this final day of the unit, you and your children will celebrate the information they have gathered, the ideas they've grown, and the traces that all this new learning has left in their lives. The concept of celebration itself suffers from a connection to firecrackers and confetti. A celebration actually denotes something far deeper, something often missed. Any thesaurus tells us: to celebrate is to mark, honor, keep, remember, and memorialize. Toward the end of the unit, therefore, the question that we might ask ourselves is "What, in this month's work of teaching and learning, is most worthy of honoring, keeping, and memorializing?"

"Nonfiction reading pushes readers into deeper connections with the very real world around us."

As you close the door on the last chapter of this unit, gather your children close together and issue them an invitation. Say, "Children, today we celebrate not only the end of this unit but a beginning, too. It's the beginning of taking this new knowledge and thinking with us wherever we go, whatever we do in the world. This is the beginning of living differently because of all we've learned."

Living Differently because of Research

CONNECTION

Share your observations about students' tremendous growth as readers, and ask them to reflect with a partner on specific ways they have grown across the unit.

"Readers, over the past few weeks, you've been inquiring into topics that are significant to you, and you have learned so much. In our last session, as you went off to research, I took a few moments to step back and marvel at your growth. It's really been tremendous." I paused to let my words sink in. "Will you think back about the ways you've grown as a reader? You might think, 'I used to be the kind of reader who . . . and now I'm the kind of reader who . . .' You can use our charts to help you."

I gave students a minute to think and then asked them to turn and reflect on their growth with their partner. I knelt down and listened in.

Invite students to see themselves as participants in a broader intellectual community of people who research their topic.

"Even though you've had your topic groups to meet with, in many ways it's felt like you were researching on your own, since your classmates were studying different topics.

"I want to remind you, though, that there have been countless others alongside you throughout this journey. It's likely people started researching your topic long before you were born, contributing to a grand conversation that exists on your topic. Each text you've read, each interview you've conducted, has been one person's contribution to that grand conversation. Imagine you were to write a book on philosophy or go and teach others all about that topic. You'd be adding to a grand conversation started thousands of years ago, by Plato and Aristotle, the first writers to write about philosophy. The same is true for your topic.

"Two weeks ago, you might not have been ready to do this work. Remember, you were just a novice on your topic. But now, you're ready to enter this conversation, to become a spokesperson for your topic, to articulate your own opinions."

◆ COACHING

In her book Mindset: The New Psychology of Success: How We Can Learn to Fulfill Our Potential, *Carol S. Dweck, Ph.D., writes about how through practice, the brain changes and grows stronger. She says, "The more that you challenge your mind to learn, the more your brain cells grow. Then, things that you once found very hard or even impossible—like speaking a foreign language or doing algebra—seem to become easy. The result is a stronger, smarter brain" (219). This reflection time supports students in recognizing the dramatic ways their brains have grown, and it helps students develop a growth mind-set.*

Name the teaching point.

"Today I want to teach you that when readers study a topic deeply, they allow the research they do to change the way they think and feel about their topic. You live differently because of the research you do."

TEACHING

Remind students that in thirty minutes they'll be traveling around the school to present their unique perspective on their research topic to other students.

"Readers, you know that today each of you will put your deep study of your topic under your arm and carry it with you into the world. I've arranged for you to head to different places around the school where, thirty minutes from now, people will be waiting to learn about your unique perspective on your topic. This means that today, you'll need to spend time preparing. To do this, you'll need to determine what you'll teach and then make a plan for how you'll teach that information."

Demonstrate how you decide what you want to contribute to the grand conversation about your topic. Set students up to watch, noticing the moves you make so they can replicate your process.

"My audience will be the third graders in Ms. Richard's science class, and I'll be presenting to them later today when you're at gym. I can't teach them everything about scientists—I'll probably only have ten minutes of their time—so I have to figure out what *exactly* I want to teach them, what I want to contribute to the grand conversation about scientists. Will you watch as I do this, noticing what I do to determine what I'll teach, so that in a few minutes you can do the same thing?

"Well, I could definitely teach them about a ton of different things that scientists research—about hagfish slime and birds that shoot vomit and feces at their prey. I bet the third graders would think that was so cool! They'd be jumping out of their seats just to see the pictures.

"But, I guess if I wanted to teach kids about that, I could just read them *When Lunch Fights Back* and *Alien Deep*. I'd be sharing someone else's contributions with them. That would be fine, but I really want to make my *own* contribution to this grand conversation. Let me think about what I could say that someone else hasn't already said." I picked up my reading notebook and modeled flipping through pages of notes. "Hmm, . . . well . . . there's all the places scientists research, but there are books about that too. Maybe . . . ."

A few students vigorously waved their hands to help me, but I continued.

"Maybe I could teach about how scientists are way more diverse than most people think. Remember how a ton of the people I surveyed described scientists as men, wearing white coats, doing research in laboratories with goggles on, and then as we were reading on, we kept seeing that it just wasn't true, that a ton of scientists were women, that scientists

The "Critical Reading" strand of the learning progression states that fifth-graders are expected to synthesize several texts in ways that support their own ideas and then to select the points that do the best job of supporting their idea. Look to the "Critical Reading" strand of the progression for more information, paying particular attention to the "Growing Ideas" strand.

Setting students up to observe your demonstration with a specific lens, in this case, watching to see what you do that they can also do, shifts them automatically into a more active role across your demonstration. Instead of just sitting back and watching, they will be noting specifically what you do, picking up on nuances they might otherwise have passed by.

worked in incredibly different conditions. I'm thinking that I could teach the third graders about how diverse scientists are."

Ask students to turn and talk, naming out the work you just did as a reader.

"Researchers, I hope you were watching closely. With your partner, talk for a minute about the work you just saw me do. What steps did I go through to choose what I would contribute to the grand conversation on my topic?"

I knelt down and listened to Dexter and Lily as they talked. "Well, first she came up with an idea of what she could teach—kind of an obvious one, one of her main ideas. And that one didn't work 'cause someone else already wrote it. It wasn't her idea," Dexter began.

"Yeah, and then she went back to her notes and flipped through to figure out what else she could teach. And what she chose was something she had thought from what she studied," Lily added.

ACTIVE ENGAGEMENT

Introduce readers to the audiences for their presentations. Ask students to reread their notes and determine what contribution they'd like to make to the grand conversation on their topic.

"Researchers, I've posted who you'll be presenting to on this chart, because you'll certainly want to ensure that your presentation makes sense for your audience." I revealed a chart that listed each student's name and the audience. "These presentations are coming up quick, so right here, even before you leave the meeting area, you'll need to begin preparing. Look back over all your research, and think about what your unique contribution will be to the grand conversation on your topic." Notes sprang open, and readers eagerly flipped through to find their contribution. I whispered in as students worked, reminding them to consider multiple options for what they could teach.

"Share what you'll teach with your topic group."

LINK

Send readers off with a sense of urgency, letting them know they'll only have a short amount of time to create their teaching plan and rehearse for their presentation.

"Readers, you've got serious work to do today. In just thirty minutes, you'll disperse down the hallway, teaching other kids some of the powerful learning you've done on your topic. That means you'll have to use every minute of reading time to get ready. Likely, you'll want to spend some time reading over your notes and creating a plan for what you'll teach."

If you feel students need additional support, you might choose to have them share out the steps they saw you go through to plan what you would teach, or you might choose to say, "I heard you say . . ." and then summarize the steps you heard students discuss. In any case, you'll want to emphasize that you sought to contribute your own ideas to the grand conversation rather than simply summarizing what you read in books.

Students worked to identify their unique perspective on their topic as part of last night's homework. They identified parts of their topic that felt particularly significant, considered the feelings they wanted to instill in others, and generated what they wanted to say to the world about their topic. Encourage students to draw on that work now as they finalize their teaching plans.

I projected a plan from a recent small-group lesson I'd taught. "It will probably help for you to record your plan so you remember what exactly you want to say. See how I jotted down what I'd teach and a bit about how I'd teach it? Your plans might look similar.

"And then, once you've got a plan for what you'll teach, spend time rehearsing, using everything you know about teaching others to make your presentation as strong as it can be."

One tip for the share of today's session: it will have more of an impact if it takes place after the teaching work that the students do out in the building.

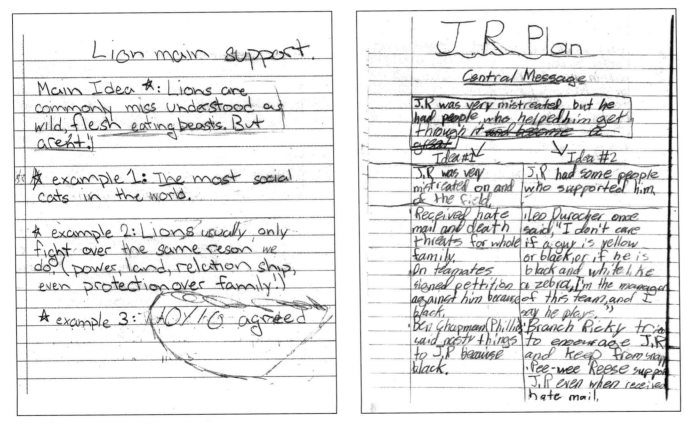

FIG. 19–1 Students generated quick plans to guide their upcoming teaching.

Tips to Strengthen Presentations

TODAY, INSTEAD OF SMALL GROUPS and one-on-one conferences, you'll want to coach in regularly around the room, offering tips to help students prepare for their upcoming presentations. Here are some tips your students might benefit from:

- Remind students to make sure everything in their presentation brings out their unique contribution. You might say, "As you're planning with your main ideas in mind, remember that your ideas will be clearer to your readers if everything you teach about fits with those main ideas. Make sure you include the most important points and visuals that fit with those main ideas."

- Encourage students to use the "To Teach Well . . ." chart from Session 4 of the unit. You might say, "As you rehearse for your presentation, use what you know about teaching others. It will be important to think about how you're organizing your information, what exactly you're teaching, and how you'll teach it—using an explaining voice, gestures, and a teaching finger. As you're rehearsing, keep these tips in mind to help you."

- Remind students to keep in mind what they know about text complexity. You might say, "Readers, remember that you now know what makes informational texts more complex and less complex. As you plan your presentation, think about ways you're helping your readers with complexity. If you're using expert words on your topic, can you weave in definitions to help you reader understand what those words mean? If you're teaching about multiple main ideas, can you keep your presentation organized so you teach all about one main idea and then all about another main idea?"

- Encourage students to use props. You might say, "Readers, you know that popular saying, 'A picture is worth a thousand words'? Use that to your advantage. Think about strong visuals you've seen related to your topic—photographs, charts, illustrations—and then look through any texts you have handy and your reader's notebook and find the visuals that will be most supportive as you teach. You can use these tools as you teach others."

To Teach Well...

- *Use the text structure to organize your teaching*

- *Know the main ideas and supporting details*

- *Use an explaining voice*

- *Use gestures*

- *Use a teaching finger to point to charts, illustrations, and diagrams to help explain*

MID-WORKSHOP TEACHING **Send Students Off to Teach**

"Readers, this is it. In just a moment, you'll open this door and head down the hallway as knowledgeable experts on your topic, armed with powerful teaching plans, ready to teach others what you've learned. Right now, gather all the materials you'll need—your plan, any books you've marked to show pictures from, your explaining voice. Now, head off, and add your unique perspective to the grand conversation on your topic!"

Thinking about How Research Changes the Way You Live

After students return from their teaching, draw the unit to a close, emphasizing that the research students did within this unit should propel them to live differently and take action.

"Today's the end of our inquiry projects, and we're celebrating all the work we've done as nonfiction readers and researchers up to this point. And there's a lot we could celebrate. But, perhaps even more importantly, I want to point out that today should be a beginning. As our inquiry projects draw to a close, we're left thinking about what we could do differently in our own lives as a result of this research. We develop reactions and take action in response to whatever we've researched.

"We let the reading work we do change our lives."

Highlight a few ways you imagine your own research will make you live differently. Ask students to share ways their research will make an impact on their lives.

"I've been thinking about how I'll live differently now because of this research I've been doing about scientists, and there are a few things that jump to mind for me. The surveys I did showed that a ton of kids think scientists are men in white lab coats working in laboratories, and I now know that's not true, that scientists can be so much more than that. So, I'm thinking that I can read books to my students, all of you this year and the kids I teach in future years, about scientists that show the diversity of scientists and all the different work they do. And I'm also thinking that whenever I see commercials that show scientists in one light, probably in white lab coats, I can point out to whomever I'm with that scientists are so much more than that. And I think I want to start researching now, so that this summer, I can sign up for some hands-on science courses at a local college. I want to experience this work firsthand!

"Will you take a few minutes on your own to think about the research you've done and how you'll live differently based on that research? In your notebook, somewhere prominent, will you jot down your initial ideas? In a few minutes, we'll share these plans with our topic groups." I gave students a few minutes to jot silently, while I jotted in my notebook.

"Gather in topic groups and share your life plans. If someone shares something you'd like to try out, jot it down. Be inspired by one another to live differently!"

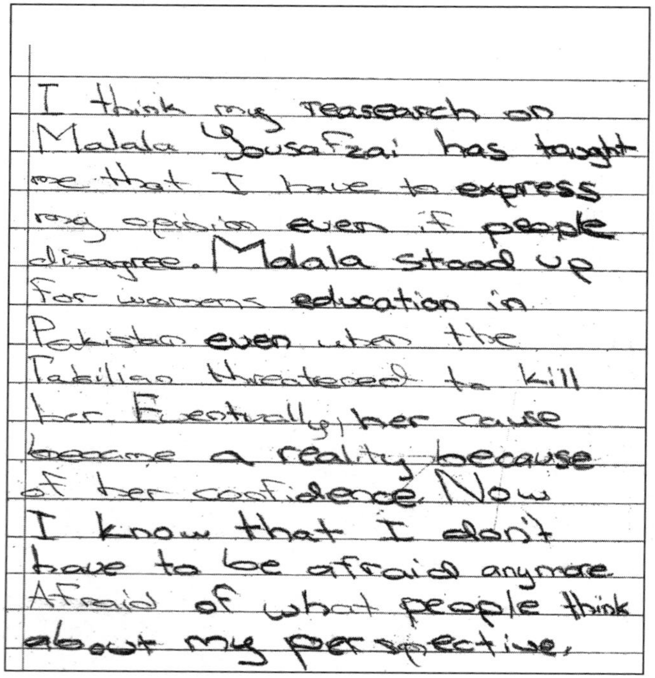

I think my reasearch on Malala Yousafzai has taught me that I have to express my opinion even if people disagree. Malala stood up for womens education in Pakistan even when the Tabilian threatened to kill her. Eventually, her cause became a reality because of her confidence. Now I know that I don't have to be afraid anymore Afraid of what people think about my perspective.

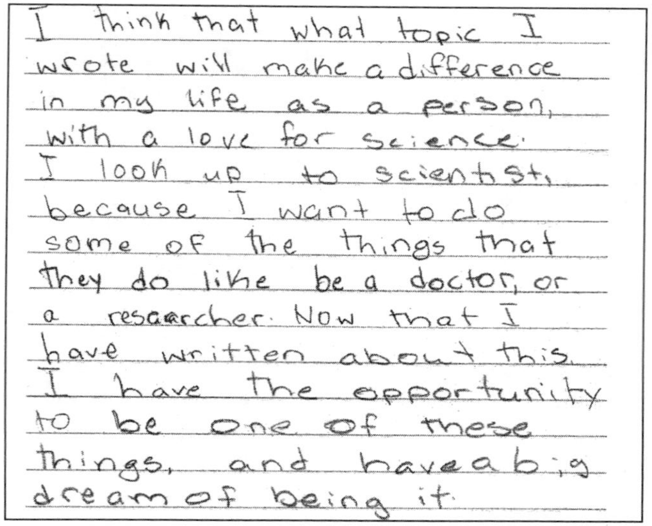

I think that what topic I wrote will make a difference in my life as a person, with a love for science. I look up to scientist, because I want to do some of the things that they do like be a doctor, or a researcher. Now that I have written about this, I have the opportunity to be one of these things, and have a big dream of being it.

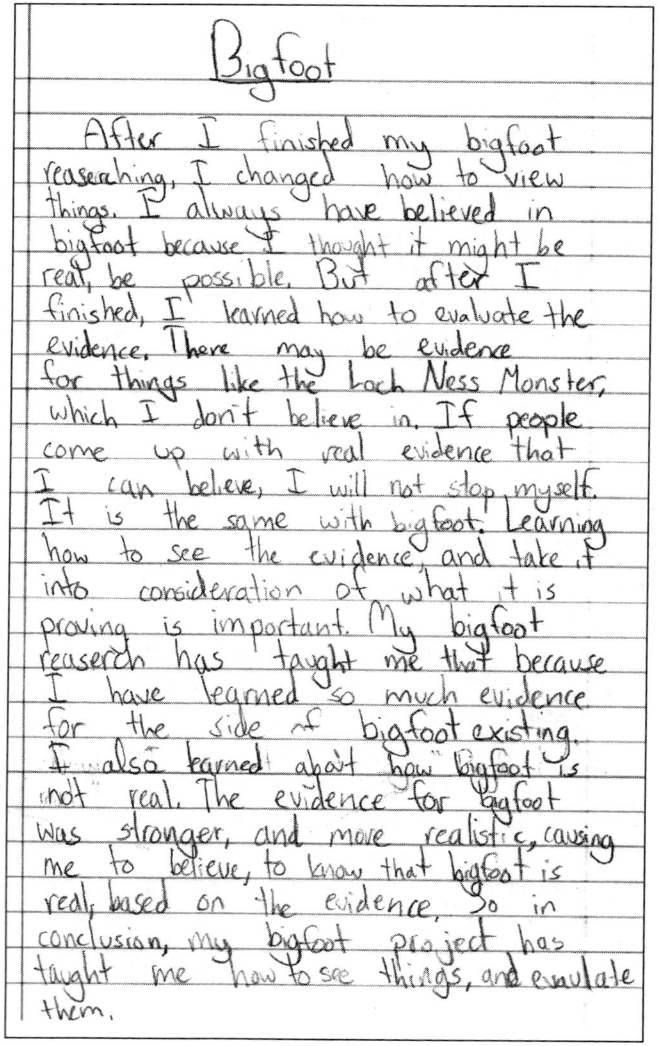

Bigfoot

After I finished my bigfoot reaserching, I changed how to view things. I always have believed in bigfoot because I thought it might be real, be possible. But after I finished, I learned how to evaluate the evidence. There may be evidence for things like the Loch Ness Monster, which I don't believe in. If people come up with real evidence that I can believe, I will not stop myself. It is the same with bigfoot. Learning how to see the evidence, and take it into consideration of what it is proving is important. My bigfoot reaserch has taught me that because I have learned so much evidence for the side of bigfoot existing. I also learned about how bigfoot is not real. The evidence for bigfoot was stronger, and more realistic, causing me to believe, to know that bigfoot is real, based on the evidence. So in conclusion, my bigfoot project has taught me how to see things, and evulate them.

FIG. 19–2 Students write long about how they will live differently because of their personal inquiry projects.

LIVING DIFFERENTLY BECAUSE OF RESEARCH

Readers, today you made your own contribution to a grand conversation on your topic. That conversation likely began long before you were born. You shared your unique insights on your topic with readers from across our community. It's important to remember that the work you did today is really just the beginning. It's the start of a whole life of living differently because of the research you've done these last few weeks. You began planning for this living differently at the end of reading workshop today. You have jotted notes about the reading you'd do. You've also jotted notes about the actions you'd take and the contributions you'd make.

Tonight, in addition to reading, will you begin the work of living differently because of your research? This goal might feel lofty, but will you find some small way to live differently? Maybe you'll gather new research on a part of your topic you hadn't explored before. Perhaps you'll refine your presentation and share it with everyone who will listen. Possibly you'll begin researching organizations that take action on your topic so you can join in and help. Remember to draw on the plan you generated in class today to help you as you take on this meaningful work. It will be up to you to decide how to begin living differently.